AMRITSAR TO LAHORE

Amritsar to Lahore

A Journey Across the India-Pakistan Border

Stephen Alter

UNIVERSITY OF PENNSYLVANIA PRESS

Philadelphia

Copyright © 2001 University of Pennsylvania Press
All rights reserved
Printed in the United States of America on acid-free paper
10 9 8 7 6 5 4 3 2 1

Published by the University of Pennsylvania Press
Philadelphia, Pennsylvania 19104-4011

Library of Congress Cataloging-in-Publication Data

Alter, Stephen.
    Amritsar to Lahore: A journey across the Indian Pakistan
border / Stephen Alter.
        p.   cm.
    Includes bibliographical references and index.
    ISBN 0-8122-3565-7 (cloth : alk. paper) ; ISBN 0-8122-1743-8
(pbk. : alk. paper)
        1. Alter, Stephen—Journeys—India. 2. Alter, Stephen—
Journeys—Pakistan. 3. India—Description and travel. 4.
Pakistan—description and travel.

DS414.2 .A55   2000   00-033800
915'.414'52—dc21   CIP

For

Urmila Law

and her

four daughters

CONTENTS

This book is a work of nonfiction. Like the words nonviolence, non-proliferation, and nonvegetarian, this suggests what it is not rather than what it is. Writing out of journals I kept during the summer of 1997, I have tried to remain as true to the facts as possible, even though I am a subjective observer. In certain instances the names of individuals have been changed to protect their privacy, but the places, conversations, and events in this book are all drawn from personal encounters. Nevertheless, it is important to admit at the outset that I am neither a scholar nor a journalist but simply a traveler who bears a longstanding grudge against borders.

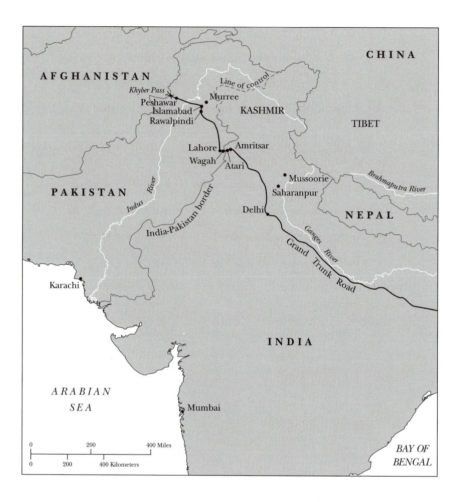

CHINA

AFGHANISTAN

Line of control

Khyber Pass

Murree

Peshawar

Islamabad

Rawalpindi

KASHMIR

TIBET

Lahore

Amritsar

Wagah

Atari

PAKISTAN

Indus River

India-Pakistan border

Mussoorie

Saharanpur

Brahmaputra River

NEPAL

Delhi

Ganges River

Grand Trunk Road

Karachi

INDIA

ARABIAN
SEA

Mumbai

0   200   400 Miles

0   200   400 Kilometers

BAY OF
BENGAL

1

NEW DELHI Union Territory

While crossing the border on August 30 in 1947, the one thing that dominated our minds was that we all knew that we were coming to India but we did not know where we'd go from there. We were part of lakhs of people who were forced to leave their homes from different parts of Punjab to save our lives. I was in my Austin car which had to be abandoned at Wagha border. . . .

No doubt there was a sense of achievement of freedom but we did not know that the freedom movement would end up in the partition of Punjab and that we would have to leave our birthplace. But then the agony and pain of leaving the home town was shared by all. The pain is lessened if it is shared.—JAG PRAVESH CHANDRA, former chief metropolitan councillor of Delhi, *Times of India*, 25 July 1997

For most travelers the journey from India to Pakistan begins on an unpaved sidewalk in Chanakyapuri, New Delhi's diplomatic enclave. Situated on Shanti Path, the Avenue of Peace, Pakistan's High Commission has a huge dome the color of lapis lazuli. The compound where Pakistani diplomats live is surrounded by a high cement wall, the top of which is encrusted with shards of broken glass. A police encampment guards the main entrance — three sagging canvas tents and a dozen or more Indian constables dressed in khaki uniforms, leaning on their rifles. It is hard to tell if they have been posted there to protect the High Commission or to keep watch on the diplomats inside.

Early in the morning, just after dawn, crowds of travelers begin to gather, arriving in minibuses and autorickshaws. Most of them are Indian Muslims who have relatives in Pakistan. They congregate under a line of pipal trees along a side street next to the High Commission. For most of the day these travelers wait in the shade while their visa applications are processed. None of them are permitted entry to the compound, and the only means of communication with the Pakistani authorities is a single, square hole in the wall, shoulder high and much too narrow for anyone to crawl inside. The travelers queue up in front of the opening and pass their documents through the wall like supplicants at a shrine. Under the spreading branches of the pipal trees, freelance clerks sit at rickety wooden desks, where they fill out cyclostyled forms, scribbling furiously in English and Urdu, riffling through passports and affixing photographs. Most of the travelers come from rural towns and villages across North India, and many of them are illiterate. The visa fees are minimal but the paperwork is laborious and complicated. The slightest mistake or omission leads to the papers being rejected. One man I spoke with said that his visa application had been turned down three times already.

The Partition of India and Pakistan was intended to create a homeland for Muslims throughout the subcontinent, but once the first wave of migration ended the borders snapped shut, and it is now virtually impossible for Indian Muslims to emigrate. Only those who can prove that they have family on the other side of the border are granted one-month visas, and their movements in Pakistan are severely restricted. Pakistanis face similar challenges when traveling in the opposite direction. Yet the persistence and patience of the people who make this journey is remarkable. Unlike the lone European backpacker I saw fidgeting in the queue outside the High Commission, these travelers endure humiliation and frustration for a chance to reconnect with their families. Against all odds they defy the existence of a border that has divided the subcontinent since 1947. Each applicant who passes a sheaf of papers through that hole in the wall commits an individual act of defiance against the injustices of history, against the tangled red tape of bureaucracy, and against the hatreds and suspicions that continue to arouse tensions on either side of the border.

Having already gotten my visa for Pakistan from the consulate in New York, I had no practical reason to visit the High Commission in New Delhi. As I wandered through the crowds, however, I felt for the first time the proximity of the border, even though it was over five hundred kilometers away. It may have been the broken glass at the top of the wall or the police pickets standing guard, but a feeling of uncertainty and alienation was palpable in the midmorning heat. Despite the cheerful exhortations of hawkers selling roasted peanuts, channa, and pakoras, and the grinning cartoon characters painted on an ice cream trolley, most of the travelers seemed worried and pensive, waiting together in clustered groups.

The blue dome of Pakistan's High Commission and its futuristic minarets mirror the silhouettes of mosques and mausoleums in other parts of the city — the sandstone grandeur of the Jumma Masjid or the marble dome of Humayun's tomb. Delhi was once the capital of Muslim dynasties, the Tughlaqs, the Lodhis, and the Mughals. Many of the ruins from those periods are preserved as national monuments. Yet today the architecture of Pakistan's High Commission seems out of place and under siege, not only from the crowds of travelers who gather outside its walls, but from the Hindu majority in India, which is increasingly antagonistic and hostile toward the country's Islamic heritage.

At the stroke of midnight, on 15 August 1947, the British left India divided. After half a century of Partition the subcontinent is still torn by the same religious tensions and conflicts which originally led to the creation of two separate countries. During this period India and Pakistan have fought three wars, the last of which brought about the secession of Bangladesh in 1971. Since then an uneasy peace has been established, but gun battles continue over disputed areas of Kashmir while communal violence, refugees, and separatist insurrections remain a constant source of animosity and recrimination. These tensions have worsened with the recent testing of nuclear weapons in both countries.

Some have argued that the Partition of India was the final, desperate act of an empire collapsing under the weight of its own ambivalence. Others have blamed the freedom fighters for playing politics with volatile religious hatreds, in order to carve out their own areas of influence and power. Whatever the reasons for those arbitrary lines drawn upon the map in 1947, there is no doubt that recent history, as well as the future of the subcontinent, has been delineated by its borders.

As an American who was born and raised in India, I have an abiding personal interest in this part of the world. Growing up during the 1960s and 1970s, I was acutely aware of borders because of the wars that were fought during that period. For many years I was unable to visit Pakistan because it would have jeopardized my status as a permanent foreign resident of India. Yet I have always wanted to see what lies on the other side of the border. My wife Ameeta's maternal grandparents and her mother, aunts, and uncles originally lived in Lahore. In 1947 they resettled in Jalandhar as refugees, then later moved to Delhi. My own grandparents, who came to India as missionaries in 1916, lived and worked for most of their lives in an area of the Punjab that eventually became part of Pakistan. Though I cannot say that I share the same sense of dislocation as the refugees who were displaced, I have always felt that the border which divides the Punjab has separated me from towns and villages where our family once lived.

During the summer of 1997 I was finally able to make the overland journey from India to Pakistan. In the course of my travels I interviewed a variety of people and compiled a range of opinions, stories, and beliefs regarding the existence of the border. I recorded the memories of those who remembered the events of 1947, but I was equally interested in the views and comments of a younger generation, as they reflected on the meaning of national identity. What interests me most are the subtle and insidious ways in which a country is confined by its borders, whether it be the mosaic of rubber stamps that smudge my passport, the enigmatic language of road signs, or the euphemisms and innuendos that are often used to describe persons who belong to another nation, creed, or caste.

Most of the ethnic and religious strife in Pakistan and India has been generated by a combination of historical circumstances and the cynical manipulation of power within each state. These forces undermine and betray a genuine desire for peace and coexistence on the part of most people who live in South Asia. Nationally enforced identities and citizenship are often at odds with a much more basic human impulse for cross-cultural understanding. Few writers have articulated this problem more clearly than Edward Said in his book *Culture and Imperialism*:

> No one today is purely *one* thing. Labels like Indian, or woman, or Muslim, or American are not more than starting points, which if followed into actual experience for only a moment are quickly left behind. Imperialism consolidated the mixture of cultures and identities on a global scale. But its worst and most paradoxical gift was to allow people to believe that they were only, mainly, exclusively, White, or Black, or Western, or Oriental. Yet just as human beings make their own history, they also make their cultures and ethnic identities. No one can deny the persisting continuities of long traditions, sustained habitations, national languages, and cultural geographies, but there seems no reason except fear and prejudice to keep insisting on their separation and distinctiveness, as if that was all human life was about.[1]

The relationships between the different peoples of South Asia are infinitely complex and contentious, particularly for those who were uprooted by Partition and forced to become refugees. It is extremely difficult for citizens of one country to travel to the other and the military authorities and police keep a strict watch on travelers who cross the border. An irrational level of paranoia exists within each government and this inflames communal hatreds. More often than not, it is the state that imposes and reinforces a false sense of homogeneity within its borders in order to defend itself against the "enemy" that lies outside. This leads to heightened tensions and the fear of exclusion or domination amongst minorities.

During the fifty years following Partition, a rash of separatist movements have emerged in the region, each with a besieged sense of ethnic identity. V. S. Naipaul, a regular observer of South Asia, describes this dangerous situation in his book *A Million Mutinies Now*:

> To awaken to history was to cease to live instinctively. It was to begin to see oneself and one's group the way the outside world saw one; and it was to know a kind of rage. India was now full of this rage. There had been a general awakening. But everyone awakened first to his own group or community; every group

thought itself unique in its awakening; and every group sought to separate its rage from the rage of other groups.[2]

Yet in contrast to the prejudice and vindictive violence that result from this rage, there are deep-rooted social and cultural bonds that have been forgotten or ignored in the fervor of separatist rhetoric and actions. As I traveled back and forth across the border, I heard many tirades of bigotry and intolerance but I also heard voices of reason and reconciliation. Despite their divisive history, most people in South Asia share an enormous curiosity and fascination for that which lies across the border, whether it be the problems of poverty and political freedom, or the latest film or ghazal recording.

Many South Asian novelists and poets have struggled with the question of borders. The events of Partition inspired writers such as Saadat Hasan Manto, Bhisham Sahni, Qurratulain Hyder, Kushwant Singh, Intizar Hussein, and Bapsi Sidhwa, to name just a few. Salman Rushdie, one of South Asia's best known and most maligned writers, has explored the uncertain territory of borders and identities throughout much of his work. In the title essay of his book *Imaginary Homelands*, Rushdie writes about the problems of an expatriate novelist from the subcontinent. His sentiments could just as easily apply to any contemporary writer living and working in Pakistan or India.

It may be that writers in my position, exiles or emigrants or expatriates, are haunted by some sense of loss, some urge to reclaim, to look back, even at the risk of being mutated into pillars of salt. But if we do look back, we must also do so in the knowledge—which gives rise to profound uncertainties—that our alienation from India almost inevitably means that we will not be capable of reclaiming precisely the thing that was lost; that we will, in short, create fictions, not actual cities or villages, but invisible ones, imaginary homelands, Indias of the mind.[3]

The act of Partition made all individuals in South Asia exiles in their own homeland and the resulting sense of alienation has been a catalyst for creative expression. In the same essay, Rushdie goes on to argue that literature can change the world by redescribing it, "particularly at times when the State takes reality into its own hands, and sets about distorting it, altering the past to fit its present needs."4 Too often the histrionics of politicians and the clamor of patriotic voices, make it impossible to hear the individual, whether it be an outspoken novelist or an unknown refugee who has an equally compelling story to tell.

The fiftieth anniversary of Independence and Partition offered a unique moment in which to explore the meaning and relevance of South Asia's borders. Coincidentally, many of the former colonial powers in Europe, including Britain, have been attempting to eliminate their own national boundaries. It seems that those intractable lines of ink which were once drawn with such authority upon the maps of former colonies need to be seen for what they are: temporary barricades which choke the flow of rational dialogue and discourse.

In 1947 the city of New Delhi changed dramatically with the arrival of Hindu and Sikh refugees from the Punjab. Though nobody has ever been able to establish an accurate figure for the number of people who were uprooted at the time of Partition, estimates range upwards of ten million and it was unquestionably one of the largest mass migrations of all time. Hundreds of thousands of people were killed in the sectarian violence which accompanied this sudden transfer of population. Many of the refugees found their way to New Delhi, which was then a quiet, colonial suburb of the old city. Designed and built in the 1920s under the direction of Edward Lutyens, Delhi's stately government buildings, broad avenues, and exclusive bungalows were constructed on a monumental scale. The British envisioned it as a modern, imperial city, a symbol of viceregal power. For all its pomp and grandeur, however, the capital had an uninspiring reputation. Compared to Calcutta or Bombay, New Delhi was considered a dull and colorless backwater, populated by civil servants and government clerks.

For the refugees, however, one of the primary attractions of New Delhi lay in the fact that there were huge tracts of undeveloped land to the south and west of the city. The resettlement colonies where this displaced population rebuilt their homes are now prime properties, and the capital has expanded to four times its size in half a century. Most of the wide avenues of New Delhi are still there, and many of

the spacious bungalows continue to house political leaders, top bureaucrats, and military brass. Beyond this exclusive domain of privilege and power lie new development areas and enclaves that have
spread beyond the municipal limits. Even as the city continues to
grow, New Delhi retains the edgy, opportunistic atmosphere of a
refugee colony and the lingering tensions of dislocation. Sunil Khilnani, in his book *The Idea of India*, describes some of the changes that
have taken place in New Delhi:

> Partition introduced the first serious strains into this urban
> world. It imported a new threat into the public spaces of the
> modern city. In the past, religious conflict had been restricted to
> the "old" parts of the city: now it stalked through every street.
> And it brought with unparalleled speed large numbers of uproot-
> ed people into the cities. In a society where there was very little
> spatial mobility (in 1931 less than 4 percent of the Indian popula-
> tion lived outside the state or province of their birth), Partition
> unleashed the largest transfer of population in human history. . . .
> Delhi became a Punjabi city.[5]

Amrita Pritam, a leading Punjabi fiction writer and poet, came to
Delhi in 1947. Fifty years after her arrival she looked back on those
events and her preconceptions of the city which would become her
home.

> Before Partition, when we were in Lahore, we admired Delhi a
> lot. We saw it as a great city, a city of serenity and silent historic
> memories, where the famous monuments spoke quietly and
> calmly about their time of glory and heyday to whosoever was
> willing to listen. . . .
> After Partition, when we came here and when the realization .
> struck us that this city is going to be our new home, the perspec-
> tive and the picture that we had nurtured somewhat changed.
> The dreamy, romantic image that we had of Delhi considerably
> paled when we came face to face with reality. Those days, for
> refugees, it was a question of survival. We had no choice, we had
> to live in whatever space we could find and do any work that we
> could get. I was not at all disillusioned, in fact I was very thank-

ful. We were exiled in our own country, and Delhi and the people here gave us another home.[6]

The influx of Punjabi refugees was soon followed by other migrations from the rural areas of North India, landless farmers and villagers in search of jobs. Driven by economic need rather than political or religious struggles, these new residents compounded the tensions within a growing population and put enormous pressure on New Delhi's fragile infrastructure. Each wave of urban migration brought with it the inevitable conflicts of class and caste as the new arrivals sought to compete with those who had preceded them.

Connaught Place is the city center of New Delhi, a circular hub of expensive shops and boutiques, glass fronted offices and five-star hotels. But where there is wealth there is also poverty. At eight o'clock in the morning, before the swarms of commuters arrive, pavement dwellers crouch in circles on the sidewalks. A beggar sits on the steps of a pedestrian underpass, one hand raised, her face hidden beneath a cowl of tattered cotton. A young boy in ragged shorts runs up to greet me, pulling at my sleeve and asking for money. Other children are playing with the shattered remains of a coconut shell while an elderly couple burn scraps of paper to warm themselves, even though the temperatures are in the nineties.

An inescapable sense of discontentment crowds the streets of New Delhi and there are signs of protest everywhere, posters on the walls announcing opposition rallies and demonstrations. In 1997 the main venue of protest was Jantar Mantar, an ancient observatory which the newspapers referred to as Delhi's Hyde Park. Instead of soap boxes there were makeshift tents with hand-painted banners demanding everything from the separate state of Uttarkhand to the dismissal of corruption charges against Laloo Prasad Yadav, chief minister of Bihar. A group of New Delhi municipal employees were holding a hunger strike. As I walked past, a squad of riot police were standing by, sweating under their tin derbies and padded vests, but there didn't seem to be any immediate possibility of trouble. Most of the protestors were squatting in the shade or dozing on the sidewalk. A police inspector was chatting with a group of activists from Bihar. Nailed to the trunk of one of the neem trees was a painted sign proclaiming the

World Unification Movement, which advocates the reunification of
Pakistan, India, and Bangladesh. When I stopped to ask if I could
speak to the organizer of this movement, one of the men in a nearby
tent said that he had gone home for breakfast.

The high fence that surrounds Jantar Mantar kept the protestors
out. With its plush lawns and flowering trees, frangipani, and jasmine,
the park remains a quiet triangle of green in the center of the city.
Wandering through the gates I stopped to read a marble plaque that
commemorates the construction of the observatory by the maharajah
of Jaipur in 1710. Almost three hundred years old, Jantar Mantar exhibits a surreal geometry — angular staircases and platforms, curved
walls of plastered masonry, painted with pink lime wash. Marble slabs
are etched with calibrated markings and cryptic numerals. Two circular observatories with radial spokes and pools of water are part of a
complex arrangement of structures by which the state astrologers
measured the movement of the stars and predicted the fate of maharajahs and other potentates. Today these enigmatic structures seem to
offer no secret visions of the future, no forecasts of power; they are
simply curiosities of the past. Ironically, though Jantar Mantar was
constructed to study the night sky, the park is now closed between
sunset and sunrise.

The Congress Party, which has been in power for all but five of India's
fifty years, has always staked its claim to the ideals of religious tolerance, as articulated by Mahatma Gandhi. Under Jawaharlal Nehru,
the first prime minister, India established itself as a secular democracy.
For this reason religious minorities, particularly Muslims and Christians, tended to support the Congress Party. Even today, within a large
and diverse segment of the population, secularism is still revered as a
cornerstone of modern India. Despite the continuing distrust and friction between Hindus, Sikhs, and Muslims, most politicians, aside
from rabid fundamentalists, adopt the slogans of religious coexistence
and reconciliation. "Communalism," a catchword for religious bigotry
and violence, is generally denounced. But rhetoric does not always
translate into action and in the past fifty years most of the major towns
and cities of India, including the capital, have experienced communal
riots.

Sudhir Kakar, a psychiatrist based in New Delhi, has studied the social dynamics of religious conflict in India and explores the question of communal identity in his book *The Colours of Violence*:

> The awareness of belonging to either one community or the other — being a Hindu or Muslim — has increased manifold in recent years. Every time religious violence occurs in India or in some other part of the subcontinent, the reach and spread of modern communications ensure that a vast number of people are soon aware of the incident. Each riot and its aftermath raise afresh the issue of the individual's religious-cultural identity and bring it up to the surface of consciousness.[7]

The facade of secularism began to erode in the late 1970s — some would argue earlier. Following the Emergency, Indira Gandhi had been thrown out of parliament but with the help of her son, Sanjay, she was willing to do anything to reclaim control of the government. Though Indira Gandhi and her cohorts continued to pay lip service to secularism, the Congress Party began to pit one religious community against the other, in states like Assam where an influx of Muslim refugees from Bangladesh threatened to sway the balance of power. Perhaps the most obvious example of the shift away from secularism was in the Punjab, where Congress Party officials helped boost the influence of religious militants like Jarnail Singh Bhindranwale, in order to split the political power of the more moderate Sikhs. These efforts backfired and Bhindranwale's campaign escalated into a fiery separatist movement, which ultimately precipitated the Indian army's attack on the Golden Temple in Amritsar. A full-scale military assault on this, the most sacred shrine of the Sikh religion, further undermined the myth of secularism. Less than a year later Indira Gandhi herself was assassinated by two of her Sikh bodyguards, in retaliation for that attack.

A reluctant heir to the family dynasty, Rajiv Gandhi, attempted to reclaim the mantle of secularism but many members of the Congress Party had already abandoned any pretense of religious neutrality. Several of the Congress leaders were accused of inciting crowds of Hindus to kill Sikhs in the riots that followed Mrs. Gandhi's death. The communalism which had hidden away within the pleats of Indira's sari, emerged in all its vindictive fury. The Bharatiya Janata Party

(BJP), which espoused the agendas of Hindu nationalism, was rapidly gaining popularity. Instead of countering the voices of hatred and bigotry with the traditional mantras of tolerance and understanding, Congress politicians attempted to coopt the BJP's pro-Hindu stance. Combined with a damaging corruption scandal, this betrayal of Mahatma Gandhi's secular vision alienated the minorities and eventually led to another Congress defeat.

The party reclaimed power only after Rajiv Gandhi died, the victim of a human bomb detonated by Tamil extremists. Narasimha Rao, one of Mrs. Gandhi's loyal sycophants, was able to cobble together a government out of the shattered remains of the 1991 elections. An erudite but enigmatic man, he was eventually brought down by further corruption scandals, though not before he presided over one of the most shameful episodes in Indian history. Narasimha Rao will always be remembered for his inability to stop Hindu extremists from destroying the Babri Masjid in Ayodhya. Through apathy and inaction, Rao and his fellow partymen allowed the pyre of secularism to burn out of control. On 6 December 1992, Congress leaders showed complete indifference as mobs of Hindu zealots attacked and tore down a mosque that was said to have been built on the site of the birthplace of Ram. The dispute in Ayodhya had been festering for centuries, but until this point it had been successfully contained by local authorities. The Hindu-Muslim riots which followed the destruction of the Babri Masjid claimed over two thousand lives in cities all across the country.

Once again religious prejudice, combined with the cynical opportunism of politicians, led to the destruction of not only a religious shrine but a national ideal. As each stone of the Babri Masjid was torn apart by saffron-clad members of the Vishwa Hindu Parishad, India's claims for being a secular democracy were reduced to rubble.

After years of monolithic dominance by the Congress Party, the political equation in New Delhi has changed dramatically and the central government is now a fractious succession of coalitions and alliances. In 1997 Inder Kumar Gujral became prime minister, representing the United Front coalition. In many ways, it seemed appropriate that on the anniversary of India's Independence and Partition, the country's leader should be a former refugee. I. K. Gujral was born in the town of Jhelum, now in Pakistan. As a young man he was active in the Quit

India movement and found his way to Delhi in 1947. He entered politics through the New Delhi Municipal Council and was involved in the resettlement of Punjabi refugees. For many years he was a member of Indira Gandhi's inner circle but fell out of favor after a dispute with her son Sanjay during the Emergency. Leaving the Congress Party he joined the Janata Dal. At seventy-eight years of age, Gujral is the last of a generation of politicians and public servants who came of age during the freedom struggle. Earlier he had served as India's foreign minister and in this capacity made serious efforts for a rapprochement with Pakistan. Perhaps his most forceful statements as prime minister reiterated this desire to establish a lasting peace between the two neighbors. But even as he came to power his authority was tenuous at best and most people didn't give him much chance of holding office beyond the fiftieth anniversary. Though Gujral is generally acknowledged to be a man of integrity, the reputations of his political allies were not as clean. During a speech to the central committee on the Jubilee celebrations he decried corruption in the government but said that there was little that he could do about it because his "hands were tied." The most damaging scandal involved one of Gujral's supporters, the chief minister of Bihar, Laloo Prasad Yadav, who was accused of embezzling a fortune in public funds connected to a government fodder scheme.

From 1982 through 1986, my family and I lived in a residential colony of New Delhi known as Nizamuddin East. We were there when Indira Gandhi was killed, and I witnessed the riots that followed her death on 31 October 1984. Within an hour or two of her assassination the news spread throughout the city, and Delhi braced itself for the inevitable violence. The streets were alive with a collective sense of anxiety and fear. As soon as word got out that the assassins were Sikhs, members of that community were attacked. Even the president of India, Giani Zail Singh, was threatened by a Hindu mob outside the hospital where Indira Gandhi died.

That evening, driving home to Nizamuddin with my family, I passed barricades on the road with burning tires and groups of young men carrying crowbars, pipes and bamboo lathis. Our car was stopped and the rioters surrounded us, peering in through the windows.

"Don't worry," they said, laughing and waving us past. "It's only the Surds [Sikhs] we're looking for." At the side of the road I saw taxis and cars in flames, their windows shattered. The Delhi police were nowhere in sight.

When I went up onto the roof of our house the next morning, I could see columns of smoke rising all across the city. Just north of Nizamuddin East lay Humayun's tomb; its white marble dome was shrouded in a sooty gray pall. In the opposite direction I could hear what sounded like gunfire, a staccato popping sound. Later I learned that these were truck tires bursting. A transport depot off Mathura Road had been attacked and the vehicles, most of which belonged to Sikhs, had been set on fire.

Our landlords, Dr. and Mrs. Amolak Ram Mehta, lived downstairs from us and they both kept saying that it was just like the riots during Partition, except that it was Sikhs who were being attacked in Delhi instead of Muslims. Like so many others in Nizamuddin East, the Mehtas had come to Delhi from Lahore. Wild rumors had already started to circulate and Mrs. Mehta got a phone call from a friend of hers warning that the city's water supply had been poisoned. There were reports that a train had just arrived at Nizamuddin railway station and all the Sikhs on board had been killed. No newspapers were available and on the television there was only somber music and images of Mrs. Gandhi's body lying in state.

Around ten o'clock that morning I heard shouts and cries outside our flat. Going up onto the roof again I saw a crowd of fifty or sixty men coming down the street. They were dragging pipes and lathis that made grating sounds on the pavement. When they reached the park in front of our house the rioters stopped. Our neighbors were watching from all the roofs around and the rioters called to us and told the men to come outside, so that they could make sure there were no Sikhs among us. Many of the nameplates on the gates in our colony had been taken down so that the rioters could not identify which houses belonged to Sikhs.

When I went downstairs and out onto the street, I was able to observe the rioters more closely. All of them were Hindu men in their twenties, most of whom appeared to be day laborers from the juggi colonies beyond the railway tracks. Afterward the newspapers and magazines in Delhi referred to these rioters as "lumpen masses," implying that they were motivated by more than just political anger or religious animosity. The public outrage over Indira Gandhi's death was fueled by frustration and discontentment that had been pent up for years. Many of the juggi colonies had been established as a result of government construction projects, flyovers, and stadiums that had been built for the Asian Games in 1982. During this period, laborers from all over North India had flocked to the city. In the interests of efficiency the municipal authorities turned a blind eye on illegal slums. The vast majority of these laborers had migrated to the city in the hope of sharing some of the capital's prosperity, but after the construction projects were finished they found themselves unemployed. Having served their purpose, by providing cheap labor for government contractors, they were no longer welcome in the capital. Though Mrs. Gandhi was as much to blame for their plight as anyone, she had always appealed to the poorer classes, with popular slogans like "Garibi Hatao!" (Get rid of poverty!). Her sudden assassination ignited communal tensions that had been building up for years. The Sikhs, many of whom were prosperous businessmen — some of them government contractors — provided an obvious target for mob anger. In most cases, though, it was the poorer members of the Sikh community who suffered the most, because they had nowhere to hide.

Perhaps the greatest share of guilt for the riots lies with those who took advantage of this anger and manipulated it for their own vindictive purposes. The Congress Party and other politicians often elicited the support of the so-called lumpen masses. Whenever there were political rallies in the capital, busloads of supporters were gathered up and herded together to provide an audience for campaign speeches. Free transport, money, and food were offered as incentives. After the riots it was clear that some of the party leaders rallied the same constituency in their campaign of violence against the Sikhs. In some cases the rioters were even provided with voter lists to help identify their targets. Added to this was the complete collapse of Delhi's municipal administration and police force. Those officers and constables who were expected to keep the peace were either too frightened to intervene or simply turned a blind eye on the atrocities because of their own communal prejudices.

Standing outside the gate of our house in Nizamuddin, I watched the rioters milling about. Nobody seemed to be in charge, though one or two of them were more excitable than the rest. From time to time they shouted slogans in honor of Indira Gandhi, but having found no Sikhs in our immediate neighborhood the rioters seemed at a loss for what to do next. More than fifteen minutes passed as we stared at them and they stared back at us. I could see the hostility in their eyes but it seemed, at least for the moment, as if they had forgotten why they were there. Several of the rioters squatted down in the shade, smoking cigarettes or bidis. They looked bored and indolent. One of our neighbors tried to reason with them, telling the rioters that they should leave innocent people alone, but before he could finish we heard the sound of a gun being fired a few blocks away. Immediately the rioters picked up their weapons and set off running in the direction of the shots, like a roaming pack of predators.

Hannah Arendt, in her book *Eichmann in Jerusalem*, has referred to the "banality of evil," but I had never encountered it until that day. Those rioters who ordered us out into the street may have been motivated in part by the injustices of caste and class, but in essence they were a mindless mob. As they squatted on the ground or strutted about impatiently, brandishing their lathis, the rioters reminded me of extras on a film set waiting for their cue. These were the men who set fire to cars and buses, who doused their Sikh victims with petrol and set them alight, who raped women and murdered children. But during that quarter of an hour, as the rioters loitered about on the street, I was struck by the utter banality of that scene, a brief hiatus in the rampage.

Twelve years later, I was reminded of those rioters by a similar crowd in front of the Sheila Cinema. I was waiting in line to buy a ticket for an afternoon showing of the Hindi movie *Border*. A disorderly queue stretched out onto the street, mostly men in their twenties or thirties. At that hour on a weekday afternoon, they seemed to have plenty of time on their hands. The temperature outside was a hundred degrees in the shade and the humidity was oppressive. Inside the cinema it was air-conditioned and a fifteen-rupee ticket was a small price to pay for two and a half hours of climate control and a celluloid escape from reality.

On the eve of the fiftieth anniversary of Independence, *Border* was one of the most popular films showing in the cinemas of Delhi. It was based on an episode from the 1971 war against Pakistan and the release of this film had been timed to coincide with the Jubilee celebrations. Fervently patriotic, *Border* portrayed the heroics of a small contingent of Indian soldiers who defended a frontier post called Longewala against an invading force of Pakistani tanks and troops.

This movie had opened two months before I arrived in India and its release had been marred by tragedy. On 13 June an electrical fire had started in the Uphaar Cinema, another theater in Delhi. Fifty-nine people were killed in the blaze. Although the accident cast a shadow over the film, this did not stop the crowds from packing the cinema halls. One of the reasons for many of the deaths at the Uphaar Cinema was the lack of adequate emergency exits. In the aftermath, Delhi's newspapers were full of condemnation for the management of the Uphaar Cinema and there were calls for more effective regulations and building codes, but at the Sheila Cinema there didn't seem to be any extra precautions and only one entrance and exit that I could see.

The cinema may not have met the basic standards of safety, but it did advertise digital sound, which was turned up to full volume during the battle scenes in *Border*. As for the story, it followed a somewhat predictable formula, with all the touches of a Bollywood blockbuster. The multistar cast of characters was stereotypical: a Sikh commanding officer played by Sunny Deol, an anglicized Wing Commander (Jackie Schroff), a Rajput Border Security Force captain (Sunil Shetty) who slept in the sand and called the desert his mother, and the baby-faced teen idol Akshaye Khanna playing an untested lieutenant who had joined the army only because his father had been killed in an earlier war with Pakistan. These male characters each had their women back home — the terrified wife who tried to persuade her husband not to fight, the village sweetheart whose engagement was forestalled by the outbreak of war, the young bride whose husband set off for battle the morning after their wedding night, and the widowed mother in a requisite white sari, who was literally blinded by her own tears. Each of these individual narratives led up to the impending confrontation, when the Indian troops — vastly outnumbered — defeated the Pakistani invaders with guile, determination, and heroic sacrifice.

Though the film attempted to present the tragic contradictions of war, with songs like "Hamara Dushman, Hamara Bhai" (My Enemy, My Brother), the director, J. P. Dutta, kept doubling back on his own ironies with a fiercely antagonistic attitude toward Pakistan. The film made a conscious effort to depict solidarity between the Hindu and Sikh soldiers in the face of a Muslim threat. As a symbol of national integrity the border itself was something that had to be defended unto death. Sitting in the cavernous hall of the Sheila Cinema, I could sense that these messages were getting through to the audience. Every time the Sikh commander, Kuldip Singh, exhorted his men to fight until death, there was an audible murmur of approval, and whenever a Pakistani tank blew up, the gallery whistled and applauded, like unruly spectators at a football match. In this way, the idle frustrations of that cinema crowd — unemployed young men on a weekday afternoon — were infused with violent fantasies. Honor and service to the nation were equated with the sacrificial bloodshed of war. The enemy were clearly the Muslims and through the deceptive magic of the cinematographer's lens those boundary markers which stood along the border were transformed into national shrines, commemorating the dead.

2

MUSSOORIE Maps and Mountains

CHAUKAS POST (Line of Control — Kashmir): . . . On May 16, four Indian soldiers were injured while on patrol in this area in a blast caused by an Impro-
vised Explosive Device (IED) planted by militants aided by the Pakistanis.
"We decided on a fire assault to teach them (the Pakistanis) a lesson," narrated
the Brigade Commander, Brig. J. S. Lidder.
  "On the morning of May 19, we treated them to a super dose," said Brig.
Lidder. The 'super-dose' was actually a no-holds-barred firing of artillery
shells, missiles, rockets, grenades and from machine guns . . . Predictably, the
Pakistanis responded two days later, on May 21, with incessant firing which
led to partial destruction of an Indian bunker containing a vintage Zu-38 anti-
aircraft gun which, however, was unaffected. Since then, relative peace has
prevailed.
  "The lesson was to be clear-cut. We will respond to every act of firing and
killing with compound interest. If you kill one, we will kill five. That's the
message," says Brig. Lidder.—DINESH KUMAR, *Times of India*, 25 July 1997

I reached New Delhi railway station at six-thirty in the morning, well
before the Shetabdi Express was scheduled to depart. A porter bal-
anced my suitcase on top of his head and led the way through streams
of travelers. The metal staircases and walkways were layered with dust
and grime and there was a sour, greasy odor of coal smoke and diesel
in the air. The tracks were littered with scraps of paper and plastic, as
well as piles of human excrement. Passengers for other trains had
spent the night at the station, camped out on the platforms with their
luggage. One man was bathing under a spigot at the side of the tracks,

his body lathered white with soap. He interrupted his ablutions and stepped aside for a shunting engine to go past.

The Indian Railways are the largest system of public transportation in the world, a complex network of tracks that carry over a million passengers a day. Traveling by train is one of the easiest means of moving about the country and often the cheapest. Station platforms in India offer a temporary shelter for passengers who are changing trains. Tea stalls, food carts, and other hawkers provide the basic necessities of life. Despite the transient atmosphere of railway stations — loudspeakers announcing departures or delays — there is a feeling of community on these platforms, a neutral territory where everyone is equal. In a very real sense the Indian Railways serve to unify the nation, kilometers on kilometers of tracks stitching together various parts of the country, cutting through linguistic and regional barriers and bringing together travelers from far-flung states and remote districts.

As I waited for my train to arrive, an inquisitive gentleman in a loose green kurta and spotless white pajama approached and greeted me in English. He had obviously singled me out because I was a foreigner and, discovering that I came from America, he told me that he had visited Atlanta, ten years earlier.

"At present I am traveling to Hardwar," he said, "just for the weekend. My daughter has finished college and we are going to give prayers of thanks."

Within the space of five minutes he had asked me my destination, my age, my marital status and occupation. He had also invited me to stay with him at his house on my return to Delhi. An ingratiating smile revealed a line of tobacco-stained teeth and the impulsive offer of hospitality made me uneasy. When the train pulled up to the platform I quickly said goodbye and hurried off to find my seat.

Those who have money in India have always found ways to isolate themselves from the less fortunate crowds — the Shetabdi is proof of that. My "Executive Class" ticket took me off the soot-smeared platform, away from the flies and filth, and into an air-conditioned carriage with reclining seats and tinted windows. A uniformed attendant offered me a bottle of Yes brand mineral water, chilled and free of germs. A recorded voice with a pretentious accent welcomed us aboard and announced that our journey would cover a distance of 320 kilometers in five and a quarter hours. Rolling out of the station we soon passed over the Jumna River, and before we reached the other side of the bridge two waiters moved down the aisle handing out thermos flasks of tea. The Taj Mahal tea bags and Amul dairy whitener couldn't quite match the flavor of station tea, brewed over a kerosene stove and tempered by the earthy taste of a clay kullar. Even though I was grateful for the comfort of the Shetabdi and the air-conditioning I felt a churlish irritation at the insulated luxuries, especially the tinted windows that wouldn't open. I could look out but nobody could look in.

The carriage wasn't full and the seat beside me was empty. Across the aisle were a couple of college students, overweight and with a dazed look of privilege in their eyes. A bearded retiree in a Lacoste polo shirt sat in front of them reading the *Financial Express*. Ahead were two Europeans wearing suits, accompanied by a Sikh businessman in a starched red turban.

Through the window I could see factories and lower-income housing colonies on the outskirts of Delhi, geometric clusters of colorless flats surrounded by juggis. After we passed through the industrial towns of Gaziabad and Modinagar the scenery improved dramatically. The monsoon rains had been plentiful and the fields were verdant with new crops of millet and sugar cane, rice paddies and vegetable gardens. The Doab, the land between the rivers Jumna and Ganga, is one of the most fertile regions of India; virtually every square foot of arable land provides at least two harvests a year. The rain had washed everything clean and brought out the contrasting colors in the landscape — a mud-walled hut decorated with yellow blossoms on a cucumber vine, the sleek black hide of a buffalo standing in a flooded ditch, the water emerald green with algae, a white egret taking flight from the bank of a canal, two men harvesting lotus stems in a pond covered with lily pads and pale pink blossoms, stacks of orange bricks at a wayside kiln that looked as if they were still glowing from the fire, and an iridescent peacock picking its way along the margins of a freshly plowed field.

Breakfast was served promptly an hour after our departure. We be-

gan the meal with Kellogg's cornflakes — just one example of the recent arrival of multinational corporations in India. The cereal was
made in Mumbai and served with a bowl of hot milk. Soon afterward
the waiters passed down the aisle repeating the familiar refrain: "Veg?
Nonveg?" I chose to be nonvegetarian and regretted my decision immediately: besides bread and jam there was an aluminum dish containing two hard-boiled eggs, limp french fries, and a serving of
cooked peas that hadn't fully recovered from dehydration.

The Shetabdi stops only twice along its route to Dehradun. The
first station is Saharanpur, where a few of the passengers got down to
have a cigarette and stretch their legs. The humidity sucked me out of
the carriage. Flies were hovering around a pool of yellowish liquid on
the platform. Hawkers walked by, selling tea and snacks. This could
easily have been the same platform in New Delhi, from where we had
departed two-and-a-half hours earlier. Saharanpur is an important
junction where the railway lines from Delhi and Calcutta converge
and continue across the Punjab. In a few days I would return to this
station and catch the train which would take me to the border. Famous for its mangoes and wood-carving industry, Saharanpur is one
of many towns in the state of Uttar Pradesh which has a sizable Muslim population. Though many of the Muslims from this region left for
Pakistan in 1947, others stayed behind and they remain the largest minority community in India. Numerically there are more Muslims in
India than in Pakistan, though Kashmir remains the only state in
which they form the majority of the population.

On the railway platform in Saharanpur there were Muslims as well
as Hindus. Some of the women were draped in bourkas, with only
their faces showing, and a few of the Muslim men had white caps on
their heads. Other than the clothes they wore, or the cut of their
beards, it was impossible to tell them apart from the Hindu travelers
at the station.

The Shetabdi continued on toward Hardwar, which is regarded by
Hindus as one of the holiest cities in the subcontinent. It is here that
the river Ganga leaves the mountains, flowing out into the plains of
North India. The monsoon is a season of pilgrimage, when millions of
Hindus travel to Hardwar and carry water from the Ganga back to
their homes. As an act of devotion, many Hindus make the return

journey on foot, walking for several weeks and stopping along the way at roadside temples and dharamshalas.

Whenever the railway line ran parallel to the road I could see a procession of pilgrims from the window of the train. Gangajal, the sacred river water, is carried in small vessels enclosed in bamboo baskets. These are suspended from a bow-shaped yoke that rests on each pilgrim's shoulders. The baskets and the yoke are ornately decorated with tinsel and ribbons, as well as pictures of Hindu gods and goddesses. Most of these pilgrims are men, called kavar or kavarian, and they often chant prayers and slogans as they walk along. This pilgrimage has gained popularity in the past two decades, undoubtedly a result of the growing force of Hindu revivalism. When I was a boy I would see a few thousand of these pilgrims on the road between Delhi and Hardwar but now there is an endless stream of devotees, a river of Hindus carrying Gangajal on their shoulders. At places the crowds of kavarian are so numerous that the traffic on the main highway has to be diverted for their annual migration.

At Hardwar the railway station was full of pilgrims. Many of the devotees were dressed in yellow and wore cotton shawls printed with the names of Ram and Sita. Near a fence by the side of the tracks I watched a group of saffron-clad mendicants, rubbing marijuana leaves between their palms and collecting hashish resin to fuel their spiritual quest. Probably more than any other religion, Hinduism is a faith that relies on public rituals and pageantry, a kind of spiritual exhibitionism. Though the temples and bathing ghats of Hardwar provide a focus of worship, acts of devotion spill into the streets, and even the railway station is included in the sacred precincts of the city. An old pipal tree, growing out of a hole in the cement platform, had been turned into a shrine with incense sticks and garlands of marigolds. Brass pots of Gangajal are available for sale at several of the stalls, though most of the pilgrims collect the water themselves before beginning their homeward journey, back to the towns and villages from which they came.

In most of us there exists a homing instinct that guides us back to the place of our birth. I was born in the hill station of Mussoorie and spent most of my childhood in that town. Though I have lived outside

India for nearly twenty years, I continue to call Mussoorie home. For this reason I made a detour up into the mountains before setting out to cross the border.

From Hardwar the Shetabdi took me on to the railhead of Dehradun. Here I got a seat in a taxi up the hill to Mussoorie. The road climbs steadily, over a distance of thirty kilometers, winding its way up the ridges to an elevation of 7,500 feet. Mussoorie is a summer resort, where tourists escape the heat of the plains, a town of hotels and restaurants that stretch along the mall. The busiest time of the year is May and June, before the monsoon, but even at the end of July traffic jams still clog the narrow streets and the bus stands are full of tourist coaches. Unlike the pilgrims in Hardwar, who project an aura of piety and self-sacrifice, the crowds of middle-class tourists in Mussoorie come up the hill to enjoy themselves.

Garhwali porters scuffled with each other to take my suitcase from the luggage rack. I could have paid the taxi driver to take me farther, but it was a clear day and I was looking forward to walking through the bazaar. Passing familiar shops along the mall, I felt a comforting sense of recognition. Only a year had passed since I was last in Mussoorie but there were changes — the Jubilee Cinema had been turned into a hotel, and the clock tower sported a fresh coat of pink and blue paint, rising above the rusting tin roofs.

After climbing Mullingar Hill, where the motor road corkscrews up the ridge between two lines of tiny shops, I left the bazaar behind. This part of Mussoorie is known as Landour and much of the ridge is forested. The peaked red roofs of summer cottages poke out among the trees. Oakville, our family home, lies at the eastern end of Landour, one of the last buildings on the ridge. From the bus stand it is a five-kilometer walk, along the Tehri Road, past the hospital where I was born and past Woodstock, the mission school which I attended as a boy. By the time I reached home my legs ached and I was out of breath because of the altitude.

The main house at Oakville was built in the 1840s by a British garrison engineer who used it as a hunting lodge. The design is much like colonial bungalows on the plains, with four central rooms, surrounded by deep verandas. Over the years several extensions have been added that give the house a rambling, disorderly appearance, corrugated tin roofs slanting down at uneven angles, as if the white-washed walls had settled in upon themselves.

Coming back to Oakville provokes mixed feelings in me. The place itself is idyllic, with a view of the Dehradun Valley to the south and to the north the snow mountains of Garhwal, Himalayan peaks that rise over twenty thousand feet above sea level. Our house is surrounded by deodar trees and oaks. In the monsoon the garden runs wild, a miniature rain forest of hydrangeas, gladioli, dahlias, and agapanthus lilies. My parents still spend part of the year at Oakville and my cousin owns a cottage next door, but when I arrived the house was deserted, lights off and the rooms in shadow. A monsoon mist had rolled in, blotting out the sun and bringing a damp chill to the air. The place felt empty — a depressing hollowness, almost as if the house had been abandoned.

Walking up the trail from the Tehri Road I had passed several boundary pillars, which mark the limits of our property, and a painted sign at a bend in the path — an arrow pointing the way to Oakville. Here I felt the first stirrings of a territorial instinct, a proprietary impulse charged with emotions. Not only did I belong here but the place belonged to me. Ever since my parents bought the property in the mid-1980s, I have tried unsuccessfully to rationalize my own attachments to Oakville. It seems illogical to feel possessive about a few acres of land that have been in the family for less than two decades. In the past hundred and fifty years the property has had a dozen different owners. And if you consider the centuries over which these mountains and forests were formed — some of the trees are older than the house — the idea of owning this land is nothing more than a symptom of acquisitive human arrogance. The boundary pillars are a vain attempt to claim and control a section of the hill. Yet even on the precipitous slope of that mountain, where the contours of the ridge defy any attempt to draw straight lines, I couldn't help but feel that I was crossing a personal border, stepping into a secure and demarcated space.

Given the panoramic views, it is easy to understand why Mussoorie is a town where maps were made. Looking out across the Dehradun Valley, the plains of North India stretch toward a distant horizon, every contour and physical feature of the landscape etched in precise detail. On a clear day, when the monsoon clouds have lifted, there is an unobstructed view of the River Ganga to the east and the Jumna to the west. The forests, fields, and villages that lie between are like the colored areas on a map, contrasting shades of green and brown. At night you can see the lights of Dehradun, Hardwar, and Saharanpur, more than seventy kilometers away.

The Survey of India has its summer headquarters in Mussoorie at the Castle Hill Estate. Sir George Everest, who conducted the first trigonometrical survey of India and after whom the world's highest mountain is named, came to Mussoorie in the 1830s and lived for a time near Cloud's End. The official benchmark for the first accurate maps of the Himalayas is located at an observatory on the north side of Camel's Back Hill. During the period of the "Great Game," when the British were seeking to extend their empire into Central Asia, survey parties set out from Mussoorie for Tibet, disguised as wandering shepherds.

Cartography has always been one of the prerogatives of empire, mapping out the subjugated regions of the globe. The British were by no means the first to capture their dominions on paper but they were certainly the most fastidious and determined surveyors to ever wield a theodolite. As the accuracy and level of detail in map making increased during the nineteenth century, the development of advanced printing processes made these images accessible to the general public. The power and authority of maps increased enormously and more than any other colonial power the British understood their value. These two-dimensional representations of geographic features and political boundaries became a source of legitimacy for the empire. The scale of British conquests could never be fully appreciated without looking at a map of the world and seeing how that tiny island, off the coast of Europe, had expanded its influence across both hemispheres. By the first half of the twentieth century, these elaborate diagrams of domination were to become the pieces of a modern jigsaw puzzle, as the sprawl of empire gave way to the borders of newly independent nation-states.

At Oakville our family has a collection of old maps, some of which belonged to my grandparents and date back to the 1920s. Most of these were printed before Partition, and a large scale road map depicts the subcontinent as it was under the British, the external borders of India extending up to the Khyber Pass. Unfolding the map and spreading it open on the dining room table I could trace the route I was going to follow, the railway line from Delhi to Saharanpur and on to Amritsar. But there was something disconcerting about a map that did not include the present boundaries. The railway tracks continued, without interruption, toward Lahore, Rawalpindi, and Peshawar. Each of these towns is also located along the Grand Trunk Road, connecting the dots, I tried to imagine where the border now lies. My finger traced an invisible line that ran between Amritsar and Lahore, then circled north into Kashmir.

Without their maps and census data, the British could never have carried through with Partition as swiftly and decisively as they did. The Survey of India provided a geographic and political template for Sir Cyril Radcliffe, who was assigned the task of delineating new borders in 1947. Radcliffe had never been to India before; in fact he had never traveled outside Europe. His ignorance of the subcontinent provided some measure of impartiality, but he was also blind to the realities of the situation. Given just over a month to complete his task, this bookish, bespectacled Englishman never once visited the contested territories of Punjab and Bengal. Locked away in one of Delhi's government bungalows, poring over his maps and charts, Radcliffe carried out his task entirely with pen and paper.

Secrecy was fundamental to the success of this project, and even the viceroy, Lord Louis Mountbatten, was kept in the dark for much of the time. In most accounts of Independence and Partition it is forgotten that even at midnight, on August 14th, neither Jawaharlal Nehru nor Mohammad Ali Jinnah, the new leaders of India and Pakistan, had any idea where the borders had actually been drawn. For this reason, Nehru's ambiguous choice of words in his famous "Tryst with Destiny" speech take on a curious significance. India, he announced, had achieved Independence, "not wholly, or in full measure, but very substantially." Both Nehru and Jinnah knew that they would not be getting all the territory that they had hoped for, and Jinnah later referred to his country's share of the subcontinent as a "moth-eaten Pakistan." The new maps of the subcontinent were not revealed until August 17, more than forty-eight hours after the British handed over power. With

all the confusion, celebrations, and anxieties of Independence, this sequence of events is often overlooked, but given the advantage of historical hindsight it is obvious that the British authorities chose to control the map of India until the final moment of freedom.

Brigadier Hukam Singh Yadav is a long-time resident of Mussoorie.
From 1945 to 1947 he served as Mountbatten's ADC and witnessed
first-hand the transfer of power. I had arranged to meet Brigadier Yadav the day after my arrival in Mussoorie and he invited me to tea.
When I reached his house, he was waiting for me on the veranda. A
tall, imposing man in a wine-red salwar kameez and embroidered
waistcoat, Yadav's eyes were full of fierce conviction. During the Second World War he fought the Japanese in Burma and later started a
school of jungle warfare. Having been a soldier all his life, he is now
retired and serves as president of the Ex-Servicemen's Association. The
brigadier showed me into his sitting room, which was full of memora-
bilia. On a side table stood a silver salver, that had been presented to
him and his wife, Ann, on the occasion of their wedding. The two of
them had met and fallen in love while serving on the viceroy's staff,
and the salver was etched with the signatures of Lord and Lady
Mountbatten. On the wall above my chair, I could see a brass insignia
in the shape of the British crown, which Yadav took as a souvenir from
Mountbatten's Rolls Royce on 15 August 1947.

"I was there at midnight," he said. "We didn't sleep for two whole
days. There was too much excitement. After listening to Nehru's
speech on the radio in Government House, the other Indian ADCs
and I organized a champagne party for the Mountbattens to celebrate
Independence. Earlier that day, we'd flown to Karachi. One of the
aides was a Muslim and he was going over to Pakistan, so we dropped
him off in the viceroy's Dakota."

When he first joined the army, Yadav was commissioned in a regiment called the Frontier Force, which ultimately became a part of Pakistan's army. After 1947 he was reassigned to the Garhwal Rifles and
later to the Grenadiers. Though an Indian patriot to the core, Yadav
staunchly defends Britain's role in the division of India.

"If it hadn't been for the British Empire there wouldn't have been
anything to partition in the first place," he said. "If you ask me, it was

the army that gave India a sense of unity. The soldiers came from all across the country and when they went back to their villages they took the idea of India home with them."

Yadav also credits the army for Independence. "The British weren't afraid of Gandhi and his satyagrahis but when the army began to get restless, that's when they knew they had to leave."

He described an incident in Rawalpindi, during March 1947, when one of the senior officers on Mountbatten's staff gave his assessment of the situation.

"'The game's up, Dicky. We can no longer trust the Indian sepoy. If we don't leave now, it will be 1857 all over again.'"

A lingering fear of mutiny had always haunted the British in India and according to Yadav it led Mountbatten to accelerate the time table for Independence.

"He decided that the transfer of power should take place as soon as possible and persuaded the government back in England to move ahead. It was the only way to keep India within the Commonwealth. The date Mountbatten set for Independence, August 15th, was a sentimental choice. It was the same day that the Japanese surrendered in Singapore and the viceroy wanted to remember those two days as one. Of course there was a slight problem with this. When Jawaharlal Nehru consulted his astrologers they said it was an inauspicious date. In the end they compromised and selected midnight on the fourteenth."

Accompanying Mountbatten on his travels around the subcontinent, Yadav witnessed the violence and atrocities of Partition. In a town on the Pakistan side of the border they saw a whole village of Sikhs who had been slaughtered.

"It was the only time I saw Mountbatten cry," he said. "Earlier we had attended a jirga at Landi Kotal village, on the top of the Khyber Pass. All the Pathan chieftains were there to meet with the viceroy and they were armed to the teeth. The Pathans are very passionate people and they said that they would never allow themselves to be ruled by Hindus. Of course, most of the men that I commanded in the Frontier Force were Pathans, but at that moment I had the unsettling realization that I was the only Hindu in their midst."

I asked Brigadier Yadav whether he kept in touch with his fellow officers in Pakistan and he said that the Frontier Force still sent him invitations to regimental dinners and annual celebrations.

"But I have to be very careful," he explained. "There's such a lot of suspicion, I can't be too cautious. The politicians would misinterpret even the most innocent contacts I might have."

The bookshelves at Oakville contain a jumble of volumes in no specific order, murder mysteries lined up beside works of theology, contemporary novels, Greek classics, travelogues, poetry collections, encyclopedias, children's stories and dog-eared copies of *National Geographic*. Many of these books I remember from my childhood; they formed an important part of my education. Picking through the shelves I eventually found what I was looking for, a copy of Kushwant Singh's *Train To Pakistan*. This novel was one I first read in high school, a cheap Fontana paperback published out of London. The cover depicts a Sikh policeman in a khaki uniform with a bamboo lathi. He is standing over a beautiful woman, who is clearly supposed to be Muslim. She is dressed in a low-cut bodice and harem pants — a British artist's clumsy interpretation of oriental costume. The blurb on the cover summarizes the contents: "rioting, bloodshed and murder on the Indo-Pakistan border."

Kushwant Singh's novel made a strong impression on me when I read it as a teenager. His depictions of the senseless violence of Partition are wrapped up in a romantic story of lovers torn apart by religious hatred. The most interesting and enigmatic character in the book is a man named Iqbal, a communist social worker who arrives at a border village, presumably to help organize support for his party. The name Iqbal, as Kushwant Singh explains for his Western readers, can belong to either a Muslim, Sikh, or Hindu, an irony that underscores the uncertainties of the situation.

The inability of the government to control sectarian violence is epitomized by the District Magistrate, a decadent Hindu, who arrives at the circuit house and ignores the mounting violence. The tragic lovers in this story are Jaggat Singh, a Sikh goonda, or thug, and Noora, the Muslim weaver's daughter. Immediately after Partition, Noora and her family flee across the border and Jaggat Singh dies a heroic death as he saves her life. Kushwant Singh writes with a lively, boisterous style, celebrating the earthy qualities of his Punjabi characters. Despite its sensationalism, *Train to Pakistan* remains an important novel because it captures in horrific detail one of the most powerful and grotesque symbols of Partition; the trainloads of corpses that crossed the border in both directions.

Kushwant Singh has also written a multivolume *History of the Sikhs*, a scholarly account of his own community's heritage. One of Delhi's best-known literary figures, he has received many national awards and was appointed as a member of the Rajya Sabha. For years Singh was a loyal supporter of Indira Gandhi, but he broke with her when she ordered the attack on the Golden Temple in Amritsar. Now in his eighties, he is a member of the first generation of what were called Indo-Anglian writers, who chose to express themselves in English. A former editor of the *Illustrated Weekly of India*, Kushwant Singh often presents himself as a cranky commentator on social and political issues. Even though he is best known for his self-professed love of Scotch whisky and dirty jokes, he has a sober eye for the events surrounding Partition. In a collection of essays titled *Kushwant Singh's View of India* he has written, "Though the English gave India its unity, they were also responsible for its disunity and ultimate break-up into India and Pakistan. They played the divide-and-rule game with little subtlety."[1]

Another book that I rediscovered at Oakville was Nirad Chaudhuri's *The Continent of Circe*. Born in a region of Bengal that became East Pakistan and later Bangladesh, he too experienced first-hand the tumult of Partition and has written about that period with strong opinions.

> I assert this with confidence that not even at the end of 1946 did anybody in India believe in the possibility of a partition of the country. Yet within six months it was announced as a policy and accepted as a proposal and in less than three months from the announcement of the plan the monstrous and unnatural partition of India became a fact. The Hindus and the British alike foreswore the principal of unity of India which they had always professed. This was made possible by a combination of three factors — Hindu stupidity in the first instance and Hindu cowardice afterwards, British opportunism, and Muslim fanaticism.[2]

Nirad Chaudhuri celebrated his hundredth birthday in 1997 — he was fifty at the time of Independence and Partition and died only recently, on 1 August 1999. Few writers can boast such a breadth of historical experience and his books have a monumental quality. He writes with a first-person perspective that literally spans the twentieth century. Even more than Kushwant Singh, Nirad Chaudhuri presents himself as an iconoclast. He has often been unjustly savaged in the Indian press because he was perceived as an apologist for British rule. Chaudhuri first gained notoriety with his *Autobiography of an Unknown Indian*, which he mischievously dedicated to "The British Empire." Only in the last few years has he enjoyed a belated rehabilitation amongst Indian critics, and a 1997 profile in the magazine *India Today* declared that "With his formidable scholarship, he combines the best of Hindu conservatism and European enlightenment."[3]

Part of the reason for the controversies surrounding Chaudhuri's books is the unrelenting criticism leveled against India's freedom fighters, particularly Gandhi and Nehru. He decries both their methods and their motivations: "Between (Ashoka's) unnecessary proclamation of non-violence in the third century B.C. and its reassertion, largely futile, in the twentieth century by Mahatma Gandhi, there is not *one word* of non-violence in the theory and practice of statecraft by the Hindus."[4] Later in the same book he goes on to say that Nehru "is by social and cultural affiliations, more a Muslim than a Hindu, so far as he is anything Indian at all. His family belonged to the circle of Islamicized Hindus. . . . Nehru had no understanding of Hinduism and not even any liking for it."[5]

An ardent Anglophile on the one hand and a traditional Hindu on the other, Nirad Chaudhuri's opinions would strike most readers as contradictory. But more than anything, Chaudhuri is fundamentally a Bengali intellectual, a role in which he relishes paradox and displays a rhetorical dexterity that can juggle a variety of contrary opinions in a most convincing manner.

Regional stereotypes are a fundamental part of Indian culture and in many ways Kushwant Singh and Nirad Chaudhuri represent two cultural extremes. Singh epitomizes the plainspoken earthiness of the Punjab, while Nirad Chaudhuri is the quintessential Bengali, a brilliant obscurantist and aesthete. Even though these generalizations could never withstand rational scrutiny, they are certainly a part of popular prejudice in India. Both geographically and culturally, Punjab and Bengal represent the parenthetical limits of the subcontinent. The two cultures are often regarded as opposites but they are also mirror images of each other and the crisis of Partition served to heighten and emphasize this contrast.

Both regions experienced a division of their soil and the inevitable migration of refugees. For Pakistan, which came into being as a country with two separate halves — like the proverbial twins separated at birth — the consequences were far greater. The tenuous links between its eastern and western territories were ultimately doomed to fail. The Muslims of Punjab and Sindh were as different in culture and outlook from the Muslims of Bengal as they were from most Hindus and Sikhs. This inherent incompatibility was exacerbated by the physical distance between the two wings of the country and the economic exploitation of East Pakistan by an oppressive regime in the west. Twenty-five years after Independence the country inevitably split in two with the liberation of Bangladesh. India aided the Bengali freedom fighters and took part in the military conflict, but the fissure which led to Pakistan's disintegration already existed from the time of Partition.

Within India as well, contrasts between the two cultures of Punjab and Bengal became even more evident following Independence. Because of the flight of Muslims across the border, a far greater homogeneity resulted in these two regions. Added to this was an influx of refugees who had lost their homes and were searching for a new identity. Faced with a truncated and displaced culture, Punjabis and Bengalis became even more acutely aware of their heritage and their homelands. For a country like India, which is sustained by the ideals of unity and integration, this kind of linguistic, ethnic, and regional chauvinism poses a serious problem. It is not surprising that during the first fifty years of India's Independence, two of the most politically volatile and troubled regions of the subcontinent have been Punjab and West Bengal.

Reading the works of Kushwant Singh and Nirad Chaudhuri, one can begin to understand some of the divisions that have existed in modern India over the past fifty years. At the same time, despite their differences, these two writers tend to complement each other, both literally and figuratively. In his introduction to *The Continent of Circe*, Chaudhuri offers a long note of gratitude to Kushwant Singh, whom he says is "the only fellow-Indian (significantly a Sikh, and not a Hindu) who has put in good words for me in print in India. This needed courage."[6] These two writers disagree with each other on many points, and offer conflicting perspectives and sensibilities, yet their books undoubtedly belong on the same shelf.

From the Railway Out Agency in Mussoorie I had been able to get a booking on the Golden Temple Mail to Amritsar. This train, which used to be known as the Frontier Mail and originally went all the way from Bombay to Peshawar, stopped in Saharanpur around midnight. I had arranged for a car to take me to the station in Saharanpur and we set off at six in the evening. Before starting his engine I overheard the driver reciting a Muslim prayer, "Bismillah ar-Rahman ar-Rahim." He was an elderly man, named Yasin Mohammed, with a cropped white beard.

"Are you catching the Frontier Mail?" he asked. Like most people he still referred to the train by its original name.

"Yes, I'm going to Amritsar, then on to Pakistan."

He didn't answer me immediately, but I could tell that he was absorbing this information.

"Where will you go in Pakistan?" he asked.

"Lahore. Peshawar. Rawalpindi. Murree."

He fell silent again, as the car wound its way around the hairpin bends.

"Have you ever been to Pakistan?" I asked.

"No. But my brother lives there. In Karachi. He came to visit us fifteen years ago. I also have a brother-in-law in Rawalpindi but we have lost touch with him."

"Your brother moved there in forty-seven?"

"Yes. He worked for the PWD and decided he could not stay here. That was his choice."

"You didn't want to go?"

Yasin Mohammed shook his head and his silence conveyed a reticence that I had noticed in others. Muslims in India are often unjustly portrayed as sympathizing with Pakistan. Hindu fanatics accuse them of everything from espionage and treason to cheering for the wrong side during cricket matches between the two countries. Though there may be some Muslims whose loyalties are divided, the vast majority have always been an integral part Indian society and culture. Because of the bitter memories of Partition and the rising fervor of Hindu fundamentalism, Indian Muslims have inevitably been put on the defensive, when it comes to questions of national allegiance.

Only the day before, when I was talking with a Muslim tailor in the Mussoorie bazaar, I had glimpsed a furtiveness in his eyes when I mentioned that I was going to Pakistan. He too had shrugged off my questions, as if I were prying into a personal matter. Just the mention of crossing the border aroused suspicion and even one of my closest friends in Mussoorie suggested that I must be working for the CIA because I was traveling to Pakistan.

"I've heard Peshawar is a wonderful place," said Yasin Mohammed. "You get dried fruit there and almonds. All of the men are dressed in salwar kameez. Nobody wears bush shirts and people walk about with an air of confidence."

The implication was that Muslims in Pakistan were free to exert their culture and their pride, unlike Muslims in India, who were kept in check by the Hindu majority. Yasin Mohammed spoke in an oblique manner, with hand gestures that told me more than his words. When I pressed him about his opinions on the threat of Hindu fundamentalism, he deliberately changed the subject.

"Things are very bad now," he said. "You cannot trust anyone anymore."

We stopped at the taxi stand in Dehradun and Yasin Mohammed explained that he would let his son, Farman, drive me the rest of the way.

"Khuda Hafez," he said. "God be with you."

By this time it was dark and after another hour of driving Farman and I came to a crossroads, where the highway from Hardwar joined our route. Ahead of us we could see lines of Hindu pilgrims carrying

Gangajal. The lights of passing vehicles lit up the mirrors and other ornaments on their baskets. Farman was impatient to keep moving and blew his horn when the pilgrims strayed onto the road.

"I have to drive slowly," he said apologetically. "If we were to have an accident with one of these pilgrims, even if it wasn't my fault, they'd kill us and burn the car."

Though he didn't say it, the fact that he was a Muslim and the pilgrims were Hindus made him even more conscious of the threat. On the outskirts of Saharanpur the crowds grew thicker and we had to keep stopping to let the pilgrims cross the road. When Farman finally drove up to the railway station, the main building looked as if it was under siege. To get from the parking lot to the platform I had to step over hundreds of sleeping pilgrims who had spread themselves on the cement floors underneath the ceiling fans.

The first-class waiting room was just as crowded and the electricity kept going off. Suffocating in the heat, I finally made my way to the opposite platform to wait for my train. Even the overhead walkways were packed with pilgrims who had camped there for the night, and I had to cross over by jumping down onto the tracks and scrambling up the other side. Several trains passed through the station before mine arrived, and each of them had pilgrims riding on the roof, carrying baskets of Gangajal. The decorative tinsel gave the carriages a festive look, like glittering floats in a parade. Over the loudspeaker system, a shrill voice kept repeating a warning that there were electric wires on ahead and that people on the carriage roofs should get down, but nobody paid any attention. On one of the station pillars, next to where I was standing, I saw a sign with a slogan in Hindi: "Kashmir sey Kanyakumari tak Bharat ek hai." From Kashmir to Kanyakumari, India is one.

3

AMRITSAR City of Nectar and Gold

Dehradun: Local police and intelligence agencies suspect the hand of some Kashmiri militant outfit behind the minor blast which took place in a coach of the Howrah-bound 3010 Dn Doon Express, near Moradabad last week. (A suspect) bears 60 percent resemblance to the features of a common Kashmiri youth. —*Indian Express*, 30 July 1997

The Golden Temple Mail was scheduled to arrive in Amritsar at six o'clock in the morning. The only other passenger in the air-conditioned compartment had been asleep when I boarded the train at Saharanpur. As we got up, the two of us nodded to each other. The man was a few years younger than I, in his mid-thirties, with thinning hair and wire-rimmed glasses pinching his face into a look of bleary-eyed curiosity. Speaking in English, he asked if this was my first visit to Amritsar. I replied that I had been there a couple of times before, but not since the late seventies. He handed me his card: Arjun Mehra, gold merchant. His family owned a small workshop in Amritsar that produced wedding ornaments, mostly for export to Indian communities abroad.

As soon as he learned that I was on my way to Pakistan, Arjun Mehra became intensely interested. He told me that his family was originally from Sialkot, a town across the border. As Hindus they had been forced to leave their home and move to Amritsar at the time of Partition. Arjun Mehra was born long after 1947 and had never been to Sialkot, even though it was less than a hundred kilometers away. He said that he had always been curious to know what it was like in Pakistan. After I explained that my grandparents had once lived in Sialkot, he insisted that I come to his house immediately and meet his family. By this time the train was already pulling into Amritsar.

A Maruti car was waiting for Arjun outside the railway station and, waving aside my protests, he had the driver load my suitcase into the boot. All the way home he kept quizzing me about my itinerary, as if the names of each of the towns I planned to visit in Pakistan were answers to a riddle that he had been worrying over for years.

His family seemed bewildered and amused by my arrival. They lived in a modern two-story house off a narrow lane, which is barely wide enough for the car. There was a heavy metal gate across the driveway and cast-iron grills on the windows. As with most middle-class homes in India, it was a joint family residence, with grandparents, parents, children, and other relatives living under the same roof. Arjun introduced me to his wife Annu and their two sons, Navin and Kapil. The boys had just woken up and were getting ready for school. The grandparents were drinking tea on the veranda, along with an uncle who was staying in the house.

After a few awkward pleasantries I was offered a cup of tea and biscuits. Arjun's father, Randhir Mehra, spoke Punjabi and a little Hindi. He was a short, stocky man, whose face showed his age, though his hair was dyed jet-black. His wife remained silent and after a few minutes disappeared. When Arjun told his father that I was going to Pakistan, Randhir Mehra showed no interest at all and asked me instead about Mussoorie. He said that he had just returned from there a week ago. Being retired he enjoyed the chance to go up to the hills every summer and escape the oppressive heat and humidity of the Punjab.

Though his father seemed reluctant to talk about their former home in Pakistan, Arjun kept pestering him to tell me details. Randhir Mehra said that they had owned a gold business in Sialkot but that everything had been lost in 1947.

"Have you ever gone back?"

"Only once," he said. "I got a temporary visa to watch a cricket match between India and Pakistan in the early fifties. We were supposed to stay in Lahore but a couple of us caught a bus and went back to visit Sialkot."

"Did anyone recognize you there?"

"A few people remembered us but we didn't stay very long. Things had changed."

At this point one of the boys switched on the television. A woman announcer, with her head covered, appeared on the screen and Arjun pointed to the TV.

"We get all of the Pakistani programs here, from across the border," he said. "Sometimes it's interesting to watch."

His father nodded.

"I enjoy listening to the Urdu ghazals and we follow some of the serial dramas," he said. "But their news is always slanted against India. You can never be sure what's true or not."

Growing impatient, the boys flipped to another channel that was playing songs from Hindi films, costumed dancers squirming to a disco beat.

After we had talked for about an hour, I asked to be excused so that I could check into a hotel. Arjun tried to persuade me to stay at his house but I could see that it would have been an imposition on the family. As I was about to leave, his father told me to wait a moment. He got up slowly and went across to a bookcase on the opposite side of the room. Pulling out a file he flipped through the contents, then handed me an old document, printed on heavy paper and torn at the creases. Most of the writing was in Urdu, with scribbled dates and numbers. The smeared patterns of ink from rubber stamps looked like purple bruises.

"That's my old ration card," he said, with a hesitant smile. "From Sialkot. Don't ask me why I've kept it."

The yellowed paper seemed ready to fall apart in my hands. A column of cryptic numerals tallied up the monthly quotas of flour, rice, and cooking oil — the basic staples of life — which had been bought more than fifty years before. Yet for Randhir Mohan the ration card had a much greater significance; it was a record of the past, a faded symbol of identity, proof of his name, his family, his origins. His reluctance to speak about Partition came from a private sense of loss, and this document I held in my hands was probably the only tangible evidence he possessed of his former home. When I returned the ration card, Randhir Mohan slipped it back into his file and carefully tucked the papers away inside the bookcase.

Punjab has always been the traditional homeland of the Sikhs, ever since their religion was founded by Guru Nanak in 1499. A wandering sage and holy man, Nanak was born in the village of Talwandi Rai Bhoe, now located in Pakistan. He was one of the Bhakti poets, part of a charismatic spiritual movement that flourished in the sixteenth century and included a number of religious reformers like Kabir, Tulsidas, and Mirabai. The underlying spirit of the Bhakti poets was one of reconciliation between religions. Influenced by the ecstatic mysticism of the Sufis, the Bhakti poets promoted an individual search for God, through worship and meditation. Guru Nanak preached an eclectic doctrine of monotheism that borrowed from both Hindu and Muslim theology. Wandering throughout the Punjab, he composed a series of hymns which form the basis of the Sikh scriptures. Rejecting the caste system and the exploitation of Brahmin priests, Guru Nanak promoted the ideals of equality and brotherhood. He declared, "There is no Hindu, there is no Mussalman."[1] The religion which he started grew and flourished under a succession of ten Gurus, each of whom helped shape the faith and doctrines of the Sikhs.

Though Guru Nanak's preachings share many of the same basic tenets of Islam, this new sect was ultimately seen as a threat by the Mughals. Under the emperor Aurangzeb, also known as Alamgir, the Sikhs were attacked and persecuted for their beliefs. The eighth and ninth Gurus, Arjun Singh and Tegh Bahadur, died at the hands of the Mughal authorities. Gobind Singh, the tenth and final Guru, rallied a Sikh army to fight against Aurangzeb and his feudal chieftains. It was during this period, the early part of the seventeenth century, that the Sikhs adopted a militaristic culture that has remained a part of their religion and identity. The Khalsa, Sikh warriors and defenders of the faith, were called to arms under Guru Gobind Singh, who established rituals of weaponry and martial emblems. According to his dictates, most Sikhs distinguish themselves from others by wearing the "five K's": kes (uncut hair and beard), kirpan (sword or dagger), kara (steel bracelet), kanga (a comb often worn inside the turban), and kutcha (undershorts that facilitate horse riding). Sikhs are also forbidden to smoke tobacco and are supposed to abstain from alcohol and other intoxicants.

The historical animosity between Sikhs and Muslims stems from the Mughal period, based in part on the martyrdom of Arjun Singh and Tegh Bahadur, as well as the murder of Guru Gobind Singh's two young sons. Over time these struggles have been synthesized into a narrative of conflict, which only added to the vengeance of Partition. Yet the truth behind these stories is far more convoluted than popular history would suggest. M. J. Akbar's study of the Sikh separatist movement in the Punjab, *India: The Siege Within*, details some of the contradictions. He writes that Guru Gobind Singh's army included a contingent of Muslim Pathans who fought with him against the Mughals and saved his life on more than one occasion. Aurangzeb's army, on the other hand, was made up of Hindu Rajputs as well as Muslim troops. And in the end, Guru Gobind Singh actually helped Aurangzeb's successor, Bahadur Shah, retain the Mughal throne. Conscious of the way in which historical truth is manipulated by religious bigotry, Akbar writes:

> Religion was only another weapon in the extensive armoury of the feudal class; one king might use it to a greater or lesser degree as his perceptions of his needs determined his decisions. The trouble with history is not the fact but the memory. A selection of incidents is funnelled into the popular imagination to serve the interests of a political elite . . . Such partial history was drummed into the Sikh psyche, particularly during the second half of the nineteenth century when the Hindu revivalists were anxious to ensure a united front against the Muslims. Till the creation of Pakistan, this suited the Sikh leadership very well too, and so the mental landscape of the community was crowded with calendar art showing blood spurting from the severed head of Guru Tegh Bahadur or, more evocatively, the death of the minor sons of Guru Govind Singh.[2]

The height of Sikh power in the Punjab came in the first half of the nineteenth century under Maharajah Ranjit Singh, who extended his domain across the Punjab. His kingdom stretched from as far north as Tibet and the foothills of Afghanistan, to the River Jumna, which flows past Delhi. Ranjit Singh wrested control of these territories from the decadent and crumbling remnants of the Mughal Empire and symbolically he ruled his kingdom from Aurangzeb's fortress in Lahore. The Sikh armies were finally defeated by the East India Company forces in 1849, but their determination and valor earned the admiration of the British. Categorized as one of the "martial races" of India, Sikh regiments were an essential element of the colonial military, fighting in both the first and Second World Wars. Even today the Sikhs are an important part of the Indian Army, serving in proportionately larger numbers than any other community.

Despite the fact that their homeland had been taken over by the British, the Sikhs retained territorial prerogatives in the Punjab. Unlike Muslims and Hindus who were scattered across the subcontinent and divided by regional and ethnic conflicts, the vast majority of Sikhs saw themselves as Punjabis, at least until Partition. It was only after 1947 that the Sikh community emigrated in large numbers and made their homes throughout India and other parts of the world. The Punjabi language is also known as Gurmukhi (language of the Gurus) and the followers of Nanak took pride in their agrarian roots, celebrating not only their martial spirit but their success as farmers. This connection with the land is an essential part of Sikh tradition, a deep-rooted affinity to the soil and the five rivers that give Punjab its name. It is significant that Punjab was the center of the "green revolution" in the 1960s when Sikh farmers were hailed as patriotic heroes, feeding the nation.

Yet more than any other community in India, the Sikhs felt betrayed and embittered by the events of Partition. In the months immediately following 15 August, 1947, the Sikhs were responsible for some of the most violent acts of retribution and vengeance against Muslims. Even the Sikh soldiers, who were still under British command, took part in the bloodshed and violence. They blamed not only the Muslims but also the Congress Party politicians who had capitulated on the issue of Partition.

The division of the Punjab created an acute crisis of identity for the Sikh community. As V. S. Naipaul has written, "The establishing of a

Sikh identity was a recurring Sikh need. Religion was the basis of this identity; religion provided the emotional charge."[3] In the violent and tumultuous circumstances of 1947, many Sikhs turned to their militant traditions rather than to the peaceful and conciliatory preachings of Guru Nanak.

> In this faith, when the world became too much for men, the religion of the 10th Guru, Guru Gobind Singh, the religion of gesture and symbol, came more easily than the philosophy and poetry of the first Guru. It was easier to go back to the formal baptismal faith of Guru Gobind Singh, to all the things that separated the believer from the rest of the world. Religion became the identification with the sufferings and persecution of the later Gurus: the call to battle.[4]

With the creation of Pakistan and the flight of virtually every Muslim from the Indian portion of the Punjab, Sikhs found themselves to be the largest minority in that region. This would inevitably lead to a confrontation with the Hindu majority. Partition also brought to the surface aspirations for a separate Sikh homeland, which had been proposed at various times during the freedom struggle. The more radical leaders of the Akali Dal, a political party which sought to represent the Sikhs, advocated much greater autonomy within the Indian union. In 1966, as a result of Hindu-Sikh tensions stemming in part from linguistic disputes, the Punjab was once again divided into two separate states, Harayana and Punjab. The former included predominately Hindu populations to the south and east, while the latter, now almost a quarter of its original size, became the center of Sikh political power. This division may have satisfied sectarian politicians at the time but it did not end the acrimony and tension between radical Sikhs and Hindu nationalists. One particular flashpoint was the city of Chandigarh, constructed out of reinforced concrete by the French architect Le Corbusier. Both Harayana and Punjab claimed Chandigarh as their capital, and a messy compromise allowed the two states to share the city for several decades. Ironically, in a region where ancient habitation is often used to justify territorial claims, some of the most emotional battles were fought over an entirely modern city that was built from the ground up in the 1950s.

The land of five rivers, which the British took away from Maharajah Ranjit Singh in 1849, had now been dismembered beyond recognition. These divisions were meant to defuse communal tensions, yet they seemed to solve nothing and led to increased upheaval and suffering. The creation of new borders and boundaries only heightened the animosity between Sikhs and Hindus, giving renewed urgency to the battle cry of Guru Gobind Singh: "Raj karega Khalsa, Baaqi rahe na koe."[5] The Khalsa will rule and nobody else will remain.

The Golden Temple, holiest of Sikh shrines, lies at the heart of the walled city of Amritsar. In the narrow, congested streets bicycle rickshaws remain the most convenient form of transport, and the drivers weave through swarms of pedestrians, ringing their bells to clear the way. I entered the walled city through Gandhi Gate, which was decorated for the arrival of the Congress Party President, Sita Ram Kesri, who was coming to Amritsar as part of the Jubilee celebrations. Streamers of gold and silver tinsel had been strung from the balconies overhead and banners had been erected every fifty feet, offering felicitations from local members of the Congress Party. But the crowds in the bazaar seemed to ignore these decorations and the market was alive with commercial activity. There were dozens of "Pugri shops," selling turbans and I saw a sign for the "Guru Nanak Computer School (for girls only)." Further on we passed a "Spiritual Museum for Character Development," hemmed in by dozens of fabric stores. Amritsar is well known for its cloth mills and my rickshaw driver assured me that it was the best place to purchase woolen fabrics. With the temperature close to a hundred degrees, however, and humidity pressing in around me like damp felt, the last thing I wanted to buy was a suit-length of heavy tweed or a woolen blanket.

A square arcade of shops and offices surrounds the Golden Temple. Most of this market caters to Sikh pilgrims and there are shops selling kirpans of every size and shape, from small daggers with a curved blade to ceremonial swords in velvet sheaths. Near the main gate is a visitor's information center, where I stopped to ask directions. The man behind the desk was a tall, dignified Sikh with an orange turban and free-flowing beard. He explained that I could take my camera inside but that I should leave my shoes and socks in a pigeonhole at the back of the office, along with any tobacco or alcohol that I might be carrying. I was also required to cover my head before entering the sanctuary.

The temple itself, known as the Har Mandir, stands at the center of a square tank of water, its gilded walls and domes almost blinding in the midmorning sun. A white marble promenade, the parikrama, surrounds the tank, with shaded galleries on all four sides. Hundreds of pilgrims were circling the temple, most of them Sikhs but many Hindus as well. Some of the men were stripping off their clothes and preparing to bathe. Dressed only in their undershorts they descended the marble steps and plunged into the murky depths of the tank. Women prostrated themselves and dipped their hands into the water to drink. This water is regarded as nectar, or amrit, from which the city of Amritsar gets its name. At several places there were trees growing at the edge of the promenade, their trunks and branches polished smooth by the hands of pilgrims. The sun baked down on the marble floors and jute carpets had been laid out so that visitors wouldn't burn their feet. The walls were covered with memorial plaques and inscriptions, many of them bearing the names of Sikh officers and soldiers who had died in the two world wars and the battles with Pakistan. From the temple a musical recitation of the scriptures, or kirtan, was broadcast over loudspeakers. A mood of contemplation and sanctity enveloped the clusters of worshippers circumambulating the tank and bathing in its sacred waters. Even the Nihang Sikhs, members of an ultramartial sect, armed with swords and bows and arrows, their blue turbans decorated with circlets of steel, seemed to be at peace.

At the eastern end of the sanctuary is a langar and dharamshala, where visitors are given free food and shelter. The kitchens are mostly staffed by volunteers. A steady stream of people were sitting down to eat, and when they finished they each stood up and took their turn helping with the cooking and serving. Mounds of wholewheat flour were being kneaded by muscular young men, while a group of women rolled the dough into balls that were then flattened between their hands to make rotis. These circular loaves of bread were tossed onto a giant griddle, almost ten feet in diameter. Another team of volunteers flipped the rotis as they cooked. All the food and fuel in the langar comes from offerings that are donated by pilgrims and wealthy benefactors. Each devotee who visits the temple contributes his or her share of the work. A young boy, six or seven years old, his long hair twisted into an unruly topknot, sat in front of a trough full of ash and sand. He was busy scrubbing stainless steel bowls and glasses that are used for drinking water and sweetened sharbat. The Sikh religion has always emphasized the importance of community service, and within the temple precincts there is an atmosphere of collective harmony.

Completely covered in gold leaf, the Har Mandir is the focus of devotion. Its gilded walls and dome were built by Maharajah Ranjit Singh, though the foundation stone is said to have been laid by a Muslim Sufi. There are no idols in the temple and worship centers around the *Granth Sahib*, the Sikh scriptures. A continuous singing of Guru Nanak's hymns can be heard over the loudspeakers and the priests, dressed in white robes and wearing dark blue turbans, sit at the heart of the inner sanctum. The gold leaf on the walls has been worked into elaborate floral patterns. The *Granth Sahib* itself is wrapped in embroidered velvet and men with flywhisks stand sentinel. Pilgrims cross a marble bridge that leads to the temple and, shuffling slowly forward, they circle a narrow balcony, peering in at the priests who sit on cushions that cover the floor. As the devotees leave the temple and file back across the bridge, they are given prasad to eat, a sweet halwa made of semolina, sugar, and ghee. Prasad is a symbol of spiritual sustenance and blessing.

Despite the peaceful atmosphere of reverence and devotion the Golden Temple has a violent history. In June 1984 this complex was the scene of an intense gun battle that killed several hundred people and left many of the surrounding buildings destroyed. At the height of the Sikh separatist agitation, Jarnail Singh Bhindranwale, who led a guerrilla war against the Indian government, took refuge in the Golden Temple along with his lieutenants and a large cache of arms. After a prolonged siege Indira Gandhi ordered the army to enter the temple. For many Sikhs, even those who did not support the separatists, this was an act of sacrilege. Most of the bullet holes on the temple walls have now been patched, and the Akal Takht, a building badly damaged in the fighting, has been completely rebuilt. For the time being the separatist agitations in the Punjab have been suppressed, though the temple still evokes an aura of martyrdom.

The roots of the Sikh separatist movement in the Punjab can be traced to the aftermath of Partition. It only came to a head during the 1980s, however, when militant members of the Sikh community, supported by expatriates in Canada and England, called for an independent nation of "Khalistan." The Indian government's response to this threat was predictably ruthless, but the irony of the situation was that Congress Party politicians were the ones who actually helped fan the flames of separatism. Indira Gandhi's stalwarts, men like Giani Zail Singh, who would later become president, provided support and legitimacy to Sikh militants in an effort to undermine the political power of moderates in the Akali Dal.

Jarnail Singh Bhindranwale, a fiery small-town preacher and activist, was propelled to a position of notoriety and influence through a political power play that went awry. He combined fundamentalist rhetoric with the rustic appeal of grassroots populism. Bhindranwale gave voice to the frustrations of Partition and the desire for an independent Sikh homeland in the Punjab. He advocated the use of violence as a means toward secession and surrounded himself with armed militants, using the martial symbolism of his faith. Adopting the title of Sant, or Saint, he took on the mantle of Guru Gobind Singh. The iconography of Sikh resistance and martyrdom became a central part of Bhindranwale's campaign, even before he took refuge in the Golden Temple.

As Punjab's law-and-order situation deteriorated in the early 1980s, and with growing support for the separatists coming from Sikh communities abroad, a tragic confrontation was set in motion. Bhindranwale's intransigence, combined with the incompetence of government, police, and military officials, allowed the crisis to escalate and erupt. Most commentators agree that until this point the majority of Sikhs did not support Bhindranwale and his fellow separatists. The campaign of terror that the militants launched in the Punjab hurt the region economically and caused many people to turn against them, even though they lived in fear of extortion and murder. But the Indian army's siege and attack on the Golden Temple (code named Operation Bluestar) was a wholesale military assault against the most sacred shrine of the Sikhs. Bhindranwale may have embarrassed and outraged members of his community by holing up in the temple precincts, but the army's desecration of the shrine led to widespread disillusionment and despair. Newspaper and television images of shattered walls and gutted sanctuaries, tanks and artillery, pools of blood on the marble floors and the bullet-riddled bodies of teenage militants left most Sikhs with a communal sense of violation. Their disillusionment and fear was reaffirmed, six months later, by the anti-Sikh riots that followed Indira Gandhi's death.

Not far from the Golden Temple is Jallianwala Bagh, a walled garden in which another massacre took place. It was here that the British general R. E. H. Dyer opened fire on a crowd of Indian freedom fighters in 1919, killing and wounding several hundred innocent protesters. This was a turning point in the struggle for Independence and a reminder of the brutal side of British rule. The garden is maintained as a memorial and here the bullet holes are carefully preserved and marked, as is an ancient well at the center of the garden into which the dead and dying fell under a fusillade of British bullets. As part of the Jubilee celebrations, the queen of England was scheduled to visit Amritsar, but a controversy arose when descendants of the victims of Jallianwala Bagh demanded that she offer an official apology for the incident. Eventually the queen's visit to Amritsar was discreetly canceled to avoid embarrassment.

The contemporary lexicon of resistance offers a number of curious paradoxes. For example, the expressions "separatism" or "separatist" do not carry the same positive connotations as "revolution" or "revolutionary." By most definitions, a separatist is someone who seeks to break away from the center and challenges the unity of a country. For many people the term suggests a resurgent form of feudalism, signaling the eventual collapse of nation states. Whereas revolutionaries once struggled to change society and brought about equality and freedom, separatists are supposedly hell-bent on fragmentation and encouraging hatred between different ethnic and religious communities. They are seen as promoting political divisions and having no interest in reconciliation or compromise. On an escalating scale of semantics, some people prefer to call them "extremists" or "terrorists," synonyms that carry an even greater note of fear and admonition.

Yet the most basic democratic ideal of self-determination is what motivates all separatists, many of whom would undoubtedly prefer to be known as revolutionaries or freedom fighters. In a sense, Mahatma Gandhi and Jawaharlal Nehru were both separatists, struggling to break away from the British Empire. Modern history has forgiven the divisive strategies of India's founding fathers, in part because they eschewed violence and were resisting the authority of British occupation. Fifty years after India achieved Independence most of us still cling to our faith in nationhood. Though we may sympathize with separatists movements in other parts of the world — the people of Kosovo resisting Serbian domination or Tibetan exiles demanding a return of their conquered homeland — most people do not want their own borders to be redrawn.

For India, the separatist demands in Punjab and Kashmir have become a challenge not only to national unity but also to democracy. Fragmentation of the country would represent a failure of the political system which is based on the concept of a diverse electorate and representative governance, wherein both the majority and the minority have a voice. The problem is that these democratic ideals are never fully put into practice and national priorities often supersede individual, ethnic, or regional interests.

In an essay titled "The Political Culture of the Indian State," Ashis Nandy explores the tensions between democracy and nationalism.

> Each democracy is an act of faith in the sense that each represents, however imperfectly, a commitment to liberal values and a trust in the political judgement of the people. Yet each is dependent on elaborate institutional arrangements to protect the values from the people. One suspects that behind the act of faith hide age-old fears: fear of the gullibility of the people, seen as all too capable of turning into mobs . . . fear of the volatility and the transient, half-baked preferences of the masses . . . fear of the emotional vulnerability of the ordinary citizens in international relations, dominated by amoral, conspiratorial powers.[6]

Once again, the paradox of democracy is that our cherished ideals of independence and liberty provide the impetus for most separatist movements. The liberal philosophies on which the constitutions of most countries like India were founded — the mantras of freedom and self-determination — inevitably give rise to regional struggles that threaten the integrity of a nation. On the most fundamental and personal level, separatism challenges our sense of who we are. The modern concept of citizenship, as a basic form of identity, is continually called into question by those who fight to create newer and lesser states.

When I returned from the Golden Temple to my hotel, I found the Mehra's car and driver waiting for me. Arjun had sent word that he was busy but he had asked his wife, Annu, and a friend of hers, Harjit, to show me around the city. The two of them were seated in the Napoli restaurant nearby and, after a cold drink, we set off to see Khalsa College and Guru Nanak University. Harjit had been a student at Khalsa College and her mother was a lecturer in the English department.

Annu and Harjit were in their late twenties, both of them vivacious and attractive young women. One was a Hindu and the other a Sikh. When I asked how long they'd known each other the two of them laughed and said that their families had been close for years. Harjit was unmarried and worked as a nutritionist, though she had taken the day off. Annu lived at home with her in-laws but my arrival had given her an excuse to get out of the house. Looking at the two of them it would have been virtually impossible to tell which was a Hindu and which was a Sikh, except that Harjit wore a thin steel kara around her wrist.

Aside from the walled city, with its frenetic bazaars and cluttered lanes, Amritsar is a quiet, provincial town. The tensions which lay over the city for more than a decade, have finally eased, even though police patrols and barricades are in evidence everywhere. Earlier I had asked Arjun Mehra what it was like to live in the Punjab during the separatist agitations. He explained that many of the Hindu residents were attacked by Sikh "extremists" and much of the "terrorism" was intended to drive them out of the Punjab. As gold traders the Mehra family would have been prime targets for extortion. Arjun told me that during this period his workshop was only open from eleven in the morning until three in the afternoon because of curfews and that no-body dared go outdoors after dark.

Though Annu and Harjit spoke briefly about the "troubles and dis-turbances" in the Punjab, they were more interested in asking me questions about America. Annu explained that she had a brother who was a doctor in New York and some day she wanted to take her sons to visit him. Harjit told me that she was thinking of emigrating.

"Why would you want to leave Amritsar?" I said.

"It's a nice place. I like it here," she said, "but it's very quiet and things have changed."

Without saying it directly she was hinting at a mood of disillusion-ment in the Sikh community. Some of her relatives had already emi-grated to England, and she was thinking of going there.

The campuses of Khalsa College and Guru Nanak University are sit-uated along the Grand Trunk Road, covering an area of five or six square miles. Guru Nanak University is a much newer institution, with concrete buildings and modern dormitories. The red-brick fa-cade of Khalsa College, however, looked more like a palace than an ed-ucational institution, with domes and cupolas, deep verandas and curving balconies. Established by the British at the end of the nine-teenth century, Khalsa college was part of a colonial effort to promote the English language and create an educated elite. The official medium of instruction at Khalsa College is now Punjabi, though certain sub-jects are still taught in English.

The buildings are examples of Orientalia at its most excessive ex-treme, constructed with a confectioner's eye. As we entered the cam-pus, Harjit explained that the architect who built this college was the same man who designed the Victoria Memorial in Calcutta. The lawns and gardens were well maintained, with spreading asoka trees and royal palms, but the classrooms were in disrepair, the wooden desks worn and broken, the lecture halls poorly lit and uninspiring. None of the rooms were air-conditioned and the tiny fans overhead seemed out of proportion with the rest of the building. The main auditorium had ceilings that rose fifty or sixty feet above the floor. On the stage a group of college women were rehearsing a play that would be present-ed as part of the fiftieth-anniversary celebrations, gesturing defiantly as they reenacted Gandhi's Salt March.

Harjit led the way up a narrow staircase to the second floor where she showed me the botany and zoology departments. A group of students sat in front of a line of microscopes, glancing up at us with amusement as we passed by. On one of the outer walls was a glass case, six feet high, containing a crumbling specimen of a tree fern. The delicate fronds had completely disintegrated into dust, and all that remained were a few bleached sections of the stem.

The vast majority of students at Khalsa College were Sikhs; Harjit explained that every year on Guru Nanak's birthday the entire student body marched in procession from the college to the Golden Temple. She had been a student during the eighties, when there had been violent protests against the central government following the attack on the Golden Temple.

"I remember watching from this balcony," said Harjit, pointing in the direction of the main road. "The police and army were lined up there and students uprooted bricks from the flowerbeds and threw them at the soldiers."

Annu and Harjit dropped me back at my hotel in the early afternoon but around five-thirty the car returned. This time the Mehra's two sons and their uncle, Mamaji, accompanied me to the border post at Atari to watch the "Beating Retreat" that is held each evening. Navin, the eldest boy, had recently written a report for school on these ceremonies. He and his brother had been to Atari several times before but their uncle and I had never seen the border. As we drove west from Amritsar, along the Grand Trunk Road, a sprinkling of rain left the asphalt steaming and put a shine on the wheat fields and kikad trees along the margins of the two-lane highway.

The Border Security Force maintains their post at Atari with all of the spit and polish for which the Indian Army is renowned. Flowerbeds of zinnias and marigolds stood at attention beside an archway proclaiming "Hamara Bharat Mahan" (Our India Victorious), and the BSF motto "Duty unto Death." A cement sculpture of two hands clasped together in friendship served as a monument of reconciliation. In a curious way, the border post reminded me of the highway rest stops maintained by the Punjab Tourism Department. There were several cold-drinks stands and young boys selling sweets and roasted peanuts. From the parking area I could see the steel gate at the border and beyond it the green and white flag of Pakistan, emblazoned with a crescent moon. On the near side of the gate was the Indian tricolor, a blue chakra, or chariot wheel, in the center of three stripes — saffron, white, and green.

Beating Retreat is an archaic military tradition that symbolizes a cessation of hostilities on the battlefield. In earlier times it was a chance for the opposing armies to collect and bury their dead at sunset. Even though their compatriots continue firing at each other across the disputed line of control in Kashmir, the Indian Border Security Force and the Pakistani Rangers put on a coordinated display of military pageantry that could only have been achieved through complete cooperation and planning on both sides. This daily ritual attracts regular crowds of tourists from Amritsar and Lahore. The BSF soldiers taking part in the parade were uniformed in khaki with starched turbans and pleated coxcombs, jackboots, gold braid, and ribbons.

Close to three hundred spectators had gathered on the Indian side of the border and the sentries kept us back about a hundred meters from the gate. As the sun began to drop behind the neem trees there was a rustle of activity and the BSF soldiers let us move forward to a reviewing stand. Those who found no room on the bleachers were made to sit in the middle of the road and watch. The ceremony began with one of the soldiers presenting arms and marching with vigorous strides to the gate and back. Orders were shouted in belligerent voices, the words virtually unintelligible. A second soldier repeated the same maneuver, stamping his boots and marching with an exaggerated goose step. He was a Sikh, his beard tinted orange with henna, while the first soldier had been a Hindu. Both men stood over six feet tall and were obviously chosen for their imposing stature and fierce demeanor. Across the border we could hear similar commands being shouted and the clatter of hobnailed boots. This posturing continued for at least ten minutes until the gate at the border was finally thrown open. On the other side we could see that an identical ceremony was being repeated by Pakistani Rangers, uniformed in black salwar kameez, with bandoliers and rifles. The two separate audiences rose to their feet and peered across at each other like the supporters of opposing football teams. All around me I could feel a bristling of patriotic sentiments as the two commanders came out to the gate and shook hands. At this point the spectators broke into applause and cheers. Two buglers played reveille and the flags were lowered in unison.

Once the Beating Retreat was over, spectators were allowed to approach within ten feet of the open gate and the painted white line that marks the border. There was a rush to get to the front and everyone pressed forward so that the soldiers had to shout and put out their arms to keep us back. Fired up by the nationalistic passions of the parade, the crowds on either side became aggressive. Shouts of "Bharat Mata Ki Jai!" (Hooray for Mother India) came from the one side and "Allah ho Akbar!" (Allah is great) from the other. For a moment it looked as if this jingoistic fervor was going to lead to a minor riot, but the BSF soldiers and the Pakistani Rangers stood between the two contingents, holding them back. Within a minute or two the hostile voices were stilled and as the muted shadows of twilight settled over Atari the spectators stood transfixed. For me this was the most remarkable and profound moment of the whole ceremony, when all of the tension and animosity, the bluster and bravado, suddenly melted into silence. For at least five minutes nobody moved and the spectators on either side simply stared at each other. Their faces were filled with bewilderment and curiosity, the kind of expressions that one sees in a crowd that leaves a cinema hall, blinking as their eyes adjust to reality.

Driving back to Amritsar, Mamaji and the two boys started laughing and joking in the back seat. As I listened to what they said I found myself laughing too, unable to wipe a foolish grin off my face. Even the driver, who had said no more than a couple of words all day, joined in the conversation. It was as if the proximity of the border and the intensity of emotions during the ceremony had animated each of us and we were overcome by an uncontrollable feeling of elation and catharsis. Both of the boys were giggling hysterically and their uncle couldn't stop talking. After a while the driver switched on the radio so that we had to shout to make ourselves heard over the sound of Hindi film music. Nobody said anything about the Pakistanis we had seen but there was an unspoken feeling in the car of having witnessed an event that signified more than just a cessation of hostilities. We had gone to the edge and back.

Approaching the outskirts of the city, we passed a banner announcing the Jubilee celebrations, along with a huge hoarding with a picture of Sita Ram Kesri, the Congress Party president. Mamaji began to make disparaging comments about Kesri's appearance, his dark skin, bulging eyes, and swollen lips. The boys were doubled up with laughter as their uncle explained that Kesri had once been a "bandmaster." By this time the traffic was growing thicker as we entered Amritsar and the driver was laughing so hard I thought he would lose control of the car. Mamaji wiped the tears from his eyes, as he told one political joke after the other.

Eventually we came to a stop near Arjun Mehra's workshop and showroom, located only a few hundred yards from the Golden Temple. The streets were so narrow that even the compact Maruti was unable to take us all the way and we went on foot through a labyrinth of gullies. On either side of us were lines of utensil shops, with brass and copper pots, aluminum bowls, and stainless steel implements hanging from the ceilings and walls. At a crossing in the center of the bazaar grew a twisted pipal tree, its branches constrained by the buildings on either side. In its roots I could see a small Hindu shrine and the stooped figure of a man lighting an oil lamp in front of a framed picture of Lakshmi, the goddess of wealth.

Arjun's showroom was on the third floor of a shabby looking building, up a dimly lit flight of stairs. Inside it was air-conditioned and comfortably furnished with chairs and sofas. As we entered, Arjun was in the process of weighing a set of wedding ornaments. He greeted us with a distracted smile and showed me a gold necklace inlaid with precious stones and pearls, worth more than Rs. 50,000. One of the assistants in the showroom was sent to bring us Coca-Colas, which we drank as Arjun finished up his work. By this time we had all recovered from our fit of laughter and the boys looked tired and subdued. I was introduced to an older man named Munshi Ram, who had worked for the family for sixty years, having come across from Sialkot with Randhir Mehra in 1947. In one corner of the showroom stood a massive safe, built into the wall, and as they put the gold ornaments away, Arjun turned one key in the lock while Munshi Ram turned another. The safe could only be opened if the two of them were in the showroom together.

Later Arjun took me downstairs to his workshop where the ornaments were made — a stuffy, rectangular room in which fifteen men were seated on the floor at low wooden tables. The craftsmen were shaping the gold into tiny flowers, their petals and leaves inlaid with rubies and emeralds. Arjun explained that all the goldsmiths employed in his workshop came from Bengal and most of them had been working for his family since they were boys. Some of the men were tapping at the ornaments with small hammers and miniature chisels the size of toothpicks. Even under the glare of a fluorescent bulb, the yellow metal in their hands seemed to glow with a light of its own. On one side of the room was a single window, which was open but secured with a line of steel bars, like a prison cell. In the distance, over the rooftops of Guru Bazaar, I could see the dome of the Golden Temple lit up against the night sky, like the bud of a gilded lotus.

4

WAGHA   This Train to Pakistan

The Punjab police today claimed to have uncovered a major plan hatched by the Inter Services Intelligence of Pakistan to eliminate top Akali Dal and Bharatiya Janata Party leaders including Chief Minister Parkash Singh Badal with the arrests of five terrorists including a Pakistan national.

Addressing a news conference, Director General of Police P. C. Dogra said one of the arrested terrorists had been motivated to be a human bomb. He said two of the arrested terrorists were in touch with the International Sikh Youth Federation chief Lakhbir Singh Rode based in Lahore.

Those arrested include Abi Saloom, a Pakistan national who is an ISI agent, Sewa Singh of Nurmahal motivated to be a human bomb, Sukhwinder Singh, Raj Singh and Balwant Singh. Balwant Singh, 66, is an employee of the Shiromani Gurdwara Parbandhak Committee working as a langri in the Golden Temple complex while Sukhwinder Singh is a kar sewak at Akal Takht. — *Indian Express*, 31 July 1997

Borders are essentially invisible and the only proof of their existence are the fences and gates, the boundary markers, floodlights and watchtowers which are constructed to provide us with a sense of physical reality. Those lines of ink on a map are not something we can actually see or touch on the ground. Though a border often corresponds to a river or a ridgeline, the geographical limits of a nation are determined by more than just topography. They represent intangible concepts — the fault lines of culture, political watersheds, and the territorial prerogatives of history. Just as nations build monuments on a battlefield to commemorate victory and locate the incomprehensible tragedy of war, so do they create borders in an equally futile attempt to demarcate the divisions between people and the land.

In an effort to reinforce and give permanence to their borders, each state erects an elaborate scaffolding of structures which represent invisible barriers and separate their country from neighboring states. Barbed wire fences and steel gates are only one part of this divisive symbolism. The complex and often contradictory procedures of travel and immigration, printed forms which have to be filled out in triplicate, customs restrictions and security checks, are each, in their own way, elements of a bureaucratic charade that gives a border its significance. Add to this the ceremonial rituals of frontier guards, the imposing sentries in their uniforms, the raising and lowering of flags, the percussive march of hobnailed boots, and it all becomes a play, a drama, a tableau that attempts to convince us that borders are something to be honored and defended. On a more mundane but equally insidious level there is the posturing of government functionaries — police inspectors and customs officials who delay and harass anyone attempting to cross from one country to another. With their intrusive questions and suspicious glances, these agents of the state demand that we acknowledge the existence of their border by opening our suitcases and handing over our passports to be inspected. Their illegible signatures and the smeared patterns of rubber stamps, bearing national insignia, are all part of an effort to give the border some kind of shape, to make it real and understood.

At the same time, borders provide the ultimate test of each nation's authority. Unlike an airport, which might be located in the center of a country, a border post is not only a point of entry and exit but a locus of friction and conflict. A certain level of ceremony and procedure attends the arrival and departure of air travelers, but land borders are imbued with much greater significance and the assertion of authority by each government along its borders is exaggerated and more apparent. Flying between Delhi and Lahore, for instance, involves far simpler procedures than crossing over by train. In part this may reflect class distinctions between those who can afford the cost of an air ticket and those who can't.

Despite the forbidding and monumental facades which each government constructs along its frontiers, there will always be those who insist on passing through these barricades. Smugglers and illegal infiltrators may pose a threat to national security, but the vast majority of people that cross a border have perfectly legitimate motives. At the same time, the very existence of a border, and efforts by government authorities to maintain and preserve its integrity, encourages individuals to challenge and subvert that proverbial line in the sand. During many of my conversations with people who had actually stood at the border between India and Pakistan, one of the recurring stories that I heard was the claim of having "put one foot across," thereby consciously defying the authority of that line. These minor acts of resistance, however, are nothing compared to the considerable determination and defiance that is required for citizens of India and Pakistan who travel back and forth across the border.

French photographer Henri Cartier-Bresson visited India in 1947 and captured a sequence of unforgettable images which document the tragedy of Partition. In one of these pictures, a refugee train from Delhi to Lahore sits at a deserted platform, waiting to move forward. All the passengers are Muslims, leaving their homes in India behind. The women are inside the carriages, while the men are perched on the roof and crowded into an open freight wagon. Their belongings are bundled around them like sandbags and the men are wrapped in shawls and turbans, only their faces visible. It has just rained and there are puddles on the platform, the carriages streaked with water. All the eyes are directed toward the camera with expressions of despair. One man holds a hookah, or waterpipe, in his hands. A boy rests his chin on his knees. Cartier-Bresson's black-and-white photograph has a stark quality that underscores the misery of these refugees. The train itself seems immobile, weighed down by the burden of passengers and luggage. The moment of departure is only a few seconds away, but time seems to have stopped and the look of resignation on the refugees' faces is frozen forever.[1]

In 1947 trains were the primary means of transport for refugees and they were also the focus of some of the worst atrocities, in which Hindus, Sikhs, and Muslims were slaughtered as they traveled in opposite directions. Railway journeys are an important part of the lore that surrounds Partition. Kushwant Singh's novel *Train to Pakistan* is only one of many works of fiction that recount these narratives. Saadat Hasan Manto's Urdu short stories contain some of the most graphic and troubling descriptions of the sectarian violence. In a sequence of fragmented episodes titled "Black Marginalia," he distills the horror of Partition.

The train was stopped.
The passengers belonging to the other community were singled out. They were pulled out of the train one by one, and shot or knifed to death. The job done, the remaining passengers who were co-religionists were regaled with halwa, milk and fruits.

Before the train resumed its journey the leader of the assassins addressed the passengers, "Brothers and sisters, we must apologize. We got the news of the train's arrival late. That's why we haven't been able to entertain you the way we would have liked to.[2]

As in many of his Partition stories, Manto never identifies the killers, allowing the reader to assign blame on either side. His work is marked by some of the darkest ironies. As a Punjabi Muslim who emigrated to Pakistan soon after 1947, Manto viewed the division of his homeland with ambivalence. He is read and admired by both Indians and Pakistanis alike because his stories transcend the religious hatreds that he describes.

Another writer who uses the railways as a metaphor of Partition, is the Hindi novelist Bhisham Sahni. His short story "We Have Arrived in Amritsar" focuses on a group of passengers in a train traveling across the Punjab. The story is set just before Partition but communal tensions are already running high and the rioting has begun. As the train moves closer and closer to Amritsar, Sahni depicts the insecurities and alienation which his characters experience. At the beginning of the story a group of Muslim Pathans begin to tease a Hindu clerk, or babu, mocking his effeminate manner. Their chiding voices are jocular at first, but as the train leaves Lahore they begin to fall silent and the Hindu, who has been swallowing his pride until that time, gradually becomes emboldened and tries to rally the other Hindus and Sikhs in the carriage. Outside the windows smoke and flames can be seen in the villages they pass, evidence of looting and bloodshed. The train itself does not stop, and Sahni's descriptions convey its relentless momentum, crossing over a border that is yet to be defined. Seeing a town where rioting has broken out, the mood in the railway compartment changes dramatically.

There was an oppressive silence in the compartment. I withdrew my head from the window and looked in. The feeble looking Babu had turned deathly pale, the sweat on his forehead was making it glisten in the light. The passengers looked at each other nervously. A new tension could now be felt between the passengers. Perhaps a similar tension had arisen in each compartment of the train. The Sardarji got up from his seat and came over and sat down next to me. The Pathan sitting on the lower berth climbed up to the upper berth where the two Pathans were sitting. Perhaps the same process was going on in other compartments also. All dialogue ceased. The three Pathans, perched side by side on the upper berth, looked quietly down. The eyes of each passenger were wide with apprehension.[3]

The train journey from Amritsar to Lahore, a distance of roughly fifty kilometers, takes almost fifteen hours. Only two days a week is it possible to cross the border, on the Samjhota Express, which originates in Delhi. Though I expected long delays, nothing had prepared me for the remarkable drama of human endurance that I witnessed. Customs and immigration procedures are handled at Atari, the last station on the Indian side of the border. An enormous shed with a corrugated tin roof covers a broad central platform. Atari Station is completely fenced in, with armed policemen standing guard.

The first step in the immigration process was to have our passports registered in a ledger before we were admitted to the platform. Each of us had to sign the register, some in English, some in Hindi, Punjabi, or Urdu. I could see that a few of the passengers ahead of me had simply put their thumb impressions on the page. When it came to my turn to sign the ledger, a policeman waved me back with an officious gesture.

"Don't go this way," he said. "You're a foreigner. You can cross by road. It's much easier and takes less time."

The others looked at me and nodded.

"I prefer to go by train," I said.

"This way you'll get to Lahore in the middle of the night. The road is hardly two or three kilometers in that direction," he said with a dismissive flick of his wrist. "You'll avoid the crowds and get across before noon."

"He's right," said another man. "You'll save yourself a lot of discomfort."

"It doesn't matter. I'm not in a rush," I said.

Reluctantly the policeman took my passport and wrote down the particulars, then turned the ledger around and made me sign.

Once inside the gate, I saw that there was a line of immigration booths on the platform. Most of these were marked "Citizens of Indian" or "Citizens of Pakistan" but there was one with a sign that said "Foreigners." When I got to the window nobody was there. After waiting a few minutes I asked for help at a nearby booth. Without looking up from the papers he was studying, the immigration officer said, "Look for the tall Sikh. He'll take care of you."

Glancing around the platform I could see at least a dozen men who fit that description, all of them in khaki uniforms. Eventually one of the men sauntered over and seated himself behind the window. His name tag read "Kashmir Singh," and the first thing he said to me was that I should go by road instead of taking the train. Once again I had to persuade him that I preferred the delays and discomfort of the train journey. With a look of suspicion, Kashmir Singh handed me an embarkation card. I was left to fill it out while he got up again and went across to have a cup of tea with two of his colleagues. Another fifteen minutes passed before he returned. When I handed him the card, he scrutinized it carefully.

"You were born in India?" he said.

"Yes."

"But you don't look Indian."

I started to explain when something on the card suddenly caught his eye.

"Here, you've made a mistake," he said, brusquely. "You've written that your birthplace is Mussoorie, in Uttar Pradesh. That's incorrect. Mussoorie is in Himachal Pradesh."

As politely as I could I said, "No. It's definitely in Uttar Pradesh. Near Dehradun."

He shook his head angrily, as if I had questioned his authority. Then rapping on the side of the booth he shouted across to the officer beside us.

"Oi, Dharamvir! In which state is Mussoorie?"

"How should I know?" came the bored reply.

Unwilling to back down, Kashmir Singh took my pen and crossed out what I had written on the form. In its place he wrote, in capital letters, HIMACHAL PRADESH. Deciding it was better not to press the issue, I waited silently as he stamped my passport.

The next step in the process was to exchange some money. The State Bank of India had a counter at the far end of the platform. I took four hundred Indian rupees from my wallet and handed them over to the bank clerk. The rest of my money was in the suitcase, but I wanted to be sure that I had enough cash for a taxi when I got to Lahore. The bank clerk made me fill out two separate forms and noted down my passport number in his ledger. The blue hundred-rupee notes which I gave him had a picture of Mahatma Gandhi on one side. What I received in exchange were green notes of the same denomination with a picture of Mohammed Ali Jinnah wearing his caracul hat. In this way I traded the founding father of one nation for the other. Even the simple procedures of currency exchange carried historic overtones.

The central platform at Atari is divided by a steel-mesh fence and the layout of the station is clearly intended to segregate passengers traveling in opposite directions. Altogether there were more than a thousand people crossing over from India to Pakistan that day. After completing immigration and customs procedures we passed through a narrow gate with a metal detector and waited on the other side of the fence. Once everybody had been processed, the gate was sealed and the police and customs officials waited for the train to arrive from Wagha, carrying passengers from Pakistan. This same train would take us back across the border.

The customs officers in their white uniforms were opening every piece of baggage. I joined one of the shortest queues and watched as bulging suitcases were thrown open and the contents picked through, everything from blankets and bedding to women's undergarments.

The customs officials probed through the luggage, thrusting their arms inside the tightly packed bundles and rummaging about with total disregard for privacy. When they were finished they left the passengers to repack their bags, which had been completely disemboweled. Most of the travelers had nothing of value, but everything was searched and customs duty was assessed. The only two items of commercial value that I noticed were gunny sacks full of tea and baskets of paan leaves. Though trade between the two countries is virtually nonexistent, I could see that this was one way of getting around these restrictions. Individual passengers, paid by merchants in Amritsar and Lahore, carried the tea and paan leaves across as part of their personal luggage. The customs officials were obviously aware of what was going on, but they must have been paid off, for they didn't bother opening the sacks of tea.

In the line ahead of me were about a dozen passengers, including a family with six children, one of whom was hardly three or four months old. As the customs official finished with the man at the head of the line he looked up and beckoned me forward. I gestured toward the others but he shook his head and told me to step out of the queue. The children watched with curiosity and their parents looked away, unwilling to complain.

Jugraj Singh, the customs inspector, was a short, stout man whose uniform seemed several sizes too small. Greeting me with a limp handshake he casually flipped through my passport.

"American?" he said. "My brother lives in New York."

I nodded, still embarrassed at having been forced to jump the queue. Jugraj Singh showed no interest in checking my bags.

"I would like to go to New York," he said, in a voice which betrayed no sense of irony. "But your immigration people, they give us such a lot of trouble."

By this time two other customs inspectors had abandoned their posts and joined us. The rest of the travelers waited patiently. Bored with their routines of harassment, the customs officers found me to be a source of entertainment and curiosity. Jugraj Singh's questions became more personal. He asked me about my wife, my children. When I told him that I taught at a university, he nudged one of the other inspectors.

"Is it coed?" he asked me, in a sly tone.

"Yes."

"Then you'll remain forever young," he said with a wink and the three of them laughed. At this point, I suggested that perhaps I should open my bags.

"What's the hurry?" said Jugraj Singh, casting his eye over the line behind me. "Once you go through the gate, you'll just have to wait over there. Besides, the girls are better looking on this side of the platform."

Half an hour had passed since he had called me forward. The tone of his conversation had gradually changed, and it was now full of sexual innuendos. He began to ask me questions about American women, then suddenly stopped with a look of alarm. From the far end of the platform three other customs officials approached us, two men and a woman in a uniform sari, the pleated pulloo pinned to her shoulder with a brass insignia.

Jugraj Singh and the two other inspectors jumped to attention and saluted. The chief customs officer was at least six inches shorter than the rest of them, her gray hair drawn back in a matronly bun. Not for a moment did she acknowledge my presence, nor did she look at any of the other travelers. Her features were stern and emotionless.

"Hurry up," she said. "Get back to work."

"Yes, madam," said Jugraj Singh. "Of course, madam."

As she turned to leave, he pointed a finger at my suitcase and made me open the zipper. I was carrying nothing but clothes and notebooks. In a sudden burst of efficiency, Jugraj Singh made me fill out a customs form, then stamped and signed my papers with an urgent flourish. Just before waving me through he asked me to write down my address for him, so that when he came to America he could pay me a visit.

Passing through the metal detector I found myself on the other side of the platform. There weren't any chairs or benches; the travelers had arranged themselves in groups on the cement floor, spreading pieces of newspaper to sit on. The temperature had been climbing since morning and it was now past noon, the air thick with humidity and flies. I found a place to sit down, next to the fence, which gave me a view of the custom's inspectors on the other side. For the next three hours I watched the lines move slowly forward as the officials put each traveler through an inquisition. There was something vindictive in the way they treated the passengers, as if these were traitors or enemies of the state simply because they were crossing the border. From what I could see all the officials were Hindus and Sikhs, while the travelers were Muslims. The tension and hostility on the platform rose with the heat. One man, the contents of his suitcase strewn on the ground, was pleading with an official not to charge him duty. At one point he bent down and massaged the inspector's leg with both his hands in a gesture of total abnegation. The customs officer brushed him aside with contempt. At other counters, I saw bribes being given, crumpled hundred-rupee notes pressed into an inspector's waiting hand.

A short distance from where I sat was a family with two sons, the youngest of whom was seven or eight years old. He was restless and irritable, fighting with his brother over a toy gun. It was made of cheap plastic and shot darts with suction cups at the end. AK-47 was written on the stock in bright green letters. The younger of the two boys finally took possession of the gun and began aiming it at other passengers, who laughed and teased him. His mischief helped break the monotony of waiting. On the other side of the fence I noticed two armed policemen with rifles slung over their shoulders. After a few minutes the boy turned his attention in their direction and pointed the barrel of his gun through the wire-mesh fence. Before anyone could stop him he fired at the policemen, who happened to turn around just as the dart landed at their feet. The boy's father grabbed him by the shoulder, a look of panic on his face. All at once the situation was charged with confrontation. The boy began to cry, realizing that he could not retrieve his dart. The policemen glared at the crowd of travelers as if someone had fired a genuine weapon in their direction. The boy's father snatched the toy gun out of his hands and angrily threw it aside. For a minute or two nobody moved and the only sound was the child's wailing. The policemen finally turned away in disdain, and a few minutes later a traveler on the other side of the fence picked up the dart and passed it back through the fence. Though the situation had been defused, a mood of anxiety lingered on.

There were a couple of food carts on the platform, selling plates of rice and dal as well as tea and soft drinks. A freelance money changer wandered about within the crowd, carrying a bundle of notes in one hand. The policemen who patrolled the platform ignored him. Many of the travelers stretched out to sleep. The most unusual looking group was a cluster of three hijiras, or eunuchs, who were seated together. The kajal that blackened their eyes and the bright red lipstick they wore contrasted sharply with their masculine features. Each hijira had his head demurely covered with a dupatta.

An old man seated nearby offered me some chewda to eat. We talked for awhile, and it turned out that he was from Peshawar, returning home after visiting relatives in Delhi. There was nothing to do but wait, while the humidity made our clothes stick to our skin. For the first time I wished that I had taken the policeman's advice and gone to Lahore by road.

Around three o'clock in the afternoon a breeze suddenly picked up and I could see monsoon clouds blowing in, dark rafts of moisture drifting across the sky. I could smell the rain before it arrived, a sweet musky odor like wet clay. The drops began to fall, each of them as large as rupee coins, spilling onto the cement platform with a silvery brightness. At first they evaporated as soon as they landed but after a minute the rain came down in a deluge. Within seconds the platform was flooded and the wind blew the rain in at an angle beneath the roof. Everyone scrambled to pull luggage under cover but it was useless, the rain spraying over us as we huddled together against the fence, clothes drenched, hair beaded with moisture. The children were the first to give up any attempt to keep dry and several ran out to the edge of the platform. One boy, five or six, stood naked under the lip of the corrugated roof and let the water cascade upon him. Immediately the temperature dropped. The storm continued for twenty minutes, by which time I was completely soaked.

When the train from Pakistan eventually rolled into the station the people waiting all jumped to their feet. The engine and carriages were a muddy green. As the passengers disembarked they pushed and shoved their way toward the immigration booths and customs counters. Still dripping from the rain, we studied them through the fence, as if hoping to recognize someone in their midst. Once the train had been emptied it was shunted around to the far end of the station and came back to our side of the platform.

After hours of waiting, the crowds of passengers hurled themselves aboard, even before the train had stopped, throwing bags through open windows and struggling to position themselves at the doors. Holding my suitcase in front of me I found myself swept inside by the momentum of the crowd. I was lucky enough to find a seat near a window. Once everyone had climbed aboard I expected the train to move, but it stood still for another hour. Across from me sat a large woman with a young boy on her lap. In the compartment to my right was the old man from Peshawar. He explained that for six months of the year the train that crossed the border was operated by Pakistan Railways. For the other six months it was an Indian Railways train, another example of the carefully measured reciprocity that exists between the two nations.

When we finally got moving it took only ten minutes to reach the border. Outside the window I could see a patchwork of fields and villages. The kikad trees and wheat fields were glistening from the recent rain, and the ditches along the railway embankment were flooded. Buffalo were wallowing in the stagnant water. A Sikh farmer was plowing his fields with a tractor, its tires sinking into the mud. The only indication that we were approaching the border was a barbed-wire fence that ran parallel to the tracks, though at one place the wires had been pried apart and a young man was squeezing through the gap with his bicycle. As the train began to slow down, a pair of mounted soldiers from the Indian Border Security Force rode up alongside. The horses were jittery as they kept pace with the carriages, which creaked and groaned against their couplings. The boy opposite me seemed excited by the sight of the horses, but his mother swatted his hand aside when he waved at them. Our train slowed to a crawl as we got to the border and the horsemen moved on ahead. Leaning out the window I could see another fence that ran at right angles to the tracks; a watchtower stood on the near side. A steel gate blocked the railway line, but it had been opened for our train. The BSF sentries stood guard at the gate and the horsemen had stopped beside the fence, watching sternly as we passed through. Strangely, on the other side of the fence there were no Pakistani sentries. The fields were cultivated right up to the border, with new wheat sprouting through the barbed wire. To have planted their fields so close together, the farmers on either side must have run their plows inches from the fence, for there was no more than a furrow's width between them.

The time difference between India and Pakistan is half an hour. Several of the people on the train reminded me to turn back my watch as soon as we crossed the border. By now it was late afternoon, five-thirty in Atari and five o'clock in Wagha. Even time must change at the border. Before 1947 the time zones in the subcontinent were somewhat fluid, with Indian Standard Time being set in Delhi, four and a half hours ahead of Greenwich. There were also Karachi Time and Calcutta Time, adjusted half an hour in either direction. The creation of East and West Pakistan was accompanied by a more formal adjustment of clocks, so that independent India (including Calcutta) remained on Indian Standard Time, while the new border demarcated the temporal as well as political divisions.

For the passengers on the Samjhota Express, who had waited patiently since early in the morning to cross the border, the time difference meant very little. Their day had been marked by a prolonged series of delays. Like so many others I had found myself glancing at my watch every few minutes. The police and customs officials, who seemed to have no concern for time, made our wait even longer and more unpleasant. Nine hours had passed since I had bought my ticket that morning, but instead of a clear sequence of events the chronology of the day seemed to have been warped, with moments of intense activity followed by extended periods of anticipation.

There was no logical reason for these delays, except harassment. The procedures and processes could easily have been completed in a fraction of the time it took. Instead there was a deliberate effort to slow us down, to stretch the process of crossing the border into a full day, as if to emphasize the political and cultural distances. The resulting sense of dislocation made the two countries feel much further apart than they actually were.

Even before our train came to a halt at Wagha station, I saw people leaping out of the carriages and racing past my window as if they were taking part in a foot race. I couldn't understand what the hurry was, until I realized that they were rushing to get the luggage trolleys, which were limited in number. At Atari there had been porters who helped haul the luggage, but in Wagha people had to fend for themselves. The trolleys were crude, unwieldy contraptions with wheels going in different directions, so the platform soon turned into a traffic jam, passengers shouting and squabbling as they maneuvered for positions in the queues.

The arrivals hall at Wagha was an enormous shed, something like an exhibition hall at a livestock fair. We were herded into one end of the enclosure where the Pakistani officials waited to process arriving passengers. Once again I had my own booth to myself, "Foreigners" written on it in red lettering. The immigration and customs officials were dressed in blue uniforms, while the policemen wore dark gray salwar kameez with black berets. Sten guns and rifles were slung across their shoulders. This time I was processed quickly, hardly a question asked and only a cursory glance at the contents of my suitcase. I was then directed to the far end of the shed, where there was a waiting area fenced in on three sides. Almost immediately passengers began queuing up in front of the exit, a steel gate that opened back onto the platform. The harassment and delays on this side of the border were no different from what we had experienced in Atari. Several customs officers roamed about, picking passengers at random and making them open their bags a second time. I had settled myself on an empty cement bench and opened a book to read, but after twenty minutes a young man approached. He couldn't have been more than eighteen, with a faint shadow of a moustache and a self-confident air. Putting a hand on my shoulder he asked politely if I would mind moving so that a group of bourqa-clad women could sit on the bench. Now that I was in Pakistan, segregation of the sexes was much more apparent. As I got up and shifted to another seat he pressed my shoulder gratefully and said in English, "Bundle of thanks."

I sat down next to one of the musicians who was traveling with the group of hijiras. The three eunuchs were seated on the ground ignoring me but the musician started a conversation immediately. He said that they had gone to Delhi for a performance, part of a cultural exchange, though he was vague about the details. The musician said that he played the tabla, and that he had fallen ill in Delhi.

"I fainted on the platform in Atari," he said. "They had to give me two bottles of glucose drip."

The hijiras were making paan, smearing the leaves with red paste and white lime, adding betel nuts and a pinch of chewing tobacco. Without a word they offered me one but I declined. The tabla player said that he had gone to America once, along with a famous Pakistani musician whose name I didn't recognize. He said that they had toured many cities but the only name that he could remember was New York.

Our conversation was abruptly interrupted by the guards opening the gate. All the passengers in the waiting area swarmed forward, crashing their trolleys into each other. Within seconds there were angry shouts and cries of panic as several policemen came rushing forward brandishing their weapons. The guards had failed to realize that there were a number of travelers still waiting on the platform to be processed. Opening the gate mixed the two groups together and it was impossible to tell who had gone through immigration and who had not. Realizing their mistake, the guards tried to shut the gate again, but it was already jammed with luggage trolleys and passengers, anxious to reboard the train. The policemen quickly formed a makeshift barricade out of a couple of steel benches.

Seeing what was taking place, I had tried to hold back but by this time were hundreds of people behind me and I was swept along with the crowd. Hanging on to my suitcase I let myself be carried toward the train. After twenty minutes of jostling and threatening gestures from the police, who waved their sten guns about with alarming carelessness, I found myself diving headlong through the door of a carriage, trampling piles of luggage underfoot. Inside the train I took the first empty seat I found. Occupying the compartment opposite me was a young girl of about fifteen who had tied her dupatta across the entrance. When anyone tried to enter the compartment she began shouting hysterically, saying that she was saving these seats for her family. At first she was successful in defending her space, but soon two other women came climbing through the window on the opposite side of the train. The girl's screams became louder and more frantic, but there was nothing she could do. By this time a couple of her family members had joined her and they were wrestling their bags under the seats and scrambling into the upper berths. An argument erupted between them and the women who had come in through the window, and when they began shouting abuse at the girl one of the men threatened to call the police.

It took half an hour for the shouting to settle down; by this time there were at least ten adults and six or seven children squeezed into the cramped compartment. As it turned out, the girl who had been screaming and her family were Pakistanis, while the intruders were Indian Muslims from Rampur. The squabble threatened to turn violent several times and other passengers in the carriage tried to calm them down.

One of these was a man named Sultan, whom I had met on the platform in Amritsar. He happened to be seated in the compartment directly behind me and we clasped hands as if we were long-lost companions who had been reunited after years. The argument between the Indian family and the Pakistanis continued for another hour and a half, while we waited to leave Wagha. The voices were no longer as shrill or full of anger and the family from Rampur began to direct their complaints against the Pakistan Railways.

"Look at this train," they said. "It's filthy. There are no fans, no lights."

One of the men began to make comparisons to the Indian Railways, proudly claiming that their carriages were clean and well maintained. Sultan joined in the discussion with enthusiasm, and the longer we waited the more he cursed the Pakistani officials for causing delays. Of course, we had waited just as long on the Indian side of the border and there was hardly any difference between the two trains, but the Indians complained about everything, from the lack of tea stalls at the station to the broken shutters on the windows. These fell without warning, like guillotines, and I nearly lost my arm to one.

It had grown dark. Outside the train I could see village lights and smell the smoke of cooking fires. A chorus of frogs was singing in the flooded ditch at the foot of the embankment while fireflies began to flicker in the darkness, pulsating brightly. The air was still and hot and the carriage was poorly ventilated. Several of the fireflies came through the windows and blinked in our faces as we waited, too exhausted to move. By nine o'clock most of the voices had fallen silent.

The two opposing families crushed into the compartment to my right had given up their battle. One of the women from Rampur twirled a bamboo fan in front of her. The Pakistani woman across from her spoke, in a low voice, a word or two of reconciliation, and together they rearranged their bedding rolls on the floor between them and laid the children down to sleep.

Half an hour before midnight, the Samjhota Express finally headed out of Wagha station on the last leg of our journey to Lahore. I woke up with a start as the carriage lurched forward and felt a slight breeze coming through the window. Gradually we picked up speed. The steady clatter of the wheels passing over the rails sounded like the ticking of a clock. Time had begun to move forward once again.

5

LAHORE   The Paris of India

Over half a million kilogrammes of Indian tea will find its way into Pakistani markets in the next two months after a successful deal between producers and traders of India and local packers and traders in a meeting held two days back. . . .

Hanif Janoo, who attended the meeting said the cost of importing tea from India can be cut down by 10 to 15 cents per kg if it is imported by rail road . . .

He added that the interaction between the world's largest tea producer — India, and the world's largest tea consumer— Pakistan, comes at a time when free market forces are dictating the trends in international commerce and trade.—AAMIR SHAFAAT KHAN, *Dawn*, 1 August 1997

I was fully prepared to be disappointed by Lahore. Having heard so many stories from Punjabi refugees in India, praising the city they left behind, my preconceptions were colored by the nostalgia of exile. "Jab tak Lahore nahin dekha, tab tak janam nahin liya," said Bari Ma, my wife's grandmother. "You haven't been born until you've seen Lahore." Others in Delhi had called it the Paris of India, with a wistfulness that echoed their loss. For most Punjabis, whether Indian or Pakistani, Lahore represents the epicenter of their culture, despite the rift of Partition.

From the middle of the fifteenth century Lahore has been the capital of the Punjab, ruled in succession by Hindus, Muslims, Sikhs, and the British. Historian Muhammad Baqir, in his book *Lahore: Past and Present*, has compiled a series of excerpts from the journals of European travelers who visited the city and extolled its opulence and splendor. In 1611, William Finch, an agent of the British East India Company, described it as "One of the greatest Cities of the East."[1] Three years late, another Englishman, Thomas Coryat, was even more effusive: "The goodly Citie of Lahore in India, (is) one of the largest Cities of the whole Universe, for it contayneth at least sixteen miles in compasse and exceedeth Constantinople itself in greatnessee."[2] Both Finch and Coryat visited Lahore during the reign of the Mughal emperor Jehangir. In 1641, a Spanish monk, Fray Sebastian Manrique, recorded his impressions:

The city of Lahore is beautifully situated, commanding agreeable views, on one side a river with crystal waters which descend from the mountains of Kashmir . . . Lahore is ornamented with fine palaces and gardens, also tanks and fountains. As to the abundance of provisions . . . the riches of the principal street (known as the Bazar del Choco), if shown to advantage, would equal the richest European mart.[3]

Lahore was famous not only for its architectural beauty and the prosperity of its markets but for its permissive and cosmopolitan society. Jean-Baptiste Tavernier, a French jewel merchant, traveled through the city in 1641. He noted that "The palace of the king is rather fine," but Tavernier seemed more impressed by the fact that "One can obtain wine in Lahore."[4] Niccolao Manucci, an Italian adventurer and self-taught physician, set up a medical practice there in 1667. In his memoir, *Storia Do Mogor* he writes of other attractions.

The walls are all of well-burnt bricks, high, and provided with bastions. The houses are lofty, some having eight stories. As to the number of people in this city, it is not easy to make an estimate, for the *kotwal* told me that he collected a weekly tax from six thousand houses of ill-fame; from this assertion careful people can arrive at the number there must be of public *filles de joie*, besides those who conceal themselves.[5]

In a footnote to this quote, Muhammad Baqir calls this "a wicked assertion,"[6] claiming that Aurangzeb had outlawed prostitution well before Manucci's arrival. Whatever the truth, it is clear that Lahore was once a city of decadence as well as a center of power and wealth.

With the decline of the Mughal Empire, Lahore began to lose some of its importance and by the beginning of the nineteenth century European travelers were mourning its crumbling grandeur. J. H. Thornton, an English military officer, wrote:

> I visited the ruins of Lahore, which afforded a melancholy picture of fallen splendor. Here the lofty dwellings and masjids, which, fifty years ago, raised their tops to the skies and were the pride of a busy and active population, are now crumbling into dust . . . all was silence, solitude, and gloom.[7]

The British, more than anyone, had a fascination for ruins and they helped contribute to the myth of Lahore as a picturesque city with an irretrievable past. Here is Charles Masson, writing in 1838:

> Lahore, the capital of the Panjab and of the territories of Ranjit Singh, is a city of undoubted antiquity, and has been long celebrated for its extent and magnificence. The extravagant praises bestowed upon it by the historians of Hindustan, must, however, be understood as applicable to a former city, of which now only the ruins are seen. To it must also be referred the current proverb which asserts that, "Isphihan and Shiraz united would not equal the half of Lahore."
>
> Without the walls are scattered on all sides the ruins of the ancient city which is still wonderful, and convey vast ideas of the extent of ancient Lahore. Numerous tombs, and other structures are still standing, some of them nearly entire; and such is their solidity that they seem, if not absolutely to foil old Time to yield to him almost imperceptibly.[8]

Though Lahore never fully recovered the reputation for magnificence that it enjoyed under the Mughals, the city did regain some of its importance by the middle of the nineteenth-century. Under Henry and John Lawrence it became the seat of British power and authority in the Punjab. These two brothers, who served as colonial administrators for the East India Company and the crown, established their headquarters in Lahore. By the turn of the twentieth century the provincial capital of the Punjab enjoyed something of a renaissance, becoming a thriving commercial hub and a center of intellectual and artistic activity. At the time of Partition, the future of Lahore, more than any other city in the subcontinent, ignited passions and was bitterly disputed.

Even during my brief stay, fifty years later, the charm and ambience of its streets, its parks and its monuments was clearly evident. Though I had prepared myself for the worst, Lahore seemed to have been spared much of the overdevelopment and turmoil that other cities in South Asia have experienced. It has grown considerably since 1947, but without losing its character, an intriguing blend of past and present. The ruins, which nineteenth-century travelers so admired, are still there but Lahore also seems to have survived and flourished as a modern city.

Several friends had recommended that I stay at Faletti's Hotel, a relic of colonial times, now managed by the Pakistan Tourism Development Corporation. Arriving in Lahore well after midnight, I checked into a room and fell asleep immediately. When I awoke around nine o'clock the next morning it took me several minutes to remember where I was. The sounds of traffic seeped in through the window despite the deafening rumble of an air-conditioner. The room was enormous and sparsely furnished. On the wall was a cheap velvet tapestry with a picture of the English countryside, a herd of deer framed by oak branches at the edge of a wood. I called room service for a pot of tea and picked up the *Dawn*, an English-language newspaper which had been slipped under my door.

"Founded by Quaid-I-Azam Mohammad Ali Jinnah," was written at the top of the front page, above the masthead. The lead story in *Dawn* announced a 10 percent rise in airfare for the Haj pilgrimage to Mecca, and next to this was a picture of Nawaz Sharif, the prime minister, who was currently on a state visit to Malaysia. Much of the news, however, was about relations between Pakistan and India. One article reported that the foreign office was opposed to India's efforts to secure a permanent seat on the UN Security Council. Just below this was the headline: "Islamabad Warns of Missile Race." The accompanying article went on to say that Pakistan had "voiced its concern over India's missile development programme, warning that it would trigger an arms race in the region."[9] Also on the front page was an article about the sale of electricity between the two countries, as well as a brief report on a bus accident that killed forty people in Bhopal. In India I had found that the newspapers also devoted a good deal of space to news about Pakistan, whether it was cricket scores or the exchange of artillery fire in Kashmir.

When a waiter arrived with my tea and a breakfast menu I ordered a "Pakistani omelette" out of curiosity. The special ingredients, it turned out, were onions, green chilies, and tomatoes, no different from the Indian omelettes I had eaten in Delhi and Amritsar.

The Mall Road was walking distance from Faletti's and after breakfast I set off on foot to find a bank. I needed to exchange money before I could buy my ticket to Peshawar. The first bank I stopped at had a machine-gun nest out front, complete with sandbags and a stone-faced policeman who kept his finger on the trigger. I was told that they didn't deal in foreign exchange and was directed farther down the road to an American Express office. The bank was on the second floor, next to a building that had a sign for the offices of the Jammu and Kashmir Liberation Front. My first impressions of Lahore reminded me of sections of New Delhi, and the buildings along the Mall Road were similar to the architecture of Connaught Place.

After exchanging my dollars I hailed an autorickshaw and asked to be taken to the railway booking office. The Tourism Development Corporation official at the hotel had told me where to go and gave me a tourist discount form that would allow me 25 percent off the regular fare. Unfortunately, by the time I got to Railway headquarters it was closed for midday prayers and I had to wait an hour until it reopened. When I finally got inside a woman at a dusty computer said that I could get a first-class-sleeper reservation on the Khyber Mail for the night of August 3rd. I showed her the discount form and she pointed me to another counter, where I waited for twenty minutes until a clerk showed up who said that I needed to take the form upstairs for signatures. "But they're closed," he said, glancing at his watch. "You'll have to come back tomorrow." Returning to the first counter I told the woman that I had decided to forgo my discount. She pressed several keys on her computer and a dotmatrix printer came to life, scrolling out my ticket on the Khyber Mail.

One of the questions that had worried me as I was preparing to cross the border was whether I would have any trouble communicating in Pakistan. The colloquial Hindi I speak, sometimes referred to as Hindustani, is very similar to Urdu. On the train from Amritsar to Lahore I had no difficulty conversing with Indians or Pakistanis. Some of them congratulated me on my Hindi while others praised my Urdu, even though these compliments were undeserved. Now that I was in Pakistan I consciously avoided specific Hindi terms and phrases. For instance I used the Urdu word, "mulk" for "country" instead of "desh."

On the streets of Lahore I overheard Punjabi being spoken but Urdu seemed far more common. Language is often a dividing factor between cultures and many borders have been drawn because of linguistic conflicts. Yet even though there are considerable differences between "pure" Hindi and "pure" Urdu, the colloquial forms are very similar and most people in North India could easily carry on a conversation with their Pakistani neighbors. In fact, there is a much greater disparity between the other regional languages of India. The primary difference between Urdu and Hindi lies in the script. Urdu is written with the same alphabet as Arabic or Farsi, its graceful curves and spirals flowing across the page from right to left. The Devanagari script, used for Hindi, is angular in appearance, with straight lines and regimented lettering. Like English, it is read from left to right. In written form the two languages look completely different, though most words can easily be transliterated from one script into the other.

Urdu is still spoken in parts of North India, particularly in areas which have a large Muslim population, but popularity of the language has declined considerably since Independence. This can be attributed, in part, to the fact that Urdu is generally associated with the Muslim minority, and as the Hindu nationalists have imposed their culture on the country, the Devanagari script is seen as a harbinger of homogeneity.

In 1947 the newly formed government of Pakistan declared Urdu to be the national language, even though less than 10 percent of the population identified it as their mother tongue. Of course, the greatest challenge to Urdu came from East Pakistan, where the majority of the population spoke Bengali. Ignoring this fact, Liaqat Ali Khan, the first prime minister of Pakistan, declared in 1948:

Pakistan is a Muslim state, and it must have its lingua franca, a language of the Muslim nation . . . Pakistan has been created because of the demand of a hundred million Muslims in this subcontinent, and the language of a hundred million Muslims is Urdu. It is necessary for a nation to have one language and that language can only be Urdu and no other language.[10]

Urdu has always been considered a lyrical language and Lahore is a city of poets. Perhaps the most famous and celebrated literary resident was Mohammed Iqbal, who is also credited as the first person to articulate the idea of a separate Islamic state in the subcontinent. Born in Sialkot, in 1873, Iqbal came to Lahore for his education and soon adopted the city as his own. Though he later traveled to England, where he studied philosophy at Cambridge, Iqbal returned to Lahore soon after completing his Ph.D. He was heavily influenced by the Pan-Islamic sentiments of the Aligarh Movement and much of his work focused on reforming the Muslim faith.

In 1930, while addressing a meeting of the All-India Muslim League in Allahabad, he made the following appeal:

I would like to see the Punjab, North-West Frontier Province, Sind and Baluchistan amalgamated into a single state. Self-government within the British Empire, or without the British Empire, and the formation of a consolidated North-West state appears to me to be the final destiny of the Muslims at least of North-West India. . . .

The idea need not alarm the Hindus or the British. India is the greatest Muslim country in the world. The Life of Islam as a cultural force in this living country very largely depends on its centralization in a specified territory.[11]

But Mohammed Iqbal was more of a poet and philosopher than a politician. In Lahore his public recitations drew enormous crowds and his verses were appreciated by people of all faiths. Influenced by the writings of Sufi masters, he began to experiment with the Persian language toward the end of his life. He also seems to have begun to question the importance of a nation-state, turning instead to a less confining concept of community.

Now Brotherhood has been so cut to threads,
That in the stead of the community,
The country has been given pride of place,
In men's allegiance and constructive work:
The country is the darling of their hearts,
And wide Humanity is whittled down into dismembered tribes:
Vanished is humankind there but remain,
The disunited nations.[12]

Iqbal did not live to see the creation of Pakistan. He died in Lahore in 1937 and was spared the violence of Partition, which his poem seemed to predict.

In the first flush of Independence, Lahore enjoyed a resurgence of Urdu literature. The Progressive Writers Association, a leftist literary movement which had been active before Partition, was energized by the creation of Pakistan and the arrival of many prominent Muslim writers from India. Intizar Husain, a leading Urdu fiction writer, described the situation as follows:

I reached Lahore in mid-November of 1947 and found myself in a city swayed by the Progressive movement, as far as literature was concerned. The Progressive Writers Association was very active. Its weekly meetings, which were held regularly, attracted a large audience and were the venue of heated discussions and emotional outpourings with reference to the contemporary situation in the newly-born country.[13]

One of the most prominent figures of the Progressive Writers Movement was Faiz Ahmed Faiz, who helped invest Urdu literature with a modern sensibility and a social conscience. Though he composed many traditional ghazals that evoked the romantic and mystical motifs of Urdu poetry, Faiz also experimented with free verse and Marxist ideology. He too wrote about the bloodshed of Partition and the suffering in voices that went unheard.

Nowhere, no trace can I discover
of spilt blood,
not on the murderer's hand nor on his sleeve;
no daggers with red lips nor scarlet-pointed swords.

I see no blots on the dust,
no stains on the walls.

Nowhere, nowhere
does the blood reveal its darkness.

Not spilt in grandeur
nor as ritual sacrifice,
it was not shed on the field of battle,
it did not raise a martyr's banner.

Screaming loudly the orphan blood flowed on.
No-one had the time or sense,
none bothered to listen.

No witness, no defence;
the case is closed.
The blood of the downtrodden
seeped mutely into the dust.[14]

Faiz was imprisoned by the government of Pakistan on several occasions because of his leftist sympathies. Shortly before his death in 1984, he lived in exile in Beirut, a vocal supporter of the Palestinian cause. Despite his conflicts with the military regimes in Pakistan, he was an extremely popular poet who seemed to represent the aesthetic and liberal values of Lahore, which are often at odds with the rest of the nation.

There were many different landmarks that I was eager to see in Lahore, but first of all I wanted to go to number 10 Sanda Road, where my in-laws used to live. Liaqat Ali, the autorickshaw driver who took me there, proudly told me that he had been named after the first prime minister of Pakistan. A voluble, inquisitive man who talked nonstop over the sputtering roar of his scooter engine, Liaqat Ali told me that he had "four sons, three daughters, and one wife." Learning that I was an American he wanted to know if I could help him get a visa for the United Sates. Even though I said I didn't know anybody at the consulate, he wasn't deterred and every few minutes returned to the subject with annoying persistence.

Sanda Road turned out to be a broad, somewhat deserted street with no visible numbers on the buildings. Dodging bicyclists and potholes, Liaqat Ali swerved back and forth, asking directions from everyone we passed. Nobody seemed to know which of the houses was number 10. We searched the length of the street several times until we finally stopped at a small tailor shop. The proprietor was seated behind his sewing machine, stitching together a child's dress. He nodded cautiously, then pointed directly across the street, where a high wall enclosed a two-story building. The upper branches of mango trees and a bougainvillea vine were visible above the top of the wall.

When I told the tailor that my wife's family used to live there before 1947 he looked skeptical.

"Were they English?" he asked.

"No, Hindus," I said.

Once again he nodded, turning the wheel on the sewing machine as the needle darted in and out of the cloth.

"Nobody lives there any more," he said. "The house was turned into a factory but it's been closed for several years."

Liaqat Ali and I walked across and banged on the gate, which was locked. Nobody answered and it was impossible gain entry. In the end I took several photographs from different angles. Two weeks later, when I was back in Delhi, I showed the pictures to my in-laws. They recognized a couple of the other buildings on the street and after studying my pictures everyone in the family agreed that it must have been their house, though the building had been completely remodeled.

I'm not sure what I was expecting to find at number 10 Sanda Road. I had imagined that there would be a Muslim family living in the house, perhaps refugees themselves, who might have welcomed me inside and told me stories of their exile. My hope had been that there might be some kind of historical symmetry to this moment, but instead it was an anticlimax as I stood there hammering my fist on a metal gate and receiving no reply.

From Sanda Road we headed on to Anarkali bazaar, which is named after one of the concubines of Akbar, the Mughal emperor. According to the legend, widely disputed by skeptical historians, Akbar enjoyed the company of Anarkali (whose name means pomegranate blossom) in his Shish Mahal, the palace of mirrors. One day his son and heir, Salim, passed by and Akbar caught a glimpse of Anarkali's flirtatious smile reflected in a mirror. Enraged with jealousy, the emperor ordered that she be expelled from his harem and buried alive. Several years later, when Salim took over the throne and assumed the name of Jehangir, he had a magnificent hexagonal tomb erected over the spot where Anarkali died. A marble gravestone is inscribed with the Persian verses:

> Ah! could I behold the face of my beloved once more,
> I would give thanks unto my God until the day of resurrection.

This was signed, "The profoundly enamoured Salim, son of Akbar." Whatever truth there may be in the story itself, which inspired a classic Bombay film, the tragic romance of Anarkali is part of the ethos of Lahore. Her tomb now lies inside the grounds of the Punjab civil secretariat. In recent years it has been used as a storage facility for government files and records. Before that, the mausoleum was occupied as a private residence by General Ventura, an Italian mercenary in the army of Maharajah Ranjit Singh, and it was also briefly turned by the British into an Anglican church.[15]

Entering Anarkali bazaar on foot I couldn't help feeling that I was walking through sections of Old Delhi. The narrow streets lined with shops were almost identical. Several of the fabric stores were called saree shops but they sold only salwar kameez. One sign I noticed advertised the Delhi Muslim Hotel. Two others read, Lucknow Tobacco and Perfumers, and, Imam Bux of Ambala. Each of these signboards recalled the names of cities across the border from where the proprietors must have come as refugees.

By this time it was just past sunset and the bazaar was crowded after evening prayers. The minarets and arches of the mosques were lit up with colored bulbs and tube lights. Scooters and bicycles were parked along the margins of the street. Every fifty yards or so a gully cut off into the shadows, barely wide enough for two people to pass. A honeycomb of tiny shops sold everything from sweets to soap, cricket bats to air rifles. There were dozens of shoe shops, each with a different name: Galaxy Shoes, Popular Shoes, English Shoes, Imperial Shoes, Italian Shoes.

After I had walked about a quarter of a mile I came to the tinsel market. Metallic streamers were strung overhead and the fluorescent lights made each of the stalls shimmer like an electric storm. Most of the shops were selling decorations for the fiftieth Jubilee. There were enormous green balloons with Jinnah's features inflated to the point of bursting, lapel pins and buttons in the shape of Pakistan's flag or with slogans in Urdu and English: I Love Pakistan, Long Live Pakistan. Everything was dyed a bright parrot-green — hats embroidered with crescent moons, crepe-paper garlands, miniature flags, and party horns. The Jubilee was less than two weeks away and the city was gearing up for the celebrations.

When I stopped to buy some of the buttons at a stall, the young proprietor shook my hand enthusiastically. Surrounded by all of these nationalistic ornaments, cheap souvenirs, and patriotic bric-a-brac, I felt conspicuous being a foreigner. The proprietor fitted one of the hats on my head and raised his thumb in a gesture of approval.

"Where are you from?" he asked.

I hesitated for a moment and then said, "India," knowing that this would spark a reaction. "I'm taking these buttons back with me to Delhi."

He stopped and looked at me in disbelief, then wagged his finger in my face.

"But you like Pakistan better, don't you?" he said.

I had no choice but to nod my head.

The following day I set out to visit the Lahore Fort and the Badshahi Masjid, both of which were built by the Mughals. The fort rises above the city, an impressive complex of buildings surrounded by high walls and bastions. The Diwan-e-Am, hall of public audience, reminded me of the customs shed at Wagha, a vast, anonymous space. The Diwan-e-Khas, hall of private audience, was a more attractive building, with intricately carved screens that provided an atmosphere of intimacy and elegance. From here I could look out over the walls of the fort and see the Minar-e-Pakistan, a modern monument built to commemorate the country's Independence. It looked like a futuristic minaret, or perhaps a ballistic missile, surrounded by an open park and public gardens.

I toured the Shish Mahal where Anarkali was said to have made eyes at Prince Salim. The residential suites are called khwabgah, literally "dream chambers," where the emperors and their courtesans slept. These are surrounded by gardens, water channels, fountains, royal baths, and a pearl mosque. Perhaps the best known of all the structures in the fort is the Naulakha pavilion, made of marble and inlaid with semiprecious stones.

Walking through the fort I felt the vacancy of history. For all of the spectacular wealth and power of the Mughals, only a shell of the fort remains, the glass mosaics of the Shish Mahal reflecting the flash of a tourist's camera, the khwabgah empty of imperial dreams. On the steps of the Diwan-e-Khas, where the emperor received only the most privileged emissaries, sat a young boy memorizing lines from a copy book. Inside the fort it was silent, though beyond the walls I could hear the low rumble of the city, a clamor of voices and engines.

The Badshahi Masjid lies directly opposite the main gate of the fort. It is an enormous sandstone and marble mosque, very similar to the Jumma Masjid in Delhi. As I walked across the open courtyard I could see two men mopping the floors with wet cloths tied to ropes, which they swung back and forth in front of them, leaving damp arcs on the polished marble. An elderly gentleman with a white beard and baseball cap was standing in the shadows. As I approached he put out a hand to shake.

"I am a Sufi," he said. "May I be your guide?"

Though I shook my head, he would not let go of my hand.

"I am also a carpet exporter, if you would like to buy some carpets, I can show you around my factory."

"No thank you," I said, trying to move away.

"You must be an American?" he said. "My son is in Oklahoma studying for his M.A. in biology. I am eighty-one years old."

As I tried to pull my hand free he smiled insistently.

"As a Sufi I believe that there should be no trouble between religions," he said. "Each of us finds our own God."

Fortunately, at that moment, he caught sight of two European women coming across the courtyard and winked at me.

"The women and girls, they trust me to show them around because my beard is white."

Releasing my hand at last he asked if I had any coins that he could give to his grandchildren.

"It's a hobby of theirs. They collect all kinds of foreign money," he explained, but when I gave him some of my Indian coins he seemed disappointed. With a wave of his hand the Sufi said, "Goodbye. God willing, some day we will meet in America and have a drink of your choice together."

Circling the mosque I felt again the monumental emptiness of the place. Several thousand worshippers could have prayed inside the courtyard, but there was hardly anyone there. Retracing my steps toward the gate I saw a sign for a museum. The entry fee was two rupees and when I went inside I found a man bowing in front of a glass case. Not wanting to interrupt him I waited until he had finished his obeisance. The case contained a wrinkled turban wrapped around a kullar cap, a twisted walking stick, and a tattered quilt rolled into a bundle. According to a label on the wall these items were "attributed to the Prophet Mohammed," though this seemed an apocryphal claim. The museum, which consisted of three small rooms, contained other similar displays, the personal belongings of seventeenth-century Muslim saints. Looking at the clothes and bedding rolls, I realized they could just as easily have belonged to any of the travelers who had been with me on the train two days before.

Next to the Badshahi Masjid is a large Sikh gurdwara that is built on the site of Maharajah Ranjit Singh's samadhi. Like most Sikh temples it combines architectural motifs from Muslim and Hindu buildings. Since Partition the shrine has not been used very much, though there is an agreement with Sikh religious leaders in India, allowing pilgrims to cross the border and visit the gurdwara on certain festivals. With the escalation of the Sikh separatist movement in the 1980s, the government of Pakistan became more lenient in this regard. Flying above the temple was a blue and saffron flag bearing the Sikh emblem of two crossed swords, but when I asked if I could go inside the gurdwara I was told that the temple was closed to tourists and other visitors.

The competing narratives of contested history have a way of garbling the past, so that dates and events often blur together. It is possible, of course, to delineate the various dynasties that ruled Lahore, to say that

Mahmud of Ghazni, the first Muslim conqueror, captured the city in 1014 A.D. and put an end to Hindu dominance. There are recorded dates for the Ghuris, the Khaljis, the Tughluqs, the Sayyids, and the Lodis, who preceded the arrival of the first Mughal emperor, Babur, in 1526. Similarly it is an undisputed fact that Maharajah Ranjit Singh established himself on the throne of Lahore in 1799 and that the British defeated the Sikhs in 1849. But beyond this historical time line, which marks the rise and fall of princes, kings, and emperors, there is the uncharted lore of the past which does not follow a linear pattern and has been consciously manipulated by those who choose to tell these tales.

Rudyard Kipling was one of those storytellers who skillfully blended history and fiction. He first came to Lahore at the age of seventeen, in 1882, and got a job as an assistant editor at the *Civil and Military Gazette*. Though he was born in Bombay, it was Lahore that captured Kipling's imagination with a blend of Indian exoticism and the social customs of colonial life. His best-known work, the novel *Kim*, opens in Lahore with a scene that places his youthful hero at the crossroads of history:

> He sat, in defiance of municipal orders, astride the gun Zam-Zammah on her brick platform opposite the old Ajaib-Gher — the Wonder House, as the natives call the Lahore Museum. Who hold Zam-Zammah, that "fire breathing dragon," hold the Punjab, for the great green-bronze piece is always first of the conqueror's loot.[16]

For all his imperial rhetoric and conservative politics, Kipling understood that the British were part of a long line of conquerors who had ruled India for their own gain. Though he celebrated the achievements of empire, he was acutely aware of the tenuous hold that Britain had over its place in Indian history.

Zam-Zammah, which Kim sat on with boyish arrogance, remains in front of the Lahore Museum but the cannon now belongs to the independent state of Pakistan. The symbolism of this ancient gun is reinforced by a far more modern weapon of self-defense, a decommissioned fighter jet displayed on a traffic island further down the street. Just as the cannon is a relic of an age when the walled city of Lahore was often under siege, the jet reminds us of the air wars fought with

India, defending the border twenty kilometers to the east.

Inside the Lahore Museum, the facts of history become even more elusive. The building itself, with domes and sculpted archways, suggests an oriental fantasy. Compared to the stolid magnitude of the fort and the austere lines of the Badshahi Masjid, the museum is a carnival of shapes, a labyrinth of intersecting rooms and disorienting passageways that only adds to the wonder and strangeness of its exhibits.

The central chamber, through which all visitors enter the museum, is lined with carved doorways from sixteenth-century Hindu homes but on the ceiling there is a modern mural in gaudy shades of blue and orange — an abstract painting of stylized hands and surrealistic sunbursts. The first gallery I entered had the sign "General" above its door. Inside was a jumble of different objects, thrown together without any sense of chronology or order. One of the cases exhibited a nineteenth-century chair with velvet upholstery, a pair of elephant tusks, and a sporting trophy presented in 1961 by Jawaharlal Nehru to the Pakistani cricket team. On the opposite wall was a display of miniature paintings from Kangra, exquisitely detailed images of Radha and Krishna making love beneath monsoon clouds. A random collection of other incongruous artifacts shared the same space in the gallery, so that at times I felt as if I was walking through the clutter of an antique shop rather than a museum.

The other galleries were somewhat better organized. I moved on to a room that was dedicated to the early Islamic period: prayer rugs and brass hookahs, chain-mail armor, ornamental swords, blue tiles, and musical instruments. Beyond this was a gallery of Tibetan art — prayer wheels and begging bowls that might have belonged to the lama in *Kim*. A life-size Buddha from Burma sat in meditation under a gilded parasol. At the opposite end of the room were Hindu statues, a marble Hanuman, his simian features stained with vermillion and idols of Ram and Sita that must have been rescued from temples at the time of Partition. There was also a marble lingam, the phallic symbol of Shiva.

The Mohenjo-daro and Harappan civilizations (2,500-1,800 B.C.) had their own separate gallery but by this time I had lost my historical bearings. The terracotta seals had pictures of a rhinoceros and elephant, miniature emblems of a culture that was here long before any of the other religions were established, a cryptic world of natural symbols and deities. But perhaps the most impressive works of art in the museum were the Gandhara statues from the Buddhist period. Excavated near Taxila and Peshawar, these statues are carved out of gray and blue schist. Though the images have distinctly Asian features, there are traces of Greek influence, from the time of Alexander. Unlike the clean-shaven Tibetan idols, these bodhisattvas sported luxurious moustaches and elaborate hairstyles. The famous statue of Buddha fasting at Bodh Gaya shows his body reduced to a skeleton, the veins and tendons visible beneath the skin, all rendered in precise anatomical detail. Nearby was a vaguely erotic carving of two figures embracing. The sign in English and in Urdu read: Sculptures of Foreign Influence.

In an Islamic society like Pakistan, which is growing increasingly conservative, idolatry and representations of human and animal forms are clearly taboo. The windowless galleries of the museum not only muddle the different eras of history but also serve as a vault that stores forbidden objects and images. One of the relics hidden away inside the Lahore Museum is a statue of Queen Victoria that used to grace the roundabout at the head of Mall Road. After 1947, the Empress of India was removed from her pedestal. In her place there is now a copy of the Qur'an.

As in Delhi, many of the colonial names of streets and landmarks in Lahore have been changed to reflect the country's independence. The largest public park in the city, once known as Lawrence Gardens, is now called Bagh-e-Jinnah, in honor of the founding father of Pakistan.

On my last morning in Lahore, I went for a walk in the gardens before the heat of the day became too intense. At the gate stood a hawker selling challi, corn on the cob which is roasted inside a smoldering mound of charcoal dust. Buying one of these for breakfast, I entered the gardens and joined the other residents of Lahore who were out for their morning constitutionals. It had rained heavily, only an hour before, and a light mist was rising off the asphalt paths. The main cricket oval in Lahore, where international test matches are played, lies at the center of Bagh-e-Jinnah. Clusters of young men and boys were playing games of cricket with rubber balls and makeshift wickets. Every few minutes there were shouts of protest or delight as someone was caught out or clean bowled.

The trees and flower beds in the park are well maintained and everything was a lush green because of the monsoon. At the far end of the garden stood a huge white building, which used to be the British club. It has been renamed the Qaid-e-Azam (great leader) library, once again in honor of Jinnah. At that hour of the morning the doors were locked, but there were bulletin boards out front, displaying the dust jackets of recent publications. One of the books was *The Crescent at a Glance,* by Shaikh Muhammad Qayyum. A list of other titles by the same author included *Indian History at a Glance (Objective).* This parenthetical qualifier was obviously meant to reassure the reader of the author's unbiased perspective.

Next to these book jackets was a poster that caught my eye:

A Workshop

LEARNING HYPNOSIS CORRECTLY
Presented by Dr. Richard Harte, Ph.D.
National Guild of Hypnotists
New Hampshire, U.S.A.

Hypnosis Is Everyone's Business

The poster went on to announce that the benefits of hypnosis included painless dentistry and chemotherapy, quitting smoking, learning how to swim, and as a special recommendation to jurists: "Judges use hypnosis for exposing sneaky advocates." The cost of the workshop was $750 in advance and $1,000 at the door. "Don't Miss It!" was written at the top in felt pen, though the date of the workshop was June 14. I had arrived a month and a half too late.

Like most of the ancient cities of South Asia, Lahore was once enclosed by high stone walls to protect it from invaders. The ruins of these walls can still be seen along the perimeter of the old city. Many of the original gates remain standing, remnants of a time when feudal armies swept across the land. While the larger, territorial claims of each regime were limited to extorting taxes or tribute from those who farmed the land, it was the cities that were fortified. Up until the middle of the nineteenth-century the borders of a kingdom were often fluid and poorly guarded, but the outer limits of a city like Lahore would have been fiercely defended. Travelers were only permitted entry if they posed no threat, and after dark the gates were closed.

Today these cities have expanded far beyond their original walls and the gates are nothing more than quaint reminders of uncertain times. With the establishment of national borders there is little need for cities to maintain their walls. The modern state has extended its envelope of power to the extreme limits of its territorial claims. In this way the security of each city no longer depends on its immediate battlements but on a distant, invisible border that lies beyond the horizon. Yet within the old cities, where vestiges of those fortifications still stand, a feeling of enclosure lingers on.

Late in the afternoon I took an autorickshaw to Delhi Gate, one of the twelve entrances to the old city of Lahore. The gate itself must have been rebuilt less than a hundred years ago, for the architectural style and brickwork did not match the original stone walls. Outside the gate were dozens of tongas, horse-drawn carriages that were the most common mode of transport in the city before the arrival of motor vehicles. The horses stood patiently, snuffling into their feedbags and occasional stamping their hooves. More than a dozen sheep and goats were tied up at nearby stalls, their wool splashed with bright colors to identify the owners. These animals were being fattened for Bakr Eid, when they would be slaughtered for the feast.

Immediately in front of the old walls stood a line of vendors with pushcarts, selling costume jewelry, cheap combs, and plastic billfolds. Delhi Gate was wide enough for a car to pass through, but the only traffic on the street was bicycles and autorickshaws, as well as pedestrians. There were shops on either side, much smaller and not as brightly lit as those I had seen in Anarkali bazaar. One shop was selling only guavas, another had bottles of pomegranate juice. Bangle merchants displayed colorful rows of fragile glass bracelets. I stopped at the Quereshi Cap Shop, where the proprietor explained that each of the hats he sold came from a different region of the country. He also had wedding turbans with starched coxcombs of pink muslin and the name of Allah embroidered on the front.

This bazaar has existed for over five hundred years, and though most of the buildings are not that old, there is an unmistakable atmosphere of antiquity. Instead of the open arcades along the Mall Road, with four lanes of traffic, the walled city of Lahore seems much more intricately constructed, with low doorways and miniature windows. Here is a city within the city, altogether insular, the streets so narrow that sunlight does not penetrate beyond the roofs. In its crowded maze of lanes there is a feeling of sanctuary. The old walls may have fallen to ruin, but the conglomeration of houses and shops still give the original city of Lahore its organic structure, like the accretions of a coral reef.

A short distance inside the Delhi Gate I came to the Wazir Khan mosque, which was built in 1634. Wazir Khan served as viceroy of the Punjab under Shah Jahan. He built the mosque around the tomb of a Persian saint. The walls of the shrine are beautifully decorated with painted frescoes, mostly floral designs, cypress trees, and arabesques. Sections of these paintings have peeled away over time and parts of the walls have fallen down, exposing rows of wafer-thin bricks. The mosque itself is virtually impossible to see from the outside because it is surrounded by other buildings, but once you step through the gate, it opens into a relatively spacious courtyard.

As I entered the mosque, a flock of pigeons took to the air, the sound of their wings like muffled applause. Immediately I saw a young boy running toward me. He was eight or nine years old and grabbed my hand in excitement.

"Are you American?" he asked, in Urdu.

When I nodded he seemed delighted.

"Then you must have seen a farishta," he said. "Tell me what they're like."

Farishta is the word for angel, but his question still puzzled me.

"What do you mean?" I asked.

"You know, the farishta you have in your country," said the boy, insistently. "Haven't you ever seen them?"

By this time five or six other children had gathered around me, all of them about the same age.

"I'm sorry, I don't know what you mean," I said. "What kind of farishta?"

The boy and his friends looked up at me impatiently. "You know, the ones we see on TV."

At this point two of the children struck a pose that finally made me understand that they were referring to the superheroes in American cartoon shows. These were the farishta, or angels, that I was supposed to have seen. For all its insularity the old city of Lahore was still vulnerable to the influences of the outside world. When I looked beyond the parapets of the mosque I could see dozens of dish antennas sprouting from the rooftops.

6

PESHAWAR   To the Khyber Pass

BHURBAN (PPI) — The Senate chairman, Wasim Sajjad, Sunday, castigated India for meddling in the internal affairs of Afghanistan, taking advantage of the infighting going on in the war-battered country. . . .

Wasim said there were hopes that Afghanistan would help promote political stability in the Muslim world after the break-up of former Soviet Union. But India is trying to become another Soviet Union by interfering in Afghanistan, which will result only in the destruction of the oppressed people of Afghanistan. . . .

The Senate chairman also referred to the issue of Kashmir and lamented that India was blatantly violating human rights in the occupied valley. He said India had converted heaven on earth into hell and was engaged in the genocide of Kashmiri Muslims to accomplish her imperialist designs.—*Frontier Post*, 4 August 1997

Seated in the sweltering refreshment room of the Lahore railway station, Syed Ibrahim fixed me with a nervous expression and explained that he was on his way to India. I had met him less than ten minutes earlier, but as we drank cups of syrupy tea under the oscillating shadows and gusts of humid air from a ceiling fan, the story of his life spilled out. He spoke in Urdu, with his voice lowered, as if he were confiding secrets. A gaunt, agitated man with restless eyes and a graying beard, Syed Ibrahim had worked as a railway employee for thirty years but now was being forced to retire.

"There is a mistake," he said. "In 1947, when I came to Pakistan at the time of Partition, all my identity papers were lost. Later, when I got a job with the railways, a doctor wrote down on one of my medical forms that I was born in 1935, but my actual year of birth is 1940."

Opening his wallet he shuffled through a wad of folded documents and produced a yellowed ID card to show me the incorrect date. Pakistan Railways, he said, would only let him keep his job if he could prove his age. But the problem was that he had been born in Jhansi, eight hundred kilometers away, on the other side of the border. Though he had a sister still living there, Syed Ibrahim hadn't been back to his birthplace for over fifty years. Pulling out his passport he pointed to the Indian visa he had been granted after three months of waiting. The next morning he was going to take the train to Delhi, then make his way to Jhansi, hoping to get a copy of his birth certificate.

Learning that I had crossed over from India three days earlier, Syed Ibrahim quizzed me anxiously, asking about customs and immigration procedures. He was worried that he might have to pay duty and bribes. Short on money, he was carrying a dozen nylon shirts, imported from Malaysia, which he hoped to sell in India, along with a new suitcase he had bought last year, while on Haj pilgrimage to Mecca.

Syed Ibrahim was in no hurry to finish his tea. Though I was catching the Khyber Mail, which left in half an hour, his train to India wasn't scheduled to leave until the following morning and he was planning to spend the night on the platform. His home was in Karachi and he had no place to stay in Lahore. He was a muhajir, as he called himself, a refugee.

"Why did you leave in forty-seven?" I asked

He looked at me with a bemused expression.

"Because I am a Muslim," he said. "After the British left, I knew there wouldn't be any opportunities for me in India. People were being killed. There were riots everywhere. For a while we were put in a camp for our protection, then I got on a train to Pakistan. An uncle of mine had decided to go and I went with him. The rest of my family stayed behind in Jhansi. I never saw my parents again. They died some years ago."

"Are you glad you came to Pakistan?"

"Yes." He nodded, emphatically. "Of course, there are problems here as well but it is all in God's hands. Just think, fifty years ago I arrived at this station by train and now I'm going back, just to get a piece of paper."

The Khyber Mail follows much the same route as the old Frontier Mail, though instead of going from Bombay to Peshawar, it starts in Karachi. The train pulled into Lahore station around eight in the evening and I found my first-class carriage without much difficulty. Once inside, however, it was impossible to locate my berth because all the lights were off. The carriage itself seemed well over fifty years old, with broken windows and the smell of dust and urine in the corridor. After I had been searching about in the dark for several minutes, another passenger struck a match and I was finally able to see my compartment number scratched into the paint above the door. Inside there were four other travelers, but I could not make out their faces even with the little bit of light that came through the windows. One of the men shifted over and made room for me on the seat as I stowed my suitcase in the corner.

As soon as the train began moving the man to my right leaned forward and spoke a few words of halting English. He seemed relieved when I replied in Urdu and told me that his name was Tosif Amjad. He was in his early thirties, with a neatly trimmed beard and a Nike baseball cap on his head. When he discovered where I was coming from he told me that he had been to India once, as a member of Pakistan's national handball team. They had played at Indira Gandhi Stadium in New Delhi. He was proud of the fact that they had won their matches but said that it was a "friendly series."

I asked him about the rivalry between the two countries and whether he had felt an added tension when playing against India.

"No, of course not," he said. "The Indians treated us very well and showed us all around Delhi. It's the politicians who create these tensions. We sportsmen are only interested in the game."

After a while we began to talk about cricket. Tosif knew the names of all the Indian players, their batting statistics, and the strengths and weaknesses of the bowlers.

"With cricket matches there's a difference," he admitted. "Whenever our two countries play against each other, it's like going to war."

As a member of Pakistan's handball team, Tosif had also been abroad to Iran, Cyprus, and Turkey. He told me that he loved to travel and that one of his ambitions was to ride the Trans-Siberian Railroad. Tosif's home was in Gujranwala, an hour and a half beyond Lahore, where he had a business selling audio and video equipment. He imported second-hand VCRs from Singapore and after dismantling them sold the components separately as spare parts.

When we pulled into Gujranwala the smell of roasting meat filled the air. Along the side of the tracks there were dozens of vendors selling kebabs. The smoke from their charcoal braziers made it seem as if the station was on fire. Tosif tried to persuade me to get off the train and spend a few days with him in Gujranwala, but despite his friendliness and the tempting odor of kebabs, I decided to continue on my way.

Later that night, I found myself wishing that I had accepted his invitation. Without electricity there were no fans in the compartment, and even though I was able to stretch out on the lower berth it was impossible to sleep because of the heat. Another two hours beyond Gujranwala, we stopped at a siding, near the station of Lalla Musa. I was aware that people were getting off the train and soon I heard a loud banging on the outside of our carriage. Someone shouted that all passengers should get down. There was no further explanation but the other men in the compartment hurriedly began to pull their luggage together.

We were half a mile from the edge of town and the siding was deserted, with no buildings or lights nearby. Eventually I found one of the conductors, surrounded by a ring of anxious passengers. He explained that there was a problem with our carriage; a wheel had fallen off and the train had almost been derailed. We were told to "adjust" ourselves in one of the other carriages because ours was going to be detached. By this time it was one o'clock in the morning and after some searching I squeezed into a second-class compartment, toward the front of the train. The eight other passengers who occupied this space cheerfully made room for me. Despite the discomfort and lateness of the hour everyone was in a surprisingly good mood. One of the passengers, a young doctor who spoke English, kept telling me that I should write up this experience and sell it to *Reader's Digest* as a "True Life Adventure."

It was impossible to sleep in the crowded compartment but after a while our conversations drifted into silence and we sat like two rows of marionettes, our heads bobbing on our necks with the rhythm of the train. At Rawalpindi station some of the travelers got out and an hour and a half later, as we passed through Taxila, the sun began to rise over the eroded hills.

In the seat directly opposite me was a tall, severe-looking man who had said very little during the night. From his moustache and the way he carried himself, I assumed he was a Pathan. He seemed unfriendly and the few times our eyes met, he looked away in disdain. When we reached the station of Attock, two armed policemen came into the compartment and we made room for them. The Pathan spoke to them in Pushto, the language of the frontier, with much gesticulation.

Soon afterward we crossed the River Indus near the town of Attock. Nearly a quarter of a mile in breadth, its waters were swollen with snowmelt. Half of the river was a milky gray color and the other half a muddy brown, as if it were two rivers in one. The current was divided down the middle and even though the Indus was flowing swiftly and churning over submerged rocks, the two streams did not mix together. It seemed as if an indelible line had been drawn down the middle, cutting the river in two. The different colors are caused by the confluence of the Kabul River and the Indus. Attock is a town that dates back to the time of the Mughals and it has traditionally been regarded as the informal frontier between the plains of the Punjab and the mountainous regions to the west.

As our train crossed over the bridge, the morning sunlight shone through the window and I took out my dark glasses, an old pair of Ray-Bans I've owned for years. Instantly the Pathan broke off his conversation with the two policemen and put out his hand for me to shake. Surprised by this sudden gesture of camaraderie, I couldn't figure out what was going on until he reached into his pocket and took out an identical pair of Ray-Bans.

Putting these on and switching to Urdu, he launched into a long lecture for the benefit of the whole compartment, explaining the merits of our sunglasses.

"You can wear them all day and never get a headache," he said. "Besides, when a man puts them on he feels like a king."

The Pathan and I were now compatriots. He had set aside his aloof demeanor and for the rest of the journey, the two of us wore our Ray-Bans proudly, while the other passengers quizzed us on where they could buy a pair. Dismissing their questions with a haughty gesture, the Pathan began to tell me about the Indus, explaining that Alexander the Great, "Sikander-e-Azam," had come this far in his conquests but finally turned back when he failed to cross the river. Half an hour later, as we pulled into Nowshera Station, the Pathan stood up and took his leave, pushing his Ray-Bans up the bridge of his prominent nose and shaking my hand in a resolute grip.

The stereotypical Pathan, or Pakhtun, is a central figure in frontier legends, a mountain tribesman who yields to nobody except for members of his own clan. He lives in the North-West Frontier Province (NWFP) and the semiautonomous tribal districts bordering Afghanistan. The British, as much as anyone, helped create this mythology, labeling the Pathans as a "martial race" and recruiting them into the colonial army.

As the inhabitants of borderlands, which form a buffer zone between Pakistan and its neighbors to the north and west, Pathans are idealized for their sense of personal dignity and honor. Traditionally, they have always resisted the concept of national sovereignty, governing themselves through feudal treaties and administering their own form of justice, known as jirga. Each Pathan clan or tribe is ruled by a council of elders who decide the disputes that come before them. While I was visiting Peshawar, the *Frontier Post*, a local English-language daily, ran a series of articles outlining the merits of jirga:

> Jirga system is one of the most time honoured institutions in the tribal world. It is part of the culture of the tribesmen who are very proud and fond of their culture. This system is not merely a judicial system like any other judicial or legal system but is also a

legislative assembly. It governs the entire tribal life whether judicial, social, political or economic in nature. Any dispute in a family, clan, tribe or inter-tribe is to be settled through it by decision based on the mixture of Shariah and Pakhtunwali, the Pakhtun code of honor.[1]

The same article made it clear that justice is administered swiftly and without hesitation. An eyewitness to an adultery case recounted, "The jirga was in progress at 9 A.M. with the accused and representatives of both the tribes. At 11:30 A.M., one tribe took the girl on the eastern slope of the hill while the other tribe took the accused towards the western slope. Four shots were heard from both slopes and two dead bodies were taken away."[2]

There is no doubt that these border regions are dominated by the rule of men. Women are zealously protected and hidden from view, even more strictly than elsewhere in Pakistan. On the special permit I was issued to travel to the Khyber Pass, there was a succinct warning: "Photography of Women Folk and Protected Areas Prohibited." Most of the tourist literature for the NWFP celebrates the masculine attributes of the Pathans. Their bravado and fearlessness is admired in Pakistan and several people with whom I spoke made a point of saying that there was much less corruption in the NWFP than elsewhere in the country. The Pathan is also generally regarded as a pious Muslim, who remains true to the basic tenets of his faith. Despite his unwillingness to acknowledge the authority of the government, this romanticized figure has become something of a national icon in Pakistan.

Like many of his generation, my grandfather, Emmet Alter, subscribed to these frontier myths. In 1937 he wrote a novel titled *Mann of the Border*.[3] The hero in the story is a missionary doctor named Ernest Mann, who works at The Good Samaritan Hospital in the NWFP, near the borders of Afghanistan. Though he is on friendly terms with the colonial authorities, Dr. Mann admires the simple dignity of the Pathans. When British troops march across the border to put down a tribal uprising, the American missionary finds himself torn between the two sides in the conflict. Disguising himself in salwar kameez and a turban he treks across the border to treat the Pathan warriors who have been injured in the fighting. With an unswerving faith in God, he risks his life to help the wounded. Despite the fact that he is white-skinned and considered infidel, Mann is protected by the Pathan codes of honor and hospitality. His own athletic prowess helps him survive in the hostile terrain and he even wins a wrestling bout with one of the recalcitrant chieftains. In the end Dr. Mann returns across the border and brokers a peace between the British authorities and the Pathans. There is also a love story at the heart of this novel. The heroic doctor returns to his mission station and is reunited with Margaret Wallace, the woman who rejected him ten years before.

All this is fiction, of course, though my grandparents worked for nearly forty years as missionaries in the NWFP and Punjab. An unabashed romantic, my grandfather borrowed freely from Kipling's stories and wholeheartedly appropriated the colonial myth of "going native." Unfortunately, Emmet Alter died before I was born, but I remember seeing his novel on our family bookshelves when I was a boy and hearing stories about his fascination for the frontier. During the 1920s he and my grandmother lived in the town of Abbottabad. We have family albums from that period, with photographs of border areas near Kohat and the Khyber Pass. One of the pictures is of an armed sentry standing beside a boundary pillar. In those days the British controlled the roads and railway lines but the rest of the territory was governed by feuding clans. As if to prove this point, there is another photograph in the album, taken at the side of the highway. A fortified village is in the distance, connected to the motor road by a long trench instead of a footpath, so that travelers could avoid being shot as they made their way home.

The romance of the frontier is a persistent and integral part of Britain's colonial narratives. For writers like Kipling, H. Rider Haggard, or John Masters, the frontier represented a region that was still ungoverned, a no man's land where colonial authority did not exist. During the late nineteenth and early twentieth centuries the British tried unsuccessfully to subdue the Pathan tribes and the disastrous results of their Afghan campaigns added weight to the white man's burden. It is precisely because the British were unable to extend their empire into these areas that the frontier became an obsession. Hollywood perpetuated these myths with films like *Drum* and *The Man Who Would Be King*, pitting the noble savagery (and dirty tricks) of

the mountain tribes against the starched manners and good sports-
manship of British officers.

When we finally arrived in Peshawar, six hours late, I got into an autorickshaw and asked the driver to take me to the Kissa Kahani bazaar.
We sped off in a fury of blue exhaust and I was soon deposited in front
of the Dubai Hotel, which the driver claimed was the best place to
stay in this part of town. I was skeptical but decided to give it a try,
and climbed up a narrow staircase to the upper floor, where the recep-
tion desk and restaurant were situated. The manager said that he could
give me a room for fifty rupees and, though the hotel appeared un-
promising, I was too exhausted to look elsewhere. My room was another three floors up, a grubby little cubicle barely wide enough to fit
a single bed. There was a fan and a window but instead of curtains the
panes of glass had been smeared with yellow paint to provide some
privacy. Previous occupants had scratched their names in the paint and
sections had peeled away, through which I could see the rooftops of
Peshawar. The attached bathroom was nothing but a closet with a single tap and a hole in the floor. Having had no sleep at all the night before, I switched on the fan, lay down on the bed, and dozed off immediately.

Four hours later I woke up disoriented. The electricity had gone off
and the fan was motionless. With the late afternoon sun beating
against the window, my room was like a solar cooker. However, the
thing that confused me most of all was that I could hear partridges
calling, even though I knew I was in the middle of a city.

Later, I discovered that many of the merchants in Peshawar had pet
black partridges, hanging in cages from the rafters of their shops.
These seemed to be a symbol of status and I was told that each bird
was worth over two thousand rupees. Every few minutes the partridges gave out a shrill cry, which carried over the noises of the
bazaar. The call of a black partridge is considered auspicious because it
sounds like an Urdu exclamation, "Subaan teri kudrat!" praising the
beauty of God's creations.

Kissa Kahani bazaar literally means the storyteller's market; it was
once a place where travelers from across the mountains gathered and
exchanged tales of their adventures or the latest news from Kabul,

Kashgar, and Samarkhand. These itinerant raconteurs have long since disappeared, but in the lobby of my hotel there was a video playing at full volume, while a group of twenty or thirty men drank tea and watched a Hindi film with rapt attention. Even here in this frontier town, television has replaced the oral traditions of the past. And the name Dubai Hotel reflects more contemporary routes of trade and travel, which now lead from Pakistan to the oil-rich emirates in the Persian Gulf.

Unable to bear the heat in my room, I headed out into the bazaar on foot. Peshawar still evokes a romantic history. It has always been located at the crossroads of commerce, and the old city has twelve gates from which the ancient trade routes radiated in all directions like the hours on a clock. Each market has its own name — Khyber bazaar, Chitrali bazaar, and the Mochi bazaar where cobblers line the streets, selling leather goods of all kinds, shoes and sandals, dog collars, saddle straps, suitcases, and cartridge belts. A couple of Afghans, who looked as if they had just returned from the trenches of Jalalabad, were wandering about the streets selling holsters and wire brushes for cleaning gun barrels.

The spice market lay near Kabuli Gate and the sharp scent of dried ginger, coriander, red chilies, cumin, and tumeric made my eyes sting. Around the corner was a line of soap merchants, their shelves piled high with thick cakes of laundry soap, a murky green color, scented with cheap perfume. On ahead I passed rows and rows of fabric shops and a tinsel market in which there were wedding decorations for sale, garlands of hundred-rupee notes with Jinnah's stern features arranged in a sunburst of gold filigree. Every thirty or forty yards I came upon food stalls and tea shops with enormous brass and copper samovars. The green tea served here comes from China, an indication of the cultural and trade links with Central Asia. Peshawar is also famous for its dried fruits and nuts. Many of the shops were selling heaps of almonds, walnuts, and apricots. On the pavement sat a streetside dentist who had spread a rug on the ground and displayed an assortment of dentures with pink plastic gums and grinning white teeth.

Unlike the bazaars in Lahore or Delhi, which are colorful but seem to have adapted to modern times, the older sections of Peshawar have a medieval quality, as if goods are still brought into the market by caravan. Of course this isn't true, but as I wandered about Peshawar I could sense the convergence of trade routes, the dusty roads from Kashgar and Kabul, Samarkhand and Khandahar, all feeding into the heart of this ancient city.

For the past two days I hadn't seen a newspaper but stopping at a stationers in Chitrali bazaar, I bought a copy of the *Frontier Post* and sat down to read at a tea shop next door. On the front page was the headline:

Americans asked not to go out in public

The newspaper contained several articles about anti-American demonstrations all across Pakistan. These were the result of an ongoing court case against a Pakistani citizen named Aimal Kansi, who was accused of shooting two CIA employees in Langley, Virginia. The government of Pakistan had helped the FBI arrest Kansi and in return the United States had agreed to pay a bounty for his capture and deportation. Many Pakistanis were already unhappy about their government's collusion with the United States. But the immediate cause of the current protests were the offensive remarks made by a state prosecutor in Virginia, Robert Horan. He was quoted as having said that America should not pay "The Paks two million dollars as they would sell their own mothers for a few thousand dollars."

The prime minister, Nawaz Sharif, had issued a statement saying that Horan's remarks were "highly objectionable and shameful and below the dignity of humanity." Meanwhile, opposition leaders were calling on all political parties in Pakistan to go on a nationwide strike. Al Ikhwan leader, Tariq Chaudhry, expressed his outrage: "Mere statements against the U.S. would not make any difference. We have to tell the Americans that we would not accept such shameful utterances." As a precaution, the foreign ministry advised "American nationals to avoid visiting public places so long as the tempers are high."[4]

Up until this point I had been moving about quite openly and I hadn't noticed any evidence of public anger. Nobody had mentioned the Kansi case to me, even when they knew I was an American. Much of the hostility seemed to be focused on the U.S. Embassy in Islamabad and the consulates in Lahore and Karachi. The reaction in Pakistan was understandable and it was more than just a matter of national pride. Horan's remarks represent the kind of racism that underlies American opinions about countries like Pakistan, with whom the United States maintains ambivalent alliances. After reading the newspaper and fortified by several cups of tea I decided that I would ignore the warnings, though I avoided flashing my passport about for the next few days, until the furor died away.

"The water in Peshawar is very healthy. It comes from the mountains. You can eat a whole kilo of meat, then drink one glass of water, and you will have no trouble with digestion."

This advice was given to me by the manager of the Dubai Hotel. I did not put his theory to the test, but I did consume a good deal of meat in Peshawar because there was little else to eat. In fact, almost everywhere I went in Pakistan the only choices on the menu were mutton, beef, or chicken. One of the restaurants in Peshawar served a breakfast buffet consisting of minced lamb, chicken jhalfrezi, and grilled kidneys with liver. The waiters looked at me strangely when all I ordered was tea and toast. Coming from India, this was one of the most striking differences I found between the two countries. Though I have no inclination to be a vegetarian, the prevalence of meat was disconcerting and seemed to verge on a dietary obsession.

The relationship between the North-West Frontier Province and the eating of meat suggests a curious equation. In the convoluted mythology of these border regions, where life is harsh and unforgiving, the slaughter of animals and the eating of flesh corresponds to a basic code of manliness. Meat is seen as an essential part of the diet for it gives a man strength and vitality. Vegetables are available in the market and obviously eaten but they seem to have no place outside the home. At one restaurant I finally found "mixed vegetables" on the menu but these turned out to be nothing more than potatoes and carrots.

The differences in dietary conventions have always been an important element in the history of the subcontinent. Some of the most volatile conflicts between Hindus and Muslims revolve around the issue of meat. The killing of cows is considered sacrilege by orthodox Hindus and beef is rarely available in India. Pork, on the other hand, is taboo for Muslims. A good many riots have resulted from the death of a cow or the carcass of a pig. Even the 1857 mutiny against the British has been blamed on animal fat that was used in greased cartridges, issued to the Indian troops.

The symbolic importance of flesh is undeniable. It can be found in everything from the cries of "Veg?" "Non-Veg?" that one hears on an airplane to the subtleties of signs on butcher shops, which advertise different methods of slaughter — halal or jatka. The first is the more orthodox technique, prescribed in Islam, where the throat is cut and the animal slowly bleeds to death, while a cleric recites a short prayer. The second is a quicker and more humane process, in which the goat or sheep is beheaded with a single stroke. Unlike in the West, where meat is usually processed and packaged beyond recognition, in Pakistan and India carcasses often hang from the doorway of a butcher's shop and customers select the cut of meat they desire.

Even in North India, where most restaurants offer a wide range of vegetarian dishes, there is still an enduring mystique about meat. Several of the five-star hotels in Delhi have restaurants which are centered around a frontier theme, serving "authentic border cuisine." The entrees have names like Kabuli Naan, Peshawari Kebab, and Khyber Chicken. These restaurants cater to the elite of Delhi, many of them Hindu and Sikh refugees, who originally came from the North-West Frontier and Punjab. Playing up the nostalgia of these lost homelands, in both their decor and cooking, Delhi's hoteliers have tapped into the frontier myth of meat and masculinity.

The importance of being nonvegetarian is a integral part of Pakistani identity. One of the most insightful books about contemporary society in Pakistan is a memoir by Sara Suleri, entitled *Meatless Days*. She writes:

> The country was made in 1947, and shortly thereafter the government decided that two days out of each week would be designated as meatless days, in order to conserve the national supply of goats and cattle. Every Tuesday and Wednesday the butchers' shops would stay firmly closed, without a single carcass dangling

from the huge metal hooks that lined the canopies under which the butchers squatted, selling meat, and without the open drains at the side of their narrow street ever running with a trace of blood. . . .

As a principle of hygiene I suppose it was a good idea although it really had very little to do with conservation: the people who could afford to buy meat, after all, were those who could afford refrigeration, so the only thing the government accomplished was to make some people's Mondays very busy indeed. The Begums had to remember to give the cooks thrice as much money; the butchers had to produce thrice as much meat; the cooks had to buy enough flesh and fowl and other sundry organs to keep an averagely carnivorous household eating for three days. A favorite meatless day breakfast, for example, consisted of goat's head and feet cooked with spices into a rich and ungual sauce.[5]

By coincidence, the day after I arrived in Peshawar happened to be a meatless day, and all the kebab shops in the Kissa Kahani bazaar were closed. The fragrance of barbecued meat that had wafted up to my hotel room in the evening had dissipated and the charcoal braziers lay cold and full of ash. Restaurants were permitted to serve only chicken, which for some odd reason is not considered meat. This was a fortunate distinction, since otherwise I might have gone hungry.

The Khyber Pass had recently been opened to foreigners, after being off-limits for several years because of the war in Afghanistan. As a precaution, however, I was required to hire a bodyguard. Special tourist permits are issued by the Political Agent of the Khyber, an administrative position that dates back to nineteenth-century treaties between the British and the Pathan warlords of this region. The Khyber Agency is one of several autonomous tribal districts in Pakistan and the police are not permitted to enter these areas. The main highway is patrolled by tribal militia, called khasedars, and the army has several forts along the route, but on either side of the road there remains a feudal world of clan and family rivalries.

The driver of the decrepit Toyota that took me to the Khyber Pass was an elderly man named Mohammed Shafi. He helped me get my permit and procure a bodyguard, who happened to be an off-duty khasedar named Zahir Shah. He was a young, red-haired teenager with a sheepish grin and a battered AK-47. As we set off from Peshawar, Mohammed Shafi told me that his father had been a noncommissioned officer under the British.

"During the Second World War he was posted to Rangoon, which is where he met my mother," he said. "That's the reason for my Chinese eyes."

Mohammed Shafi was a devout Muslim and for most of the journey he complained about American prejudices against Islamic countries, including U.S. policies in the Middle East, the war in Iraq, and the recent comments by Robert Horan. Shafi also complained about India, saying that they had no right to occupy Kashmir and that he was convinced the Hindus still planned to reconquer all of Pakistan. Zahir Shah spoke only Pashto and remained silent throughout most of the four-hour ride.

Ten kilometers outside of Peshawar we passed a large Afghan refugee camp called Kachi Gahi which has been there for almost fifteen years. Though the houses are made of mud they now have electricity and plumbing, as well as an impressive array of TV aerials. Further on we passed the Karkhana bazaar, where black-market goods are sold, everything from televisions and refrigerators to textiles from Malaysia and Singapore. This multistory complex of shops and warehouses is located about a kilometer from the border outpost of Jamrud, and much of the merchandise is smuggled over the Khyber Pass. Limited jurisdiction over these tribal areas allows for an elaborate network of corruption and commerce across the border.

Entering the Khyber Agency at Jamrud we passed a line of gun shops and arms factories at the side of the road. In the tribal districts no licenses are required for weapons and all varieties of pistols and rifles are on display. Most of these are hand-made by local gunsmiths who can copy any weapon, from a .22-caliber pen gun that fits in your pocket to grenade launchers and AK-47s. With the war in Afghanistan the trade in arms has increased and this has led to more and more violence spilling into Pakistan. When guns and ammunition are so readily available, killing naturally follows. Looking at my young bodyguard in the front seat, with the rifle nestled between his knees, I had a disturbing flashback to the little boy on the railway platform at Atari who had pointed his plastic gun at the Indian policemen.

Coincidentally, on the outskirts of Jamrud we passed a graveyard littered with slate headstones. The more recent graves were decorated with strands of tinsel that glittered in the sunlight, flecks of gold and silver in the dusty soil.

> The porous nature of the border zone and an inability to monitor it have been a mixed blessing for Pakistan. The honeycombed border has benefited the Afghan mujahideen, but it has also permitted the infiltration of the ugliness of war — weaponry, drugs, bombings and death — into the Pakistani heartland. Neither the natural nor the man-made barriers — neither the Hindu Kush nor the Durand Line — have halted the movement of Central Asian dilemmas into the subcontinent. Since 1980 men have been at war from the Amu Darya to the Indus.[6]

Mahnaz Ispahani's scholarly and insightful book, *Roads and Rivals: The Political Uses of Access in the Borderlands of Asia*, argues that most of the conflicts in this region are a result of competing national interests, struggling for control over traditional trade routes. Even in the age of jet aircraft and instantaneous communication, the northwestern borders of Pakistan are subject to what Ispahani calls, "the tyranny of terrain."[7]

In essence, a road provides access to trade and territory while a border restricts movement along that route. The intersection of these two lines on a map represents specific points of conflict. Nowhere in the world is this more evident than along the mountainous frontier of Pakistan and Afghanistan. The history of South Asia has long been dictated by the accessibility of routes across the Hindu Kush and the generally unsuccessful lines of defence that were put up to block invaders and regulate trade.

During the nineteenth century the British and the Russians competed for access to these routes in what was euphemistically called the Great Game. Essentially, this contest amounted to a series of expeditions into the mountains, from both sides, with the object of exploring and charting land routes between India, Persia, and Central Asia.

The Durand Line, named after Sir Mortimer Durand and his brother Algernon, both central figures in the Great Game, still forms the official border between Afghanistan and Pakistan, even though it is a tenuous boundary at best. Except for the few roads that wind their way through this desolate region, the importance of the Hindu Kush is more symbolic than strategic. As John Keay writes in his book *The Gilgit Game*: "High above the snowline, somewhere midst the peaks and glaciers that wall in the Gilgit Valley, the long and jealously guarded frontiers of India, China, Russia, Afghanistan and Pakistan meet. It is the hub, the crow's nest, the fulcrum of Asia."[8]

Ispahani details the political impact of the Karakoram Highway, which links Pakistan with China. The construction of this road was finished in 1978 and it follows sections of what was once known as the Silk Route, between Peshawar, Gilgit and Kashgar.

The construction of the world's highest international road has provided a powerful, visible centerpiece for the Sino-Pakistani partnership. It benefits both China and Pakistan in their political and military maneuvering in the subcontinent. Though not an ideal offensive strategic system, the Karakoram network has unnerved and discomfited its builders' rivals. It has put India on the psychological defensive in Kashmir, where to the west India now faces Pakistan, to the north, China. By connecting their own transport system with that of the Chinese the Pakistanis have complicated potential Indian infringements in the Northern Areas.[9]

These "games" of roads and borders, which are played out between the regional powers and their allies, represent an ongoing struggle for control over a part of the globe that has never been successfully governed, at least not from the outside. Perhaps the greatest tragedy in recent history has been the Soviet Union's attempt to impose its authority in Afghanistan. This led to a heavy-handed and ineffectual response from the Americans, the displacement of countless refugees, and continued destabilization that has all but leveled Kabul and plunged Afghanistan into seemingly perpetual civil war.

Hurtling down the curves and switchbacks of the Khyber Pass, several dozen men in loose salwar kameez and turbans maneuvered their bicycles around treacherous hairpin bends. A second bicycle, lashed to the carrier, fish-tailed behind each rider. Like daredevils, challenging fate at every turn, they dodged the overloaded trucks and buses which crawled upwards in the opposite direction.

Once the gateway of conquest for invaders such as Alexander the Great, Mahmud of Ghazni and Taimur (Tamerlane), the Khyber Pass has always remained an impossible place to govern and any authority over the pass eroded as quickly as the scarred brown hills and seasonal water channels that give the landscape a forbidding appearance. Today the pass has become the primary avenue for trade between Afghanistan and the rest of Asia. Some of this trade is legal but much of it is an elaborate ruse to bypass the customs barriers of Pakistan.

Imported goods are shipped from Singapore, Malaysia, Japan, and China to the southern port of Karachi. These goods are ostensibly destined for Kabul, loaded into trucks and sealed by Pakistani customs for transshipment across the country, an overland journey of nearly a thousand kilometers. Eventually the trucks make their way over the Khyber Pass and descend to the frontier town of Torkham. Once across the Afghan border, the goods are unloaded and smuggled back over the pass and into Pakistan. Heavier items such as refrigerators, air-conditioners, and television sets are carried by truck. At every checkpoint along the route bribes are paid in lieu of customs duty, until the goods are delivered to merchants in the Karkhana bazaar.

At the lowest rung of this complex commercial ladder are the bicycle smugglers who travel back and forth from Torkham, sometimes twice a day. They go up by bus, collect two or three bicycles from the warehouses across the border, then ride them over the pass. Most cyclists prefer to leave several hours before dawn, taking advantage of the coolness of the night and the cover of darkness to climb the eight kilometers to Landi Kotal village, which lies at the high point of the Khyber road. From there the remaining thirty kilometers is mostly downhill and the smugglers race each other at breakneck speed. With a second and often a third bicycle tied behind, it is hard work, particularly as they cross dry riverbeds where seasonal floods have washed away the road.

The cycle smugglers are understandably reticent to talk about their trade, but one man, Arif Khan, explained, "The dealers pay me fifty rupees for each cycle that I bring down. The police and customs officials don't bother us. They are more interested in the trucks carrying televisions. We are poor people, doing our mazdoori, for a daily wage." It is not an easy wage to earn with six or seven hours of hard pedaling, and the risk of collision, flat tires, and other dangers.

Uncertain levels of jurisdiction make this area an ideal environment for the drug trade. Many of the prosperous smugglers have built enormous mud forts along the roadside. Within these walls are lavish gardens and palatial homes where extended families of three or four brothers live together, protected by their own private militia. Some of these traders have legitimate businesses in Peshawar, dealing in gemstones and carpets but others have diversified their traditional trade and handle shipments of microwaves and air-conditioners, or hashish and heroin. Their profits allow them a lifestyle that is a far cry from the daily struggle of the bicycle smugglers who labor past their gates.

Mohammed Shafi, my taxi driver, explained the economics of the cycle trade. "Bicycles are produced in Pakistan but ours are not as good as the Chinese models. The most popular kind is known as China Number One." In Karkhana bazaar these sell for about Rs. 2,200, whereas the models made in Pakistan are priced at Rs. 1,800. Considering the distance they are transported, the profit margins are slim, but in Rawalpindi, three hundred kilometers east of Peshawar, the price of a Chinese bicycle goes up to Rs. 2,600.

Near the village of Landi Kotal, the highest point on the Khyber Pass, are the remains of a Buddhist stupa that dates back to a period before the Muslim invasions. On ahead, at a fork in the road, is a hillock plastered with the insignia of various regiments which have guarded the pass. Mohammed Shafi boasted that his father's regiment had been stationed here in the 1930s. He drove me through the cantonment, past lines of barracks and the Khyber Rifles Mess. Despite its colorful history, Landi Kotal is hardly picturesque. As we approached the main bazaar, Mohammed Shafi had me roll up the windows because of the smell of raw sewage. Garbage was piled on either side the road and the dry water channels were full of rubbish. One bridge had plastic bags wrapped like bandages around its pylons, where flash floods had deposited refuse from the village. Near the main bazaar there were several warehouses and I saw a man carrying three Sony tape players in their boxes, while two others were unloading a brand new air-conditioner.

There is a train between Peshawar and Landi Kotal, though it runs infrequently, two or three times a month. The narrow gauge line passes through dozens of tunnels along its route. Built by the British, the railway tracks used to go as far as Torkham, but sections have been washed away by landslides.

Two kilometers beyond Landi Kotal we came to a place called Michni Kandao. Here there was a signboard that read, "Foreigners are not permitted beyond this point." Though the mountains were obscured by a haze of dust, I could just see across into Afghanistan. The entire landscape was a khaki brown, except for the brightly painted buses, with bulging sides, that carried passengers to Torkham. As they made their way around the hairpin bends, the vehicles looked like gaudy beetles, crawling through the sand. Many of the trucks were also colorfully decorated, painted with floral motifs and pictures of movie stars, cypress trees, and partridges. Their mirrorwork ornaments and brilliant hues stood out in flamboyant contrast to the dull brown slopes of the mountains.

At Michni Kandao there is a VIP guest house and a flat area from where I could take pictures. There wasn't much to photograph, however, except for the ruins of British watchtowers on the surrounding hills. A cool breeze was blowing in from Afghanistan but the temperature was still above eighty degrees. Mohammed Shafi poured water into the radiator of his Toyota. Zahir Shah, AK-47 dangling from his shoulder, sauntered off to chat with some of his friends at a sentry post nearby. A ring of six string cots were arranged on the flat overlooking Afghanistan, as if a group of travelers had spent the night under the stars. Nearby was a peculiar looking sculpture, made of steel rods and shaped something like a bird cage. Hanging in the center was a dove of peace, welded out of scraps of steel.

7

RAWALPINDI AND ISLAMABAD   Across the Indus

JHANG: At least eight innocent people were shot dead in terrorist activities in Shorkot city.

Some 40 miles from here in broad day light Monday two motorcyclists wearing masks came to Haidrei Chowk where they opened fire with Kalashnikovs at a shop killing owner Khadim Hussain and his companion Sadiq Hussain. The same motorcyclists opened indiscriminate firing on the road killing two persons Ghulam Shabbir and Farzand at the spot.

These terrorists then went to the graveyard where they again opened fire and killed four persons namely Jaffar Ali, Munawar Ali, Faiz Ali and Shahid. Almost all the victims belong to Shia community, only one of these eight victims is reported to be a Sunni. Panic and harassment spread in the area and the news of this incident spread like jungle fire. —*The Muslim*, 5 August 1997

Air-conditioned coaches between Peshawar and Rawalpindi leave from a bus stand directly below the eastern walls of Balahissar Fort, which was built by the Mughal emperor Babur. As soon as I got there a conductor grabbed my arm and hustled me over to a kiosk where I purchased my ticket. "Abasin Flying Coach" was painted across one side of the bus and the conductor scribbled my seat number on my suitcase with a red felt pen before stowing it in a luggage compartment.

The bus turned out to be a video coach and the film had already started as I climbed aboard. It was a Hindi movie, a comedy of errors starring the popular Indian screen idol Govinda. The other passengers were already seated and had their eyes fixed on the video screen at the head of the aisle. Arabic subtitles suggested that the cassette had been imported from Dubai, though everyone in the bus could understand the Hindi. As I sat down next to a window, the music started and Govinda began dancing to a throbbing, disco beat. The volume had been turned up full blast and combined with the idle rumble of the diesel engine and the rushing sound of air-conditioning, the noise inside the bus was deafening.

For most of the ride, I divided my attention between the video screen and the landscape outside, but every time I lifted the curtain an elderly man in the seat across from me glared in my direction. Bus journeys, especially in a video coach, are far less convivial than the experience of traveling by train. Our route from Peshawar followed the Grand Trunk Road, a highway which dates back to the reign of Sher Shah Suri. An Afghan invader who interrupted the Mughal dynasty in 1540 with his brief but significant conquest of India, Sher Shah Suri built the first road from the Khyber Pass to Delhi. Several centuries later British engineers followed the same alignment and gave the highway its present name. Both in Pakistan and in India it is still referred to as the GT Road.

Each of the towns we passed through had a large cantonment, a military presence that was obviously intended to guard against invasions from the north. A repeated history of incursions along this route dictates a need for these defenses, especially after the Soviet Union invaded Afghanistan in 1979. In Nowshera we drove past an enormous artillery base and the headquarters of an Armored Corps regiment. Guns and tanks were displayed in front of the gates, the raw hardware of power. Compared to the dusty clutter of roadside bazaars, the army cantonments had an orderly, regimented appearance. One of the signs I saw, as we raced past, identified the Indus Cadet School. Their motto, painted on the walls: "Devote Your Present. Protect Your Future." A pervasive culture of militarism exists along the Grand Trunk Road and as we drove through the center of Nowshera I counted over a dozen arms and ammunition shops.

By this time the two lovers on the video screen had been brought together by a series of fortuitous coincidences and they declared their passions in song and dance. The actress, whom I didn't recognize, wore a chiffon sari and as she turned a pirouette her breasts jostled together seductively. Meanwhile, Govinda hopped about in front of her, flexing his pelvis with lusty enthusiasm. The audience in the bus were mesmerized by the performance, even though the men and women were seated separately. Nobody seemed at all concerned by the sexual improprieties on the screen or the fact that we were watching an Indian film. It was as if our journey down the Grand Trunk Road had been hijacked by the romantic fantasies of Hindi cinema.

As we approached the town of Attock our bus crossed over the Indus and once again I saw the two separate colors in the river, flowing parallel to each other. The source of the Indus, and all of the other major rivers in Pakistan, lies across the border in India. Forces of nature have little respect for lines on a map. Despite dams and canals that divert their flow, these waterways remain an important link between the two nations. The sharing of waters is a contentious issue, but unlike many other disputes between the two countries, a remarkable degree of accommodation has been reached. This has allowed Pakistan to construct dams on the Indus and Jhelum rivers, while India has similar projects on the Sutlej and Beas.

On the far bank of the Indus, just above the motor bridge, were the remains of ancient walls and battlements. The Mughal fort at Attock is still used by the Pakistan Army. Sections of the highway were being repaired and every few miles the bus veered off onto a detour so that we were engulfed in a cloud of dust. The driver of the Abasin Flying Coach was relatively cautious but others on the road were possessed by a collective death wish, overtaking our bus with inches to spare. Several times I found myself bracing for impact, our brakes screeching over the shrill din of the video soundtrack.

At six different places between Peshawar and Rawalpindi we were forced to stop because of police checkpoints. Each time the conductor switched off the film and two or three armed constables climbed aboard, peering under our seats or into the overhead luggage racks. It was hard to know what contraband they were looking for, but pointing with their rifles they made several passengers open bags and packages.

After each inspection had been completed the movie was restarted and we continued on our way. Just before Taxila, however, the video player suddenly broke down. We had been watching a scene in which

the heroine and her mother were praying at a Hindu temple, in front
of the idols of Ram and Sita. For the rest of the passengers, all of
whom were Muslims, this must have been a distasteful sequence, but
when the conductor failed to get the video working again there were
cries of protest and dismay. Though he fiddled with the VCR's buttons
and knobs nothing appeared on the screen except for a blizzard of static. The last half hour of the film was lost, though the ending was predictable, and I was secretly relieved.

Islamabad, the capital of Pakistan, lies ten kilometers north of
Rawalpindi. Though virtually contiguous, the two cities are opposites
of each other. Pindi, as it is often called, remains a congested, anar-
chic town of busy markets and messy streets that twist and wind their
way through crumbling neighborhoods. In contrast, Islamabad is a
planned and orderly city, constructed from the ground up less than
thirty years ago. Spacious and green, the capital is divided into num-
bered sectors and the gridwork of broad, well-paved streets gives Islamabad a feeling of discipline and conformity. Whereas the taxis and
other vehicles in Rawalpindi drive brazenly through red lights, Islamabad's crossroads are carefully patrolled by traffic police and the rules
are strictly enforced.

Though I spent time in both cities, I chose to stay in Rawalpindi
first, checking into the Al Amir International Hotel near the bus stand
in Sadar bazaar. The hotel's name was much grander than its rooms
and furnishings, which were adequate but spartan. From there I hired
a taxi to take me around the city so that I could get my bearings. Before coming to Pakistan, I had heard many stories about Rawalpindi
from Sikh and Hindu refugees in India. Though the city has none of
the gracious or romantic ambience of Lahore it has always been an important military cantonment. There are very few monuments to see
and the main attractions in the city are shopping centers. As we drove
past a cinema I saw a huge billboard with the reclining figure of a
woman who looked as if she had been dipped in gold. The film that
was advertised had an English title, *Dream Girl*, even though it was a
Pakistani production and made entirely in Urdu.

My taxi driver, Mohammed Ishaq, explained that there wasn't much
demand for cinema tickets because everyone now had a VCR. He also

told me that Hindi films were not allowed to be shown in cinema halls but all the latest releases from India were available on cassette, smuggled in through Dubai and Abu Dhabi.

Just beyond the cinema was a bazaar for gravestones, most of which were cut out of marble and etched with Quranic verses. Further on, along Murree Road, we passed a line of gold merchants selling bridal ornaments. When I stopped to look at the window displays, I saw that the jewelry was virtually identical to the necklaces and bracelets that I had seen in Amritsar at Arjun Mehra's showroom. Once again I was struck by the fact that these streets and markets were so similar to what lay on the other side of the border.

The cantonment in Rawalpindi is almost as large as the rest of the city, with numerous regimental headquarters and officers' messes. This part of town has a colonial atmosphere with spacious lawns and bungalows enclosed within brick walls. At each of the roundabouts there were tanks and artillery pieces on display. I also noticed posters everywhere, with pictures of General Zia-ul-Haq, the former president of Pakistan. Mohammed Ishaq explained that these announced a rally to be held on August 17th, commemorating Zia's death. He was killed in an air crash in 1988 and many people believe that his plane was sabotaged. A popular but controversial figure, General Zia imposed a stricter Islamic code on the country and was responsible for the execution of his predecessor, Zulfikar Ali Bhutto. Under Zia's picture on the poster was the exact time of his death — 3:51 P.M.

"For people like us, Zia did a lot," said Mohammed Ishaq. "Poor fellow, he was an honest man."

As we drove around Rawalpindi, Mohammed Ishaq rattled off a litany of complaints against the present government, most of which I'd already heard from others, a general cynicism about politicians and bureaucrats in Islamabad.

"They're all corrupt. How else could they build those huge houses, with dozens of rooms?" he said, then pointed to a gleaming new Toyota Landcruiser that was overtaking us. "You see that car. It costs twenty lakhs. Where do you think all that money comes from?"

Mohammed Ishaq was also bitter about the Afghan refugees who had moved into the Punjab. "They're bad people and their business is 'number two' (illegal). They deal in drugs — charas and heroin. They sell liquor and women, scrawny little whores that they use to keep the government officials happy."

It was clear that Mohammed Ishaq's sentiments reflected a widespread animosity towards those in power. Sometimes referred to as Pakistan's "feudal class," the wealthy and influential elite have isolated themselves completely from the rest of the populace, who struggle each day to make a living. This contrast can been seen in the two cities of Rawalpindi and Islamabad, the one with its neglected buildings and seething streets, the other with its luxurious mansions and spacious avenues. Two days later, when I was driving through the outskirts of Islamabad, I saw a small dirt road cutting off from the divided highway and disappearing into a dusty ravine. Nailed to a tree nearby was a crude sign, in the shape of an arrow, that read "Commoner's Town."

Gordon College was a fifteen-minute walk from my hotel. One of several institutions in the Punjab which were started by American missionaries, it is now controlled by the government. From 1935 to 1939 and 1946 to 1950, my grandparents worked at Gordon College and lived on the campus. From descriptions I had been given by my father it was not difficult to find the brick bungalow which had once been their home. The family who now occupied the house were Christians who had started a small primary school on the premises, called St. Andrews, Mission School. Though Gordon College is no longer a Christian institution, the freshly painted signboard outside the front gate still carries a scripture verse, "Seek and ye shall find." Above the entrance to the administrative building is a marble plaque that gives the names of two pious benefactors:

To Glorify God
Through the Christian Education of Indian Young Men
by
Eleanor C. Law
Ina Law Robertson
Chicago, USA
1902

One of the lasting legacies of the missionaries in South Asia has been the educational institutions that they established. In addition to Gordon College there is Kinnaird College for Women in Lahore, which has a distinguished list of graduates both in Pakistan and in India. Forman Christian College in Lahore and Murray College in Sialkot are two other schools that still continue to operate, though all of these have been nationalized by the government. Islamic fundamentalists have taken over Forman Christian College, where, unlike at Gordon College all of the Christian names have been erased from the buildings. Earlier, when I visited the campus in Lahore there were banners hanging from the trees, one of which read "PROUD TO BE A MUSLIM."

The Christian community is the largest minority group in Pakistan. Unlike Hindus and Sikhs who fled across the border in 1947, most Christians chose to remain where they were. Since Muslims consider them to be "people of the book," some may have felt a closer affiliation to Islam. Others were probably guided by more pragmatic impulses and a desire to hold onto the property they owned. Today, Christians in Pakistan are among the poorest and most disadvantaged citizens of the country, exploited because of their social class and their faith. With the growing fervor of Islamic fundamentalism, they have been targeted by Muslim zealots and accused of everything from proselytizing to conducting rituals of black magic. A growing number of incidents have been reported in which Christians were killed or threatened because of their religion. In India the Christian community faces similar discrimination from Hindu fundamentalists but under the constitution Indian Christians have much greater freedom and control over their own institutions.

One of the few prerogatives that Christians and other minorities enjoy in Pakistan is the right to purchase alcohol, which is forbidden for the Muslim population. In a country like Pakistan it takes a good deal of perseverance and determination to sell beer, and Minoo Bhandara, the CEO of Murree Brewery, is an unlikely candidate to take up this formidable challenge. He is a soft-spoken, unassuming man with a distracted air that makes him seem more like a professor of literature than a brewmaster battling it out with the mullahs. Seated behind an oval teak desk in his office, Bhandara recounted the early history of his company, which was founded in 1861. The brewery gets its name from the hill resort of Murree, where the clear spring waters and cool temperatures were ideally suited to making beer. An Englishman named Whymper set up the brewery to quench the thirst of British colonials who came up to the hills in the summer months. As cooling technologies developed in the 1880s, Whymper saw the opportunity for wider markets and moved his operations to Rawalpindi, which was on the railway line.

Minoo Bhandara's father, Peshotan Dhanjibhoy Bhandara, bought a controlling interest in the company in 1947. By this time the Murree Brewery had passed into the hands of a Hindu merchant, who migrated to India during Partition, taking a loan from a bank and leaving his shares as security. The Bhandara family are Parsis or Zoroastrians, a minuscule but highly successful minority community in South Asia.

"There are about twenty-five hundred Parsis in Pakistan. Ninety-five percent of them live in the province of Sind. Only a handful in the Punjab," said Bhandara, who was born and raised in Lahore though he has lived in Rawalpindi for the past thirty-seven years. Educated at Punjab University, he went on to study politics and economics at Brasnose College, Oxford. Minoo Bhandara is one of the leaders of the Parsi community in Pakistan and his sister, Bapsi Sidhwa, is a well known novelist. In books like *The Crow Eaters*, *The Bride*, and *Cracking India*, she has explored the complex nuances of a Parsi identity as well as the horrors of Partition.

Asked about prohibition in Pakistan, Bhandara responded with unexpected vehemence: "Nothing but a fig leaf," he said. "Since 1947 there's been one form of prohibition or another in this country. In the early years, Muslims were allowed to drink for medicinal purposes. Permits were issued to 'alcoholics,' and of course, Christians and Parsis were free to drink as much as they liked."

The army generals who controlled the country in the 1950s and '60s were in no great hurry to ban alcohol under their regimes, steeped as they were in the traditions of the military mess. According to Bhandara, it was only when the former prime minister Zulfikar Ali Bhutto started losing power in the 1970s that he tightened up the permit system to curry favor with the fundamentalists. From then on only non-Muslims were allowed to buy alcohol, supposedly for religious festivals. Foreign tourists are issued permits through their hotels, but buying a beer involves almost as much paperwork as applying for a visa. The conservative policies of General Zia further restricted the consumption of alcohol, as he sought to impose an orthodox Islamic lifestyle throughout the country.

Though there are three other distilleries in the country, Bhandara's company is the only brewery, producing two different kinds of lager and Murree's Export Stout. In a glass case that runs the length of one wall in his office, Bhandara displays a range of products, including Gymkhana Whisky and Doctor's Brandy (presumably for medicinal purposes). He has also diversified his operations and produces a line of fruit juices and squashes, ketchups and vinegars. Nonalcoholic beers are sold by the company, though these are also frowned on by the fundamentalists.

"Last year was the only time that the brewery was forced to close down," said Bhandara, "but it had nothing to do with Islamic sentiments."

The man behind the closure was Asif Zardari, husband of Benazir Bhutto, who stepped into her father's shoes as prime minister after Zia's death. Zardari and his associates were in the process of setting up their own brewery in Sind and attempted to put the Murree Brewery out of business by using strong-arm tactics. In response to the closure, Bhandara took out advertisements in the newspapers, protesting the action and appealing for help. Fortunately for him Benazir was soon ousted from power and her husband was locked away in jail on corruption charges. The Murree Brewery reopened and appears to be flourishing again, its gates emblazoned with rampant lions, defiant symbols of a beleaguered industry.

Clearly attuned to the uncertain and unsettled politics of Pakistan, Bhandara served as a member of the National Assembly between 1983 and 1988, first as a nominated member and then as an elected minority representative. An independent thinker, he claims no affiliation with any political party and has very little time for politicians like Benazir Bhutto. "Never got her act together," he says dismissively. The ruins of Rawalpindi jail, in which Zulfikar Ali Bhutto was hanged on orders from General Zia, lie only a kilometer from the gates of the Murree Brewery. After Benazir became prime minister, she had the jail razed to the ground and began construction of a park and memorial to her father, an unfinished monument that stands as a symbol of the treacherous vicissitudes of power in Pakistan.

Minoo Bhandara is a frequent contributor to the English-language press in Pakistan and often writes articles on Indo-Pakistan relations. Admitting frustration over the lack of dialogue between the two countries, he dismissed those who fuel these tensions as "an asinine lot." One of his goals is to lead a delegation of minorities from Pakistan to meet with minority communities in India. When I interviewed him, Bhandara said that he was encouraged by the conciliatory language of India's prime minister, Inder Kumar Gujral, and the Pakistani premier, Nawaz Sharif. He felt that both men had a sincere desire for peace. "But they're scared of the right-wingers and have to watch their tails," he added, throwing up his hands in a gesture of despair. He also approved of Nawaz Sharif's efforts to jump start the Pakistani economy. "He's a doer, a businessman, a pragmatist."

Strongly opposed to nuclear weapons, Minoo Bhandara published an article in the *Dawn* newspaper, in 1995, which sounded a note of warning and premonition:

> One of the few verities that unites the nation is the acquisition of nuclear weapons. Some hundreds of Press articles have appeared in the past two decades justifying, demanding, promoting the acquisition of nuclear weapons. The public perception is that its acquisition is vital for Pakistan's survival in a hostile world. And yet very little has appeared in the Press measuring or quantifying the consequences of a nuclear war in the subcontinent. . . .
>
> We think that in the event of a nuclear war a few expendable millions of the population will be killed. Pakistan will be saved; that Hindu India will be taught the lesson of the millennium. . . .
>
> To remove any misunderstanding of the consequences of nuclear conflict, the public needs to be informed of one conclusion which is highly probable: India and Pakistan as sovereign states as constituted at present will cease to exist.[1]

Islamabad is situated at the foot of the Murree Hills, the lowest range of the Himalayas, which rise up towards Kashmir. On a ridge about eight hundred feet above the city, there is a vantage point called Daman-e-Koh, which offers a panoramic view of the capital. It is a popular tourist spot, with a restaurant and colorful gazebos. In summer the air is a few degrees cooler and the hills are a verdant green. Looking down from Daman-e-Koh, one can see the complete layout of Islamabad, almost as if you were looking at an architectural model, with miniature streets and houses.

The capital is still being built; when I was there the prime minister's new secretariat was under construction, an enormous building that stretched for several blocks. The houses of parliament and other government offices are arranged in neatly ordered ranks, like the pieces of an elaborate board game. I could almost imagine the blueprints from which the urban planners had worked, marking out the streets and avenues with a straightedge, making sure that everything was positioned at right angles. The residential colonies were equally symmetrical, each with its own park and shopping center, as well as a neighborhood mosque. From where I stood at Daman-e-Koh, it was possible to identify the wealthier sections of the city, palatial homes with individual gardens, as well as the smaller plots of middle-class colonies. There were apartment buildings too, for government servants, but none of the congested neighborhoods or slums that are a part of older cities. Even from a distance, Islamabad conveyed an impression of power and exclusivity. Further east, beneath a haze of dust and smoke, I could see the jumbled skyline of Rawalpindi, like a gray mirage.

Scanning my eyes over the capital I tried to imagine what this landscape must have looked like fifty years ago, nothing but a deserted expanse of ravines and acacia jungles, with perhaps a few fields and villages scattered about. Much of Islamabad still contains large tracts of greenery, and to the east lies an artificial lake that irrigates the many public parks and gardens. Unlike the ancient cities of Lahore and Peshawar, with their walls and forts, Islamabad has a sprawling, open feeling that suggests a different outlook on the world.

It is significant that the leaders of Pakistan chose to construct a new and distinctly modern capital for themselves, instead of building on their historical foundations. Soon after Independence there was a protracted debate as to whether Karachi or Lahore should be the seat of power. In the end, Pakistan decided to foreswear the ruins of the past in favor of breaking new ground. The city of Islamabad reflects an optimism that may have faded over the past three decades, since the first buildings went up, but it is still a symbol of national pride. Even though the lavish villas and exclusive estates represent the corruption that plagues this country, the capital continues to stand for a vision of Pakistan's independence and modernity.

The most prominent of all the buildings that I could see from Daman-e-Koh was the Shah Faisal mosque, one of the largest in the world. It is named after the former king of Saudi Arabia who donated the money for its construction. With futuristic domes and acres of courtyards, the mosque looks more like an airport than a house of worship. The tapered minarets resemble rocket ships and the pristine white walls have a monumental but impersonal beauty. Like all mosques it faces toward Mecca, but there is more to this alignment than just religious tradition. Over the years, as Saudi Arabia and the United Arab Emirates have provided a steady source of employment for hundreds of thousands of Pakistanis, the country has grown closer to its western neighbors, both economically and culturally. After the secession of Bangladesh in 1971, Pakistan turned its back on the rest of the subcontinent, looking instead toward the Arabian peninsula for alliances and opportunities. In many ways, Islamabad's architecture and overall design is more like the new urban developments in Riyadh or Sharjah than other cities in South Asia.

PROVE YOUR IDENTITY

This sign was everywhere in Pakistan, outside the gates of military installations in Rawalpindi and stenciled onto the glass doors of government buildings in Islamabad. Of course, it meant that nobody would be admitted without showing some form of identification, though whenever I saw the sign, I couldn't help but give it a different interpretation.

Pakistan seemed to be a nation that was still struggling with its own identity. Fifty years earlier it had been created in opposition to India and the country immediately declared itself an Islamic state. From the first moment of Independence, religion and politics were inextricably linked. In most people's minds, to be a citizen of Pakistan was to be a Muslim. And yet, the very concept of a modern nation-state demanded a sense of communal identity that went beyond the bonds of faith. Democracy, however ambiguously that ideal is applied, assumes both a diversity of political affiliations and a collective allegiance to the state. In theory, this duality allows majority and minority groups within a country to participate in the national experience while preserving their own cultural and ethnic identities. The problem in Pakistan, however, is that the concept of representative democracy was never given a fair chance.

In 1958, ten years after Independence, the army took over the country and a series of military dictators came to power. They governed Pakistan in the same manner as they ruled the army, through a hierarchical chain of command which did not allow for open dissent or debate. Ultimately, this system failed because it could not accommodate the aspirations of distinct ethnic groups within the country, primarily the Bengali-speaking population of East Pakistan. The disastrous war in 1971 and the creation of Bangladesh dealt a severe blow to Pakistan's identity as a nation.

The immense loss of territory was perhaps less of an issue than the defeat of a national ideal. Jinnah and others had insisted on the creation of Pakistan as a homeland for Muslims in the subcontinent, linking their demands to a Pan-Islamic concept of universal Muslim brotherhood. By asserting their independence — with the wholehearted complicity and military support of India — the nationalists in Bang-ladesh carved out their own country while at the same time shaking the foundations of West Pakistan.

Among the immediate casualties were the generals who were temporarily trotted off the political stage. But already the idea of a cohesive citizenry had been challenged. When Zulfikar Ali Bhutto came to power in the elections which followed this debacle, he used the divisive politics of ethnic chauvinism to establish his authority. As a wealthy landowner from the southern province of Sind, Bhutto was able to garner support in those areas including the port city of Karachi. In this way he positioned himself as an alternative to the generals, most of whom came from the Punjab and North-West Frontier

Province. A flamboyant orator, with a sartorial style that was reminiscent of Jinnah, Bhutto provided a welcome contrast to the inarticulate, heavyset generals like Yahya and Ayub Khan, with their disgraced uniforms and tarnished medals.

From that point on, regional contests became the fulcrum of Pakistani politics, and the ethnic tensions that Bhutto created and exploited to great effect led to his eventual political demise and execution. Bhutto's daughter, Benazir, and her supporters further exacerbated these rifts by pitting the native Sindhi population against the muhajirs, or refugees from India. Over time this conflict has escalated into a virtual civil war in cities like Karachi. Added to this have been an increasing number of attacks on Shia Muslims by militant members of the Sunni majority. It is the darkest irony that a nation founded on the concept of unity amongst Muslims in South Asia is now torn apart by sectarian strife and violence.

India's role in the subversion of Pakistan's national integrity, goes well beyond its support for the freedom fighters in Bangladesh. As the larger and more powerful neighbor, India has forced Pakistan to remain on the defensive. The arms race on the subcontinent has helped propel military dictators to power and drained the Pakistani economy. During the Cold War, India's coziness with the Soviet Union forced Pakistan into an uncomfortable alliance with the United States and a more natural partnership with China. For the most part the foreign policies of Pakistan and India are locked into antagonistic postures. In Afghanistan, for instance, New Delhi has deliberately backed those factions which are fighting against Islamabad's allies, the Taliban.

Over the years, Pakistan has retaliated by aiding and abetting separatist movements across the border, particularly in Kashmir and Punjab. But this has done little to establish its own stability, and precious time and resources are wasted in a effort to aggravate the government of India. At heart, the problem lies in the conflicting demands of statehood, a concept which was essentially alien to the subcontinent until the British arrived. The central tenet of nationalism, as conceived by Europeans, is that an individual must relinquish his own identity for the greater good of the state. Patriotic sentiments dictate that if you are one thing — a citizen of Pakistan, for instance, or a citizen of India

— you cannot be the other. This sense of exclusivity and opposition has made it difficult for Pakistan to form its own distinct identity. There is no doubt in the minds of most Pakistanis that they are not Indians, but still the larger question, "Who am I?" remains unanswered.

For the majority of Indians this issue is less of a problem. In an essay titled "A Land of Plenty," written for the Fiftieth Jubilee, Salman Rushdie presents an optimistic vision of India's national identity.

[India] has taken the modern view of the self and enlarged it to encompass almost 1 billion souls. The selfhood of India is so capacious, so elastic that it accommodates 1 billion kinds of difference. It agrees with its billion selves to call all of them "Indian." This is a notion far more original than the old pluralist ideas of a melting pot or a cultural mosaic. It works because the individual sees his own nature writ large in the nature of the state. This is why Indians feel so comfortable about the strength of the national idea, why it's so easy to "belong" to it, in spite of all the turbulence, corruption, tawdriness and disappointment of 50 overwhelming years.[2]

As an expatriate, Rushdie celebrates this harmonious, rose-tinted sense of nationalism, but when it comes to relations with Pakistan there is an essential contradiction behind this belief. In the same anniversary issue of *Time* magazine, in which Rushdie's essay appeared, there is a brief anecdote that puts these views in perspective:

F. S. Aijazuddin, an investment banker in Lahore, recalls being on a bus in Paris when he was hailed by another subcontinental passenger. "Are you Indian?" asked the stranger. Aijazuddin, 55, said he was from Pakistan. "Oh, India-Pakistan, one and the same," replied his new friend blithely. "Then," said the banker, "can I say you're Pakistani?" The Indian man's smile faded and he turned away.[3]

Setting aside petty jingoism and patriotic sentiments, however, there is obviously some truth in the notion of South Asian plurality. Amitav Ghosh, who is both a writer of fiction and an anthropologist, put it most succinctly in a recent article about the Indian National

Army.

> The idea that individuals owe loyalty to a single political entity is relatively recent, and probably connected with the comparably recent birth of the nation-state. But human loyalties are, and always have been, diverse. People are capable of being faithful to many things at once: not just to their families, their kin, their compatriots but also to their masters, their servants, their friends, their colleagues, and, sometimes, even their enemies.[4]

This seemingly paradoxical combination of loyalty and enmity is very much a part of the ambivalent and ambiguous relationship between the citizens of India and Pakistan.

The Capital Inn, where I stayed in Islamabad, cost me about three times as much as the Al Amir International Hotel in Rawalpindi and over ten times as much as the Dubai Hotel in Peshawar. It is located in sector G-8, a predominantly residential area of the city. When I went out for a walk in the evening the streets were deserted and there was a disconcerting emptiness to the neighborhood. I wandered into a nearby park with overgrown lawns and drooping oleander bushes. It had rained earlier in the day and the air was relatively cool, but there was nobody else about and I began to feel uncomfortably conspicuous.

Returning to the Capital Inn, I ordered room service and switched on the television. Since coming to Pakistan I had watched a few programs, both in Lahore and Peshawar, but hadn't really paid much attention. There were six different channels in Islamabad and a surprising number of the programs came from India, though most of these were broadcast via Dubai or Hong Kong. On Star TV I watched a show called *Ooh La La*, with a simpering compere named Neelam who introduced musical selections from Hindi films. In between, there was an advertisement for a TV adaptation of Kushwant Singh's novel *Train to Pakistan*, which was scheduled to air in India on August 14. Flipping channels, I came to a talk show discussion about elopement, with a panel of four different couples in New Delhi who had married against the wishes of their families. Two of the couples represented interreligious marriages; in one case the man was a Hindu and his wife a Muslim, in the other case a Sikh and a Hindu. A third channel was showing the classic Hindi film *Amrapali*, starring Sunil Dutt and Vijayantimala. Like the video I had watched on the bus from Peshawar, this movie had Arabic subtitles.

Even though Pakistan now directs its antennas towards Arab neighbors to the west, many of the cultural influences invading the country still come from India. These signals are beamed across the Arabian sea, from studios in Mumbai, then transmitted back into Pakistan by satellite. All of this leads to a disconcerting interjection of cultures. In addition to the programs from India there were also shows from Europe and the United States, but here too the lines were blurred. For example, one of the programs that I watched in Pakistan was the American soap opera *The Young and the Restless*, which had been dubbed in India. The actor and actress, both of them blonde and blue eyed, were engaged in postcoital pillow talk in Sanskritized Hindi.

Despite these linguistic contortions, audiences in Pakistan could understand virtually all of what was being said. To a remarkable degree, popular culture in the subcontinent thrives on this element of translation. Bilingual puns are a part of almost every comedy script, just as they are mischievously prevalent in everyday life. (One of my favorites was a hand-painted sign on the fuel tank of a truck in India: "D- जल ." Only through transliteration — "D-jal" — could one get the joke, an inventive way of writing "diesel.") Two of the Indian TV shows that I watched in Pakistan had bilingual titles — *Just Muhabbat* (Just Love) and *Winner Mangta Hai* (Winner's Requests). The advertisements also toyed with language, using clever wordplay to sell everything from Pepsi to Colgate.

I had been watching television for about an hour, when I heard a hesitant knock at the door. One of the desk clerks, a young man named Yusuf, had brought a telephone bill for me to pay — which for some unexplained reason had to be settled in cash. I had spoken to him earlier and he had told me that he was from Afghanistan but had come across the border as a refugee six years earlier. While living in a camp outside of Peshawar, Yusuf had taken a course in English as a second language from an American volunteer named Joe and he was hoping to eventually emigrate to the United States or Canada, where he had a sister.

When I gave Yusuf the money to pay my phone bill he apologized for the interruption and closed the door behind him. A few minutes later, however, there was another knock. This time it was the second night clerk, whose name was Imran. After handing me my receipt, he asked if he could come in and talk to me for a minute. Imran was from Pakistan — his home was in Chakwal, about a hundred kilometers south of Islamabad. We spoke in Urdu and Imran explained that he had noticed on the check-in form that I had listed my occupation as "teacher."

"I also want to become a teacher," he said. "Right now I am giving private tuition for high-school students in chemistry, physics and math. But can you tell me, please, what is the secret of being a good teacher?"

The question baffled me and I gave him an incoherent answer. Imran may have been interested in furthering his education, but I got a feeling that both he and Yusuf were bored with their night shift and he had come to my room more out of curiosity than any genuine interest in pedagogical theory.

"Do you like watching Indian programs on TV?" I asked, trying to change the subject.

"Yes, of course," he said. "Who doesn't? It's much better than Pakistan TV."

Surprised by the directness of his answer, I pushed him further, asking what the difference was.

"Our shows are *thanda* [cold]," he said. "The Indian shows are *garam* [hot]. Pakistan TV hasn't changed since 1947."

Never mind that television has only been available in the subcontinent for less than thirty years, the sentiments which Yusuf expressed were similar to what I heard from others. It was obvious that national loyalties did not extend to the realm of entertainment. Later that evening, I watched part of a program on Pakistan TV, a family melodrama in which everybody seemed to be weeping, the father, the mother, and the son. It was a depressing show and I finally switched it off. The alternative, on another channel, was a Hindi version of MTV's *Singled Out*, in which a young woman with ringlets and a miniskirt was trying to choose between four young men who wanted to take her out on a date.

The blurring of national boundaries that occurs on the airwaves is an unavoidable consequence of satellites and digital transmission. Television and other media make borders all but obsolete and the fact that audiences in Islamabad or Delhi can simultaneously watch the same shows, obviously helps to erase the artificial divisions of culture. For the most part, it seems that the Pakistani and Indian authorities have conceded this fact. The only attempt that I saw at blocking Indian broadcasts was when Star TV showed a short documentary on Independence. There was a clip of Jawaharlal Nehru releasing a dove, followed by shots of the Indian flag. At this point the signal was clearly jammed, the images distorted into psychedelic squares and the sound reduced to static. As soon as the documentary finished, the screen returned to normal. Later on there was a similar documentary, from Pakistan's perspective, with pictures of Mohammad Ali Jinnah. This was followed by an ad for Pepsi, with an accompanying song, "Hum hain Pakistani! Hum Jitengey! Hum Jitengey!" We are Pakistani! We will win! We will win!

8

MURREE   Looking Toward Kashmir

India's independence day, on Aug. 15, will be observed as a "black day" by various political and social Kashmiri organizations in Lahore.

According to a decision taken at a meeting of Kashmiri organizations' representatives held here under the aegis of the Kashmir Action Committee, Pakistan, the day will be marked with protest rallies and processions against India's usurping Kashmiris' right to self-determination and atrocities perpetrated on Kashmiri people.

Through a resolution, the meeting condemned India for its brutalities in the held Kashmir and urged the Government of Pakistan not to start trade with India unless it agrees to solve the Kashmir issue.—*Dawn*, 7 August 1997

Like most hill stations in the Himalayas, Murree stretches along the crest of a precipitous ridge. The main part of the town is about seven or eight kilometers in length and spills down either side of the hill, with cottages and hotels perched on every available patch of level land. At the southeastern end of Murree is a promontory called Pindi Point, from where tourists can look out over the plains of the Punjab. On a clear day the twin cities of Rawalpindi and Islamabad are just visible beyond the receding foothills. At the opposite end of the ridge, on the other side of Murree, is Kashmir Point, which offers a panoramic view of the disputed mountains to the north.

Since 1947, Kashmir has been the primary focus of hostilities between India and Pakistan, an unresolved and festering conflict that is aggravated by historical anomalies, regional politics, and persistent dreams of paradise. The pleasure gardens of Shalimar, built by Mughal emperors in the sixteenth century, and the breathtaking natural beauty of the Srinagar valley, have elevated Kashmir to a mythical plane, on a level with fictitious places like Shangrila or Xanadu. Unlike the barren and rocky terrain of the Khyber Pass, with its frontier legends of masculinity and feudal violence, the "Vale of Kashmir" is an idyllic landscape of gentle greenery and bucolic pleasures. But the political realities of this region and the battle lines that have been drawn across these mountains dispel any fantasies which may have survived the past fifty years.

At the time of Independence, most of the "princely states" — ruled by Hindu and Sikh maharajahs or Muslim nawabs — were integrated into either Pakistan or India. Since the middle of the nineteenth-century the British had maintained subsidiary treaties with each of these states, giving the rulers prestige but very little autonomy within the empire. On the eve of their departure, the colonial authorities abrogated their treaties and left the territorial issues to be resolved by the newly formed governments. For the most part, the 362 principalities in the subcontinent fell neatly within the freshly demarcated borders. The accession of territories belonging to maharajahs and nawabs was bought with generous promises of privy purses and tax incentives. In India, the man credited with this achievement was Sardar Vallabhbhai Patel, who combined shrewd political guile with a streak of administrative genius. But the complex choreography of Partition was not without several missteps. In 1947 three of India's princely states failed to accede to the union. The small coastal kingdom of Junagadh was quickly taken over by Indian troops without much protest, even though the nawab preferred to join Pakistan. Hyderabad, located in the center of the subcontinent, was somewhat more difficult to subdue, given its large territory, a sizable Muslim population, and the nawab's intransigence. But here too the army was sent in and any resistance to India's territorial claims was summarily quashed.

The problem of Kashmir, on the other hand, was not so easily resolved. Maharajah Hari Singh was a Hindu but the vast majority of the population in the valley were Muslims. The southern section of the kingdom, near the town of Jammu, was predominantly Hindu and there was also a scattered Buddhist population in the northern areas of Ladakh.

There had always been some question as to the exact extent of territories ruled by the maharajah of Kashmir. Traditionally the river Indus served as a convenient border, but Hari Singh's ancestors laid claim to some of the lands beyond, though their authority over the valleys of Gilgit and Chitral was hardly secure. John Keay, in his book *The Gilgit Game*, describes the ambiguity surrounding the western boundaries of Kashmir.

> Whether or not the Indus ought to be the frontier of Kashmir was a debatable point. But, for a certainty, such authority as the Maharajah of Kashmir wielded in the lands beyond was of so tenuous a character that he was in no position to guarantee the safety of any traveller there.
>
> All this country west of the Indus and as far as distant Afghanistan was usually lumped together under the title of Yaghistan, meaning the land of the ungovernable, of the savages. The Kashmir government's experience of it more than bore this out.[1]

Even within the Srinagar Valley, the maharajah faced challenges to his rule. From the early 1930s, Sheikh Abdullah, popularly known as "the Lion of Kashmir," had spearheaded the freedom struggle in this region. He was opposed to both British rule and to Maharajah Hari Singh, who put him in jail on several occasions. When Jinnah and other members of the Muslim League demanded a separate Muslim state, Sheikh Abdullah rejected this idea as "suicidal" and preferred to ally himself with secular India. In September of 1947 he made a speech in which he said, "Pandit Jawaharlal Nehru is my friend and I hold Gandhiji in real reverence . . . we shall not believe the two-nation theory which has spread so much poison. Kashmir showed the light at this juncture. When brother kills brother in the whole of Hindustan, Kashmir raised its voice for Hindu-Muslim unity."[2]

In 1947 Nehru seemed to recognize a kindred spirit in Sheikh Abdullah and supported his opposition to Maharajah Hari Singh, who had grandiose illusions of turning Kashmir into the Switzerland of Asia — a neutral, independent, landlocked state. There are differing accounts as to the specific chain of events that led to the occupation of

Kashmir. One writer has suggested that toward the end of August 1947, hardly ten days after Partition and Independence, Mohammad Ali Jinnah decided that he wanted to take a holiday in Srinagar. The fact that Kashmir's future was still uncertain, and that there were on-going riots in Punjab and Bengal, did not deter him from his desire to escape the summer heat of Lahore. Hearing of Jinnah's intentions, the Maharajah thwarted these vacation plans by refusing to let the founding father of Pakistan set foot in his kingdom. Denied entry into paradise, Jinnah decided that he would take Kashmir by force. Supposedly in a fit of pique, he authorized a contingent of Pathan tribesmen to attack the valley and oust the Maharajah.[3] British historian Percival Spear describes the events which followed.

> The Hindu ruler played for time and had still not acceded to either side in October (1947) when a Pathan irregular force from the old frontier burst in and raced towards the capital Srinagar. In a panic the ruler acceded to India whose airborne troops saved the situation in the nick of time. From that time India has stood on the legal ground of accession, branding Pakistan an aggressor since the Pathans came from her territory. Pakistan called for a plebiscite to which initially Nehru agreed in principle. But he was never able to accept any proposals for carrying it out. A brief war flared up between the two dominions, settled by a United Nations truce in 1948.[4]

This UN-mandated ceasefire has remained in effect, with varying degrees of success, for the past fifty years. It established a "Line of Control" that runs through western sections of Kashmir and up into Baltistan, Ladakh, and the Siachen Glacier. In 1972, as part of the Simla Pact following the Bangladesh war, Indira Gandhi and Zulfikar Ali Bhutto signed an agreement to conditionally accept the Line of Control as a de facto border. This helped ease some of the tensions but did not fully resolve the issue of Kashmir. Until today, the two armies remain at hair-trigger readiness on either side of the "LoC" and hardly a week goes by without some sort of incident. These encounters range from the exchange of small arms fire to full blown artillery barrages.

Until now India has succeeded in maintaining control over the bulk of Kashmir, including prize territories in the Srinagar Valley. On the opposite side of the Line of Control, sections of the former principality, still held by Pakistan, are known as Azad Kashmir (Free Kashmir). Nehru may have agreed to the principle of a plebiscite, but it is unlikely that he had any intention of handing over the territory to Pakistan. For one thing, Kashmir was his ancestral home. Though a pragmatist in many respects, he was also a romantic at heart, and the rose gardens of Shalimar were not something that he was willing to surrender. Nehru once described Kashmir as a "supremely beautiful woman, whose beauty is almost impersonal and above human desire. . . . It was like the face of the beloved that one sees in a dream and fades away on awakening."5 Since 1947, Kashmir has become a symbol of national pride and unity in India, reinforced by Hindu extremists who denounce any hint of negotiation or compromise.

For the first six years of Independence, Sheikh Abdullah ruled Kashmir as the chief minister, but his faith in the Congress Party and the motives of secular India, were gradually being eroded. As he began to push for greater autonomy and demand some form of referendum on the future of Kashmir, Abdullah was betrayed by his old friend and ally Jawaharlal Nehru. In 1953, the Indian government threw the Lion of Kashmir in jail, on the pretense that he was pro-Pakistan. During the years that followed, the populace of Kashmir were kept within the union through the repeated imposition of central rule and a combination of generous economic subsidies. As Nehru once promised the Sheikh, "We will bind you in chains of gold."6

Kashmir enjoyed relative prosperity throughout this period. Despite the border dispute and the two wars between Pakistan and India, tourists flocked to the valley, staying in luxurious houseboats on Dal Lake and holidaying in the mountain resorts of Gulmarg, Pahalgam, and Sonemarg. The Hindi film industry helped to promote the myth of paradise, using the picturesque valley as the backdrop for a series of romantic films like *Kashmir Ki Kali* (The Flowerbud of Kashmir). In the late eighties and early nineties, however, militant separatist agitations surfaced and the Indian Army began a ruthless campaign which backfired into civil war. The tourists departed quickly and the local economy was severely affected. Various Kashmiri separatist groups, located in Pakistan and England, stepped up their support for militants in the valley and tensions along the Line of Control grew increasingly worse. Just as the border which divides the Punjab has been a constant source of antagonism and animosity, the ceasefire line in Kashmir has become the focal point of hostilities.

The word "ceasefire" is a misnomer. Perhaps the greatest absurdity of this conflict can be found in the high altitude regions of the Siachen Glacier. At eighteen thousand feet above sea level, in a forbidding moonscape of rock and snow, Indian and Pakistani troops face off across this river of ice. Somewhere between them lies the Line of Control, snaking its way invisibly though shifting crevasses. Soldiers on both sides risk the dangers of frostbite and acute altitude sickness to defend a territory that literally moves each day. With barely enough oxygen to breath, they fire at each other, lobbing artillery rounds through the thin mountain air. Since the first skirmishes occurred here in 1984, hundreds of lives have been lost; all of this in defense of territory where nobody can survive for more than a few weeks at a stretch. Military authorities may argue that the Siachen Glacier is of strategic importance, particularly with the Karakoram Highway nearby, but in essence it represents a pointless and arbitrary conflict, goaded by national pride and an absurd belief in the efficacy of boundaries on a map. If Kashmir symbolizes heaven on earth, then the Siachen Glacier can only be the dark side of that myth — an icy, intractable hell.

As Amitav Ghosh has written in his book *Countdown*, "To visit the Siachen glacier is to know that somewhere within the shared collective psyche of India and Pakistan, the torment of an unalterable proximity has given birth to a kind of deathwish, an urge that is rising ever more insistently to the surface."[7]

The road map of Pakistan, which I had purchased in Lahore and carried with me for the rest of the journey, had a misspelled disclaimer printed at the bottom: "Boundaries & Other Infrmation Are Not Authantic." All of Jammu and Kashmir was shown as part of Pakistan, a pink expanse which disappeared inconclusively beyond the margins of the map. The province of Punjab was colored green and the NWFP was a khaki brown. The Siachen Glacier was not labeled but the

Karakoram Highway was clearly marked. There was no Line of Control on the map. Aside from the disclaimer, the only other indication that things were not quite as they appeared were the words "Disputed Area," printed in one corner of Kashmir, which seemed to have been added as an afterthought.

In Delhi I had bought a similar map, which showed all of Kashmir as part of India, including the town of Muzzafarabad, and the territories of Chitral and Gilgit. On the Indian map there was no mention of disputed territory, though the Line of Control was faintly marked inside the original boundaries of Jammu and Kashmir. As I compared these two maps I came to realize how unreliable they were in other ways as well: the omission of towns, the areas left blank, the twisting borders which should have fit together like pieces of a jigsaw puzzle but failed to match the other country's profile. In my naïveté I had assumed that maps like these were meant to assist a traveler on his journey, furnishing landmarks and distances, but these were documents of another kind, conflicting diagrams in which the scale and contours mattered less than symbolic inaccuracies, those intentional flaws which define the political landscape of South Asia.

Cartography has always been an inexact science, a process of miniaturization in which miles and kilometers are reduced to inches and centimeters. In this way the specific details of terrain and topography are lost. What is projected onto paper is inevitably an approximation and for this reason is easily manipulated. Even with satellite photography there will never be a perfect map, one that we could put under a microscope and enlarge to reveal the true facts on the ground. No matter how carefully they are surveyed, these fluid lines of ink should never be seen as definitive. Symbols of invisible boundaries, created out of conflict and compromise, they will always remain open to dispute.

When I arrived at Murree's Kashmir Point, after walking four kilometers uphill from my hotel, the view of the mountains to the north was obscured by monsoon clouds. The only other person around was a young boy selling roasted ears of corn at the side of the road. He was fanning a makeshift brazier with a piece of cardboard. I asked him if I was at the correct place and he nodded, then pointed casually into the mist.

"Kashmir," he said, as if it was right there in front of me and I just hadn't noticed.

The mist enclosed us in a damp, gray shroud. The wet air was so thick, it felt like fine rain. My hair and clothes were beaded with moisture and I was disappointed because there was nothing to see. It was still early in the morning, around eight o'clock, and there were no other tourists about. Leaning over the metal railing, where the road ended, I looked out into a pale, impenetrable blur. I could hear sounds coming up out of the clouds, invisible vehicles on the road below, a truck horn, voices from a nearby house which I could not see, even though it was less than a hundred meters away.

Though I waited for almost an hour at Kashmir Point, the mist and clouds did not disperse and I finally retraced my steps. By this time tourists were beginning to stir; as I approached the Mall Road I could see groups of people out for their morning promenade. Though the sky remained overcast the mist had finally started to lift. The similarities between Murree and my home town, Mussoorie, were uncanny — identical sounds and smells, the same architecture — tea shops and hotels opening onto the winding streets, rusty, corrugated tin roofs, crows calling in the mist, and the soapy, sour odor near a public tap where an old man was scrubbing a blackened cooking pot. There were differences, of course, but these were so subtle I felt that if only I walked a little further along the mall I might even find my way home.

Part of the reason for this curious sense of deja vu may have been that earlier that morning I had passed six or seven American missionaries on my way to Kashmir Point. One of them, an earnest-looking man with thinning blonde hair and a sunburnt face, had stopped and spoken to me. He explained that he and his colleagues worked in different parts of Pakistan but came up to the hills for summer language study, and to be with their children who were enrolled at Murree Christian School. Before Partition, all the missionaries in North India sent their children to Woodstock, the boarding school I attended in Mussoorie. In 1947, with the imposition of the border, families in Pakistan were forced to set up their own school in Jhika Gali, a small set-

tlement on the outskirts of Murree. For years I had known about the
school and my grandfather actually helped purchase one of the properties that now serves as a dormitory.

Visiting Murree Christian School was like stepping back into my
childhood. Though the buildings were quite different from Woodstock — including an old British garrison church that had been converted into classrooms and an indoor basketball court — I recognized
voices on the playground, where a dozen or more white children were
chasing each other about in a frenzied game of tag. Standing there I
felt an all too familiar sense of isolation and insularity. Very few missionaries remain in Pakistan, and the school has about a 125 students.
It is inevitable that their numbers will continue to dwindle, for the
missionaries are no longer welcome in a country where Islamic fundamentalism is on the rise. Though I wandered about the campus for
fifteen or twenty minutes, I began to feel strangely uncomfortable and
left without speaking to any of the students or teachers. Despite the
familiarity of the setting and perhaps because of my own connections
with the missionary community, I was overcome by an uneasy sense of
estrangement. More than anywhere else in Pakistan, it was at Murree
Christian School that I felt conspicuously a foreigner.

By the time I got back to my hotel the sun had come out and Murree seemed to erupt with a carnival atmosphere, boisterous crowds
milling about the restaurants and souvenir shops. Rooftop signboards
advertised the Red Onion Pizza Parlor, Mr. Food, and the New Khyber Restaurant. There were video arcades and playgrounds, open air
pavilions painted blue and yellow, a Martyr's Park with hawkers ped-
dling soft drinks and peanuts. One vendor, selling an assortment of
cheap toys, was blowing soap bubbles in the air, which drifted overhead, catching the sunlight in transparent rainbow colors. Another
man was selling wild raspberries in funnels made out of chestnut
leaves. There were ponies for hire and porters with hand carts pushed
children up and down the mall. Being summer, the Pakistani tourists
had come to Murree to escape the heat of the plains, though the hill
station provided a poor substitute for Kashmir. The air was considerably cooler than in Rawalpindi and Islamabad, but it was not cold

enough for the bulky sweaters and fur caps that were for sale at many of the shops.

Men and women seemed to mix more freely in Murree than elsewhere in Pakistan, though segregation of the sexes remained in evidence. There were lots of families with children and even a few honeymoon couples who strolled about self-consciously. But there were also clusters of young men, who moved back and forth along the mall like schools of fish patrolling the margins of a reef. They followed after similar groups of unmarried women, dressed in colorful salwar kameez, hair half-covered and eyes hidden behind oversized sunglasses. Watching these men and women, I was aware of a complex and co-ordinated pattern of movement, as each group eyed the other with surreptitious glances and furtive gestures that tested the distances between them. In many ways it was like observing an elaborate dance or courtship ritual in which the young men and women wove in and out of the crowds on the street, coming closer every time but never actually touching. On the parapet walls in Murree I found plenty of lovelorn graffiti, written with colored chalk and bits of charcoal, that revealed unrequited passions and secret romances: "R.M. Loves Shahnaz." "Love you, Tasleem."

Every few hundred yards along the mall there were shooting galleries, where tourists could test their marksmanship with air rifles. For a couple of rupees you got three shots, and the galleries seemed to be doing a brisk business even though the air rifles didn't promise much accuracy. Most of the shooters were men but I saw a few women taking aim as well. The majority of these stalls had cardboard targets with rows of colored balloons to pop. Some of the shooting galleries were more inventive and one booth even had a line of green plastic soldiers, about two inches tall. A group of tourists, college students by the look of them, were taking turns firing at these targets, squinting fiercely as they aligned the rifle's sights. Several of the toy soldiers had already been hit by lead pellets, their miniature bodies mangled and twisted out of shape.

From Murree I continued on to Nathia Gali, another hill station thirty kilometers to the west, from where I did get a view of the mountains of Kashmir. The ridges dropped away steeply into the Jhelum Valley and were heavily forested with fir trees and pines. As the crow flies, the Line of Control lay only a few kilometers away, but there were no soldiers in sight except for armed sentries outside the governor's residence. Unlike Murree, which is located in the Punjab, Nathia Gali lies in the North-West Frontier Province and it is a much more exclusive resort with none of the middle-class crowds.

Most of the property in Nathia Gali is owned by the provincial government, the army or wealthy families from the plains. Strict regulations limit the construction of new buildings and there were only a few hotels, all of them expensive. The cottage where I spent the night belonged to Minoo Bhandara's family. He had offered to let me stay there when I met him in Rawalpindi. Nobody else was at the house, except for a caretaker who let me in. It was an attractive cottage, with raspberry canes and sweetpeas in the garden and potted hydrangeas on the porch. Nearby was a small wooden church, with a peaked tin roof and arched windows shuttered tight. The town itself had a colonial ambience and the few tourists I saw were either riding horses or roaring about in their Toyota Landcruisers. Green's Hotel, at the northern end of Nathia Gali, advertises itself as a ski resort in winter. The lobby was full of pictures of mountains covered in snow, with wealthy Pakistanis posing in winter fashions, as if this were Grenoble or Gstaad. In fact, the only ski slopes in Nathia Gali were the hotel lawns which fell away gently for a couple hundred feet, beyond which there was a dense forest of pines.

I had gone to Green's Hotel in search of dinner at seven o'clock but found that their restaurant didn't open until eight-thirty. Along the way I'd passed a smaller hotel called Holiday House and I headed back there to see if I could get something to eat. The manager immediately took me into the dining room and offered me an elaborate menu, though he explained apologetically that the only dish available was chicken curry. There were fifteen other tables in the room but I was the only person in the restaurant. After taking my order, the manager brought me a copy of the *Dawn* newspaper to read.

The front page carried a lead article about "sectarian attacks" in the Punjab. Eleven people had been killed. Eight of them had been shot at a mosque in the town of Multan while three others had died when a bomb exploded in Lahore. The newspaper deliberately avoided identifying the specific community to which the killers and their victims belonged, but it was obvious that those who had died were Sunnis and that their assailants were Shias who were taking revenge for a similar attack at a mosque in Shorkot three days earlier. There was a related report on the front page with the headline: "Nawaz hints at new measures to curb crime." It quoted a statement from the prime minister's cabinet which said that the government "could not remain indifferent to the complicating law and order situation, which has grown from bad to worse."[8]

The *Dawn* was full of other articles about killings in different parts of the country — a trader shot dead in Lahore's Anarkali bazaar because of his brother's political connections, six people gunned down in Karachi, three others in Larkhana, all as a result of communal animosities. It was depressing reading but there were an equal number of articles calling for reconciliation. In Muzzafarabad, the prime minister of Azad Kashmir had given a speech the day before condemning the "sectarian violence and racial prejudices."

He called upon the people from all sects and shades to frustrate the nefarious designs of the anti-Pakistan forces by demonstrating unity, faith and discipline in their ranks and files. He said his government was endeavouring hard to turn Azad Kashmir into a true Islamic state. "We want to enforce here the laws in consonance with the teachings of the holy Quran and Sunnah so that a society having peace, brotherhood, justice and equality, can be established in the liberated territory," he vowed.

About the liberation movement in the held valley, the premier said the unprecedented sacrifices being rendered by the people of Kashmir were aimed at overthrowing the cruel and non-Muslim Indian rule there.

He said the Indian occupation forces were desecrating the holy places of the Muslims and molesting their womenfolk due to which the Kashmiris had started a Jihad in Kashmir.[9]

I set the newspaper aside when my dinner arrived, though the descriptions of violence and the angry rhetoric kept running through my mind. At times like this the situation seemed hopeless and those ideals of "peace and brotherhood" seemed far removed from the religious and sectarian conflicts that seemed to be tearing the country apart.

Half an hour later, as I was walking back to the Bhandara's cottage, the monsoon clouds above Nathia Gali parted for a few minutes and I could see the dark profiles of the Pir Panjal, those mountains which rim Kashmir. Above me in the sky was the narrowest sliver of a moon, framed by the sheltering branches of the pines. This slender white crescent is the emblem which dominates the flag of Pakistan. But hanging there above me in the darkness it seemed to represent something more than just religious or national aspirations. It symbolized the purest part of Islam, a faith that has been abused and corrupted over the years but which still preaches peace and reconciliation. The delicate beauty of that crescent moon, suspended over the mountains of Kashmir, made the conflicts and tensions in this region seem petty and perverse.

James Buchan, a British journalist who has covered the conflict in Kashmir echoes these same sentiments:

> In all the time I have lived as a newspaper correspondent in the Muslim world, I imagined a place in Asia where, cut off by mountains or some other barrier from the bullying of the Christian West and its allies, Islam could be as peaceable, hedonistic and humane as I felt it was meant to be. Kashmir seemed to me, on my visits to be a paradise: not in any metaphysical meaning, but in the sense of the Persian word that the Greeks transliterated into paradise: a park or garden enclosed from the desert, planted and watered, a place for pleasure, conversation and love affairs; which, as the supreme achievement of Muslim domestic culture, became a notion of timeless delight. Paddling about my cedarwood boat on Dal Lake, or fishing the high streams, my mind immersed in water, I sensed that I was missing something; that the valley had been invaded and ruined times without number, and could not remain insulated from the revolutions of the Muslim world or the sibling hatreds of India and Pakistan.[10]

Before Partition most travelers to Kashmir followed a motor road that ran along the Jhelum River, north of Nathia Gali, but that route is now inaccessible because of the border conflict. In the twenties and thirties, when my grandparents used to spend their summers in Kashmir, this was the road they traveled. My father was born in a British mission hospital on the outskirts of Srinagar, and I have heard accounts of the majestic chinar trees in Nasim Bagh, where he and his family camped for several months each year. On the walls of our family home in India there are watercolors which my grandmother painted of the gardens in Srinagar, flowerbeds awash with colors. All this contributed to my own imagination of Kashmir as an unspoiled world of placid lakes and alpine meadows.

In the 1970s I visited Kashmir with my family on two occasions, trying to recapture some of those romantic memories of my father's boyhood. The landscape was still seductive — avenues of poplar trees and trout streams draped with willows, mountain vistas that seemed too perfect to be real, like photographs that had been touched up to hide the flaws. But for all its beauty there was an embittered, discontented mood in Kashmir that I did not fully understand at the time. I could feel it in the relentless haggling of the houseboat owners, with whom we negotiated our stay, and in the curio shops piled high with cheap imitations of traditional handicrafts, suggesting a culture that had been robbed of its genuine treasures.

The last time I visited Kashmir was in the summer of 1980, when I drove there by motorcycle. I was living in Mussoorie at the time and it took me two and a half days to reach Srinagar, by way of Pathankot and Jammu — a much more arduous journey than the old motor road which follows the Jhelum River. Along this route the first view of the valley lies at the end of the Banihal Tunnel, a dark, claustrophobic passage almost three kilometers in length. Emerging from the dripping bowels of the mountain, I could see the Vale of Kashmir spread below me, a lush tapestry of green fields, meandering streams, and scattered villages.

From this vantage point at the end of the tunnel the valley seemed peaceful and undisturbed but driving into Srinagar, an hour later, I rode directly into a street protest on the main road near Nedou's Hotel. A mob of two or three hundred Kashmiris were shouting slogans and throwing bricks at a line of Indian policemen dressed in riot gear. As I made a quick U-turn in the middle of the road, a couple of tear-gas canisters shot through the air. Though these protests were mild compared to the insurgency and bloodshed that would follow, it was obvious that the romantic dreams of paradise would soon turn into a nightmare.

From Srinagar, I continued by motorcycle toward Ladakh. For years this region had been closed to foreigners because of the border conflicts with China and Pakistan. But in 1980 it had recently been opened up to tourists and Leh, the capital of Ladakh, had become a popular destination for adventurous travelers. It was a two-day journey by road, and the first twenty kilometers beyond Srinagar and Sonemarg was almost impassable, because of landslides. As soon as I got across the Zoji La Pass, however, the highway was well maintained by the Indian Army's Corps of Engineers.

Though there were no military installations in sight, the presence of the army was evident throughout Ladakh. At regular intervals along the road there were whitewashed plaques commemorating the deaths of soldiers who had lost their lives during the construction and defense of the highway. Cliffs at the side of the road fell away steeply into the valley, beyond which lay the territories held by Pakistan. More than once I passed convoys of military vehicles carrying supplies into Ladakh, though for long stretches the road was completely deserted.

About twenty kilometers beyond the town of Dras, I noticed that the air in the rear tire of my motorcycle was low. Though I was carrying a pump, I soon discovered there was a problem with the valve and my attempts at refilling the air only made things worse. Within a few minutes the tire was completely deflated and I was stranded at the side of the road. Cursing myself for not carrying a valve wrench I waited to flag down the next vehicle that went by. At that time of day, however, there seemed to be nobody else on the road. The mountains on either side of me were desolate and barren, with no villages or towns in sight.

After I had been waiting for ten or fifteen minutes, a movement on the hill above me caught my eye. Half a minute later I saw a head pop up and then another. Two Indian soldiers emerged from their foxholes on the ridge overlooking the road. Rifles slung over their shoulders, they approached me with cautious expressions. Neither of the soldiers said very much, but after I explained that I needed a valve wrench they told me to follow them. We walked down the road, about a hundred meters or so, until we came to a shallow ravine where an unpaved track cut off to the right. Following the dirt road, we came around a corner and there in front of us was an army workshop, where jeeps and trucks were being repaired. The entire encampment was hidden under a canopy of camouflage netting. As we entered the workshop there were at least a dozen mechanics, dressed in greasy coveralls, who looked at me in amusement. After overcoming my initial surprise I explained the problem. Immediately, as if they had rehearsed this moment, each of them reached into the pockets of their coveralls and produced a valve wrench, after which I was escorted back to my motorcycle. Tightening the valve and refilling the tire, I continued on my way.

This experience occurred almost twenty years ago but I often think back on it when I read about hostilities along the Line of Control. The military presence in the mountains, those soldiers in their khaki uniforms, the fox holes and camouflage seemed to emphasize the proximity of that border even though none of it was visible from the road. In a similar way the ambiguities of the conflict in Kashmir are hidden behind those barren ridges. If it wasn't for the flat tire on my motorcycle I would have driven by without any knowledge of what was there.

One of the largest military cantonments in Pakistan is located in Abbottabad, a town that lies near the border with Kashmir. After spending the night in Nathia Gali, I hired a car and driver to take me there. It was only a forty-kilometer drive but the journey took over three hours because sections of the road had been washed away by monsoon rains. We passed through several small villages but much of the area was unsettled and heavily forested. The driver of the car was named Qayum, who told me that his village was in Azad Kashmir. When he learned that I had come from India he immediately asked me if it was true that the Indian army was killing all the Muslims in the Srinagar Valley. I replied that I wasn't sure exactly what was going on, for I hadn't been there in many years, but from what I'd read the situation was very tense.

"If only India and Pakistan would leave us alone," he said, in an exasperated tone. "What's the harm in allowing Kashmir to become a separate country? That's the only way this problem will be solved."

Qayum was in his mid-thirties and had never been to Srinagar. He kept asking me questions about the valley and I tried as best I could to describe for him the houseboats on Dal Lake, the floating gardens, Shalimar Bagh, the Hazratbal mosque. After awhile he shook his head in despair.

"It is surely the most beautiful place on earth." he said, then whispered the Farsi word for paradise, "firdaus."

After that Qayum remained silent for several kilometers, before opening the glove compartment. He took out a cassette tape and fed it into the music system.

"You don't mind some Hindi music, do you?" he asked.

I shook my head and a few seconds later, a familiar melody filled the car. As the volume increased I recognized the lyrics: "Ghar kab aogey?" — When will you be coming home?

Startled, I looked up at Qayum.

"Do you know which movie this song is from?" I asked.

"Some picture called *Border*."

"Have you seen it?

"No."

"I watched the film in Delhi two weeks ago," I said. "It's about the war between India and Pakistan. How can you be listening to it here?"

Qayum looked at me with a puzzled expression, then laughed.

"So what?" he said. "I like the tune."

For the rest of the drive we listened to the theme song from *Border*, again and again. At one point I asked to see the tape and it was clearly a copy made in Dubai. Every time the song finished, Qayum immediately rewound the cassette and by the time we reached our destination he must have played it at least a dozen times. Listening to the refrain, "When are you coming home?" I wondered what it meant to him. Was he thinking of Kashmir?

Abbottabad is located in a broad river basin and surrounded by ridges on all sides. Driving into the town, I saw that the main road was lined with military compounds, mess halls, parade grounds, and rows upon rows of barracks. I had several reasons for going to Abbottabad but primarily I wanted to see the town because it was a place where my grandparents lived in the 1920s and '30s. My father and his brothers had always reminisced about their time in Abbottabad. The black-and-white photographs in our family albums showed pictures of colonial bungalows and flower gardens, as well as four young boys wearing khaki shorts and pith helmets.

I had no idea where to look for the house in which my grandparents once lived, but as we approached the main bazaar I saw a sign for the United Presbyterian Church. It was hidden behind a row of shops. As I entered the gate I immediately recognized the building from one of the photographs in my grandparents' albums. The church has a distinctive appearance, with high stone walls, an outside staircase, and tiny windows at the top. Originally it was built as a squash court and later remodeled into a house of worship. None of the other buildings in the area seemed to match the pictures I had seen and the only person around whom I could ask was a boy, fourteen or fifteen years old, who had no information about the history of the church or the missionaries who used to work there.

My own personal curiosity and search for the places where my grandparents once lived may seem irrelevant to a larger discussion of borders and the territorial politics of South Asia, but underlying these digressions is a basic human impulse to reclaim ancestral lands, even if only in a transient manner. Most of us have an instinctual need to physically locate the past, to set foot on the ground where our forefathers once lived. For this reason, our inner compass leads us back to those places which were once our home, even if that home was abandoned before our birth. Being an American who was born and raised in post-Partition India, my own sense of family history is inextricably tied to geography. When I visited the mission compounds in Pakistan where my father once lived, I felt something of the same emotional pull as I do when I return to my own birthplace in Mussoorie, or even to my mother's childhood home in Pennsylvania. If these bonds with the land are as strong for someone who has willingly moved from country to country for most of his life, as I have done for the past twenty-five years, how much more powerful must they be for those refugees who are forcibly uprooted and denied the opportunity of returning home.

A friend in Delhi had given me the address of her family home in Abbottabad. She still had relatives living there and continued to stay in touch with them. Because of the border, however, my friend had only been able to go back to Abbottabad for one short visit in fifty years. At the time of Partition, half of her family had moved to India, while the rest remained in Pakistan.

I had written down their address, which was on Circular Road, but there seemed to be no logical pattern to the numbering of the streets. After several circuits of the town we kept coming back to the place where we had started. At one point Qayum and I stopped outside a military officer's mess, which had a huge sign that read: "Home of the Baluch." A turbaned sentry, with impressive sidewhiskers, was standing at attention. When I approached him he gave me an exaggerated salute, but for all of his military bluster, he could not help us find our way.

By this time I was ready to give up but Qayum seemed determined to help me find the place. Eventually he asked a shopkeeper in the bazaar, who happened to recognize the family's name. He pointed us in the right direction and we located the house. It was a graceful, tin-roofed bungalow, enclosed within a walled garden at the center of which was a spreading chinar tree.

I had not been given a telephone number and had no way of calling ahead. When I arrived at the gate a man and a woman were sitting in the garden. It took a few minutes for me to explain who I was and how I had got their address.

"Welcome. Most welcome. My name is Khan, S. M. Khan," said the man, who had an Oxbridge accent. "And this is my cousin, Ayesha."

Without hesitation, they invited me into the house and offered me a cup of coffee. The living room was furnished with comfortable armchairs and littered with Kashmiri carpets. For the first ten or fifteen minutes S. M. Khan tried to explain to me the various family relationships, but in the end he threw up his hands helplessly and laughed.

"It's all very confusing," he said. "Cousins marrying cousins, you know . . . though I'm a bachelor myself."

When I mentioned that my grandparents had lived in Abbottabad during the late twenties his eyes lit up.

"I was here in those days. Abbottabad was a much smaller town back then. The British kept it very clean. You wouldn't find so much as a cigarette butt on the street."

"Have you ever been to India?"

"Yes, of course. Before Partition I was a student at Aligarh Muslim University. From there I went on to Oxford . . ."

Ayesha, who was quite a bit younger than S. M. Khan, had been silent through most of the conversation but at this point she interrupted him.

"I've never been," she said, "But I would love to go. There's a train in India, which I've heard about. It's called the Palace on Wheels, made up of all the old carriages that used to belong to the maharajahs."

A little later Ayesha explained that she taught English literature at a government college in Peshawar and was only visiting Abbottabad for the summer holidays.

"Our grandfather bought this property at the beginning of the century," said S. M. Khan. "He was the chief revenue officer on the staff of Colonel Durand, after whom the Durand Line is named — the border with Afghanistan. On their way up to Gilgit they camped in Abbottabad and when my grandfather saw how beautiful it was, he decided that this was where he wanted to settle. Our family has been here ever since."

9

ATARI   The Grand Trunk Road

Chandrapur, Aug 10: Although the country is celebrating its golden jubilee, there are students here who do not know the name of the country. When Sudhir Mungantiwar, BJP MLA, visited a Zilla Parishad school at Kavadjai village some students said India had become free in 1972, one said he did not even know the name of the country. —*Indian Express*, 11 August 1997

From Abbottabad I headed back into the Punjab and continued my journey by bus along the Grand Trunk Road. Much of this route runs parallel to the railway line that I had traveled in the opposite direction, and I passed through the towns of Gujar Khan, Jhelum, Kharian, Lala Musa, and Gujranwala, before finally arriving in Lahore. The air-conditioned bus was a rattletrap Toyota Coaster with black velvet curtains on the windows. These made me feel as if I was riding in a hearse and the unsettling awareness of my own mortality was heightened by the dangers of the road. Our driver, who had a bunch of plastic grapes hanging from his rearview mirror, along with laminated cards bearing verses from the Qur'an, kept the accelerator pressed to the floor and seemed determined to overtake every vehicle in sight. The drive was a six-hour slalom through heavy traffic, our bus swerving from one side of the road to the other at eighty kilometers per hour, with only a shrill horn and the dangling scriptures to get us through.

At the side of the highway I saw the remains of at least a dozen acci-

dents, including a Suzuki Mehran which had been crushed like an aluminum can, the twisted metal compacted into an unrecognizable
shape. On ahead was a truck which had veered off the road and lay up-
ended in a ditch full of weeds. Both of its axles had been ripped off the
chassis and the wheels were scattered over a hundred meters apart.
The truck had been carrying bags of lime which had burst open and
the entire area — the road, the trees, and the nearby buildings — were
white with chalk dust, as if a freak snowstorm had struck in the middle
of summer.

I was relieved to arrive in Lahore unscathed. The sun was just setting when we reached the bus station and I saw a sign for the Clifton
Hotel, where I decided to spend the night. The next day I would be
crossing the border, leaving Pakistan behind and returning to India.
Writing down my passport and visa numbers in the hotel register, I
began to feel the first pangs of anxiety, as I anticipated the checkpoints
and customs barriers, the immigration forms and police procedures.

That evening I ate my last beef curry and naan in Pakistan, at the Pa-
keezah Restaurant, on the ground floor of the Clifton Hotel. The dining room was full of men, fifty of us altogether, and not a woman in
sight. Suspended from the ceiling was a television set on which there
was a Hindi movie playing, *Ek Phool Do Mali* — One Flower, Two
Gardeners. It was an old film that I had seen in the early 1970s, starring Balraj Sahni and Saira Banu. The dance sequences were not as
sexually provocative as in the newer films, but the scenes of the heroine dancing on the meadows of Kashmir had a seductive quality. The
hero of the story is a mountain climber and toward the end of the film
plants an Indian flag on the summit of a Himalayan peak. At this
point in the movie there wasn't a word of conversation in the crowded restaurant. Everyone in the room, even the waiters, was transfixed,
not by the politics or irony of the situation but by the melodrama in
the scene.

During the course of my journey, many of the people I met in Pakistan
and India expressed a curious combination of affection, indifference,
and animosity toward their neighbors across the border. At first this
seemed to be a contradiction but more and more I began to recognize

it as a symptom of the profound ambivalence that exists between the peoples of the subcontinent. The border divides them but it is also a seam that joins the fabric of their cultures.

Having spent most of my life in India I had always thought of the border as an aberration, an arbitrary line which the British drew across the map before retreating to their sovereign isle. Amongst most Indians, especially Punjabi refugees, I had sensed a wistful hope that some day this border might be erased and people could cross back and forth unhindered. "Partition was not a solution; we should have created some sort of federation," was the common refrain, which I had come to accept, as a preferable alternative. But in Pakistan my assumptions were severely tested. Virtually every person that I met asserted the importance of that border, no matter how cynical they were about the current state of affairs in their country. For the citizens of Pakistan, Partition from India was a far more important event than Independence from Britain. In that division lay their identity as a nation and the border was something to be jealously guarded.

This justification of national boundaries, however, doesn't mean that most Pakistani refugees do not share the same sense of loss and separation that is felt by their counterparts in India. Similar sentiments are evident in the words of poet Ahmed Rahi, who was born in Amritsar but moved to Lahore in 1947. In an interview for the British television documentary *A Division of Hearts*, he said, "One forgets things from the past as time wears on but the partition is something one cannot forget. It has hurt me deeply. I still remember my home which I had to abandon. I was young, 23 or 24, an age which inspires dreams. I left most of my dreams in Amritsar." Rahi later revisited the city of his birth, where he recited one of his poems:

> People of my own land, I come to you as a foreigner comes
> People of my own house, I come to you as a stranger comes
> In the womb of this land my mother lies asleep
> To the waters of this land my tears flow
> My love grew and wilted in this sun once
> I search for the grave of my mother in this land
> I search for the bones of my brother in this land

> Once we believed it was human beings we would become
> Today it is Hindu, Sikh and Musalmaan we have become.[1]

Communal conflicts may well have been the primary cause of Partition but curiously enough it is often religious beliefs that help to bridge the border. Situated about a hundred meters inside Indian territory, near the village of Khem Karan, is the tomb of Baba Sheikh Braham, a sufi mystic who was a contemporary of Guru Nanak. His "samadhi" has been turned into a shrine that is visited by devotees from both sides of the border. Even during the two wars in 1965 and 1971, when pitched battles were fought in the region, the Baba's tomb was left unharmed. Muslims, Sikhs, and Hindus worship at this shrine and annual fairs are held to celebrate his birth. In a newspaper article in the *Indian Express*, the shrine was described as an "oasis of peace and amity," and a Border Security Force officer was quoted as saying, "Since Partition, there has been a tacit understanding between the two countries to allow Pakistani devotees into the Indian territory up to the shrine without any restrictions."[2]

In many parts of Punjab the tombs of other saints are also revered by Muslims, Hindus, and Sikhs alike. The mystical traditions which surround shrines like the grave of Baba Sheikh Braham are not a part of organized religion and represent a popular, less regimented faith that reaches back several centuries before Partition. Today however, the Baba's tomb is a curious anomaly, an example of the way in which borders and religious prejudices can be subverted and perhaps become even a symbol of hope.

Spontaneous expressions of unity, on the other hand, have often led to frustration and disappointment. On 14 August 1996, a group of about a hundred Indian activists, intellectuals, and artists went to the Atari border post, hoping to "fulfil a long-cherished objective by groups in the two countries: Indians and Pakistanis would stand, in roughly equal numbers, on each side of the border and sing songs for peace."[3] As this group discovered, their idealism was challenged by the physical barriers at the border and they were kept apart by security forces on either side. One year later they tried again. Led by Kuldip Nayar — former high commissioner to London and himself a refugee

— they turned their backs on the Jubilee celebrations in Delhi and traveled to Atari instead. Initially this group had hoped to cross over on the night of August 14–15 and meet with a similar gathering of Pakistanis in Lahore. At the last minute, however, their visas were denied. Instead of making a symbolic crossing, Nayar and his compatriots were forced to conduct a candlelight vigil on their side of the border.

> The cold response from Pakistani counterparts of Indian peacemakers and advocates of Indo-Pak friendship didn't dampen the spirit of hundreds of people who last midnight participated in the candlelight vigil. . . .
>
> Chaos prevailed on the border throughout the function. The Punjab police and BSF cane charged people who were pushing forward towards the LoC. The cultural programme which began around midnight was discontinued abruptly at 1 AM due to power failure. Hans Raj Hans, a Punjabi folk singer, enthralled the audience.
>
> He began with a song, "Eh Punjab vee mera hai, oh Punjab vee mera hai. Eh Satluj vee mera hai, oh Chanab vee mera hai, Jisam mere do do tukre jod jeyo, eh hadan tod deyo sarhanda tod deyo" (The Punjabs on both sides belong to me, the rivers of Satluj and Chenab also belong to me. Join the two parts of my body, demolish the boundaries and the borders).[4]

A large part of the problem with these attempts at reconciliation lies in conflicting perceptions on either side of the border. While most rational citizens of Pakistan would undoubtedly prefer an amicable and peaceful relationship with their neighbors, they are unwilling to deny the reality of Partition. On the other hand, those in India who seek to promote unity tend to express their beliefs and emotions by directly challenging the existence of the border. For this reason, even in the most compassionate exchange of rhetoric, there is a fundamental dispute between coexistence and cohesion.

From all accounts, it was obvious that the authorities in Pakistan did not share the sentiments of those Indian activists who gathered at Atari, seeking to promote a sense of unity and brotherhood. The choice of the border as a venue was clearly cause for suspicion, and their well-meaning overtures were interpreted as an effort to reclaim a lost homeland. Rather than erasing the boundaries created by Partition, the manner in which Kuldip Nayar and his compatriots were rebuffed reasserted the existence of that border.

Though the concept of a modern nation-state depends upon the acceptance of these territorial symbols, it must be understood that virtually every national boundary leads to some form of dispute. The line that was drawn between Pakistan and India in 1947 is particularly contentious because it carries completely different meanings for the two opposing sides. In India the border represents a source of national regret, something to be rejected as a falsehood, a tragic mistake of history. In Pakistan it is a symbol of identity and pride, the bulwark of their republic and a cause for defiant jubilation.

Customs and immigration offices at the border opened at nine o'clock in the morning and closed at noon. I was anxious to get an early start, but before I could leave Lahore I needed to change some money to settle my bill at the hotel. Because of foreign-exchange regulations, the desk clerk had told me, he couldn't accept dollars, but he explained that there was a street nearby, where I could buy Pakistani rupees. At 7:00 A.M. I hired a taxi to take me there, though I was skeptical about finding anyone at that hour. When we got to the street, however, there were five or six currency traders already in position, and without even getting out of the taxi I was able to exchange twenty dollars. The whole transaction took less than a minute and gave new meaning to the concept of drive-through banking.

When the taxi driver learned that I was going to the border, he offered to take me there and we negotiated a fare. His name was Ahmed Rusool. He was a young, clean-shaven man who was dressed in a gray salwar kameez.

"If you had spoken to me in English I would have asked for three hundred rupees," he said, as we set out. "Instead I'm only charging you a hundred and seventy-five, because you spoke to me in Urdu."

We headed out of Lahore along the banks of the Upper Doab Canal. The day was already hot and dozens of young boys were splashing about in the muddy current.

"This water comes from India," said Ahmed Rusool.

The canal is diverted from the Ravi River, which flows to the north of the city. Its source is in Lahaul Spiti, beyond Kashmir, and like the other five rivers of the Punjab the Ravi eventually drains into the Indus. As we joined the Grand Trunk Road, Ahmed Rusool pointed out Lahore's Shalamar Gardens. The waters of the Ravi still irrigate the flowerbeds and lawns which were planted by the Mughals.

"This is where lovers come in the evening," he said. "Men and women. Here they have some privacy. They can hold hands and nobody says anything. In the city they dare not meet. But here nobody cares. Love is something you cannot stop. It always finds a way, when you are young."

I asked Ahmed Rusool how old he was.

"Twenty-eight," he said, laughing. "But I'm still not married."

As we headed east from Lahore he began to talk about India.

"Here in Pakistan, we have no problem with the Sikhs," he said. "It's the Hindus that are our enemies."

Ever since the separatist movement gathered force in the 1980s, Pakistan has sided with the Sikhs, even though the territorial ambitions of Khalistan include Lahore and sections of the Punjab on both sides of the border. I asked Ahmed Rusool if he knew of any Sikhs still living in Lahore.

"No," he said at first, then corrected himself. "Maybe there are five or six, but they keep out of sight. During November pilgrims from India come to the gurdwara in Lahore. At that time you can see them on the street."

Approaching the border, the GT Road was less congested and there were farms on either side. Near the edge of a village I saw a stagnant, green pond in which six buffalo were wallowing among the water hyacinths like obese matrons at a spa. One buffalo had a tuft of hair between her horns, which had been dyed orange with henna as if it were the latest fashion.

Only one other person besides myself was crossing the border by road that day, a Japanese backpacker who had hitchhiked all the way from China. Because of tensions in the Punjab, citizens of India and Pakistan were only permitted to travel between the two countries by air or train, which left the road crossing almost deserted.

Three Pakistani porters were squatting near a sign that read Immigration and Anti-Smuggling Office. One of these men picked up my suitcase and led me to a line of mustard-colored buildings. I waited for about five minutes, when a thin, flustered looking official came in and sat down at his desk. He took my papers impatiently, as if there was a queue of people waiting, and recorded my name and passport number in a ledger, as well as the visa numbers, place of issue, expiry dates, and so on. In the process of crossing the border that day, this information was written down nine different times — three times on the Pakistan side and six times in India, not counting one entry that was made on a computer.

The porter had changed into a bright parrot-green shirt, which he wore over his clothes so that the police and border guards could easily identify him. He led me on to the building next door, which was a customs shed. The inspector seemed uninterested in my bags, giving them a cursory glace. The only question he asked was, "Any magazines?" I shook my head, even though I was carrying a collection of newspapers from Pakistan and a copy of *Time* and *India Today*. Scribbling on a receipt book, which had sheets of carbon paper interleafed between the pages, he issued me a gate pass. Earlier the porter had quietly told me not to give the immigration or customs officials any of my Pakistani currency.

"I'll exchange it for you," he said.

When I explained that I had only enough rupees to pay him for his services, the porter seemed disappointed.

"Give it to me here," he said. "Before we get to the gate. Otherwise the guards will want their share."

From the customs shed, we had to walk about two hundred meters to the border. The main road passed through an area that looked like a park or public garden, not all that different from Shalamar Bagh. In fact, at sunset, when the Beating Retreat ceremonies are held it is a popular place for family outings and picnics. A few buildings and sentry boxes were visible but mostly there were tall shade trees, jamun, mango, neem, and shesham, that must have been planted around the time of Partition. About twenty meters from the border we passed through a tall archway decorated with a crescent moon and the words "Pakistan Zindabad" written in Urdu. Two army Rangers greeted me cheerfully, despite their bandoliers and rifles. Taking the gate pass, they waved me through with a casual gesture, like ticket collectors at the entrance to a tourist site.

At that hour of the morning the metal gates at the border were open and I could see through to the line of bleachers, where I had watched the Beating Retreat ceremonies two weeks earlier. The flags of both countries were flying on opposite sides of the gate but there was none of the military bluster or bravado that I remembered from the parade. The Pakistani porter, in his loose green shirt, carried my suitcase on his head. Walking up to the gate he stopped on one side of the painted white line that marked the border. From the other side I saw an Indian porter hurrying towards us. He was a Sikh, dressed in bright blue shirt, the color of the Khalsa. With ceremonial precision the two porters positioned themselves on either side of the line, their toes no more than eight inches apart. Neither of them said a word, but as I crossed over, my suitcase was passed simultaneously from the head of one porter to the next, so that it never touched the ground.

One of the questions that I asked people in both India and Pakistan was what they thought the border actually looked like. Descriptions varied from images of concrete bunkers, barbed-wire fences and machine-gun nests to less forbidding visions of checkpoints and customs barriers. Nobody had described it as a park or garden, though most people mentioned the existence of a no man's land, a buffer zone between the two countries through which all travelers must pass. The concept of this neutral strip of territory suggested both the uncertainties and ambiguities that are often associated with borders, as well the idea of transience. By crossing through this supposed no man's land a person entered an intermediate space, a world between worlds, where none of the rules of nationality applied.

The phrase "no man's land" often suggests a forbidden zone which is fraught with danger and anarchy. But it is also a curiously reassuring image, implying that somewhere along the border there is a strip of land that remains undivided — in some ways like the shrine of Baba Sheikh Braham. It is neither a part of Pakistan, nor a part of India. Instead, this territorial myth provides a curious metaphor of unity, regardless of the political realities of Partition.

My own preconception of the border included a no man's land. Part of the reason for this was a short story by the Urdu writer Saadat Hasan Manto. "Toba Tek Singh," is a grim, satirical tale of Partition, in which the governments of India and Pakistan agree to a mutual exchange of "lunatics." All of the Muslims in Indian asylums are traded for their Hindu and Sikh counterparts across the border. The main character, Bishan Singh, cannot decide where he belongs and is distraught by this dilemma. At the end of the story he symbolically collapses and dies in a neutral territory between the two countries.

One of the great disappointments of my own journey was to discover that there is no such thing as a no man's land. At both the railway and road crossings, the territory of each country is entirely contiguous. Nothing separates these two nations, except for manmade structures like fences and gates. There is no buffer zone, no transitional swath of land to keep the two countries apart. Unlike the tribal regions along the North-West Frontier, where national authority and borders are blurred, at Wagha and Atari, Pakistan ends precisely where India begins.

And yet, the persistent image of a no man's land seems to represent the ambivalence with which many people view the border. In Manto's story, which was written shortly after Partition, he expresses this uncertainty through the behavior of the "lunatics":

As to where Pakistan was located, the inmates knew nothing. That was why both the mad and the partially mad were unable to decide whether they were now in India or in Pakistan. If they were in India, where on earth was Pakistan? And if they were in Pakistan, then how come that until the other day it was India?

One inmate had got so badly caught up in this India-Pakistan rigmarole that one day, while sweeping the floor he dropped everything, climbed the nearest tree and installed himself on a branch, from which vantage point he spoke for two hours on the delicate problem of India and Pakistan. The guards asked him to get down; instead he went a branch higher, and when threatened with punishment, declared: "I wish to live neither in India nor in Pakistan. I wish to live in this tree."

When he was finally persuaded to come down, he began embracing his Sikh and Hindu friends, tears running down his cheeks, fully convinced that they were about to leave him and go to India.[5]

Through this story, Manto suggests that everyone in Punjab, at the time of Partition, was living in a no man's land. The boundaries were still fluid, even though the concept of two separate nations had officially been conceded. It is interesting that fifty years later some of those same ambiguities remain, at least in people's imagination of the border.

As I crossed over into India, the atmosphere at the Atari checkpoint was quiet and peaceful. There was a languorous stillness to the morning, the heat and humidity tempered by the scent of flowers and wet earth. Jasmine bushes were in bloom. Border Security Force soldiers, whom I had last seen on parade, loitered about with a nonchalant air, actors awaiting their next performance. Mynahs and ring-necked doves were calling in the jamun trees that leaned across the electric fence. At the side of the road I noticed a small Hindu temple, freshly whitewashed. A foreigners registration officer sat under a frangipani tree with a wooden desk in front of him. As he noted down my passport particulars the fragrance of the white blossoms helped dispel any sense of anxiety I might have had.

The Sikh porter led me into a customs and immigration hall which looked as if it had recently been built. A dozen or more officials were sitting around drinking tea; when the Japanese traveler and I entered the hall, they looked up at us with indifference. Immigration formalities were completed in a perfunctory manner and everything went smoothly until the customs officer who was leafing through my passport asked if I was carrying Indian currency. Without thinking, I nodded my head and instantly his bored expression changed to a look of interrogation.

"How much money do you have?" he asked.

"Just enough for a taxi," I said. "Eight hundred rupees."

The inspector raised his eyebrows and looked at me with astonishment and accusation, as if this were a fortune. Shaking his head disapprovingly, he pointed to a line of plastic chairs and told me to wait while he called his supervisor. Eventually the inspector and another man in a white uniform came up to me, acting as if they were going to throw me into jail. The supervisor waved a pamphlet in front of my face which had a list of customs regulations, including one which said that tourists were forbidden to take Indian currency in or out of the country. When I tried to look appropriately admonished, saying I hadn't realized I was doing anything wrong, there was an awkward pause.

After a few moments the inspector leaned closer and his voice took on a gentler tone.

"A taxi to Amritsar costs much less than eight hundred rupees," he said.

Realizing they were waiting for a bribe, I continued to play dumb until the officials made their intentions absolutely clear.

"Make us happy and we'll let you go."

Hesitating, I reached into my bag and slipped them each a hundred rupees. Suddenly the situation changed and we were friends. Escorting me to the door the two customs officials shook my hand vigorously and wished me a "happy journey."

One more checkpoint remained, which was manned by the Punjab police, and after that I passed under an arch with the words "Welcome to the World's Largest Democracy" painted overhead. Beyond this was a parking lot and bus stand, where I was surrounded by a circle of hawkers selling bottles of chilled beer. They obviously catered to travelers who had worked up a desperate thirst in Pakistan. Several taxis were waiting at the bus stand and with some haggling I was able to get a ride to Amritsar with plenty of rupees to spare.

Putting the border behind me I had a strange feeling that I had never left India at all. The landscape was virtually unchanged, kikad trees and verdant fields, the two-lane asphalt highway, buffaloes wallowing in pools of rainwater by the side of the road. It was the same country, as far as I could see, though instead of Ahmed Rusool, who had brought me to the border from Lahore, my taxi driver was named Pritpal Singh. There was no denying that I had been back and forth across that line. In my passport I had the entry and exit stamps to prove it. At the same time, though, I felt no immediate sense of dislocation, even as I adjusted my watch half an hour forward.

During the past three weeks I had consciously searched for the differences between Pakistan and India, making comparisons in every town and city that I visited. There were plenty of contrasts, at least on a superficial level, and yet, as I returned to India it was difficult to say exactly what separated these two nations.

In the epilogue of his book *The Idea of India*, Sunil Khilnani raises intriguing questions about the ways in which we locate and identify a country.

> Where in the world is India? Historical precedent suggests that it is possible to be wildly — if profitably wrong about its geographical location (remember Columbus). And there is a venerable tradition that has insisted on seeing India as a conceptual rather than a physical space. "A country", as Rabindranath Tagore put it, "is not territorial, but ideational"; or, in the more demotic cadence of the tourist board poster, "India is a state of mind".
>
> It may well be. But since 1947 India has existed as a precisely mapped, counted, and bounded territory governed by a sovereign political authority, as a state, a recognized member of the international state system.[6]

The border which I crossed at Wagha and Atari has existed for fifty years, long enough to prove its resilience. Unlike the Line of Control in Kashmir, there is no real contention over its validity, at least not on the level of international relations. In my mind, I could still picture the string of lights which I had seen from the airplane window when flying into Delhi, my first sighting of the electrified fence India has constructed to keep "infiltrators" and separatists at bay. I also remembered the Beating Retreat ceremonies, the BSF soldiers with their motto: "Duty unto Death." Recalling the fifteen hours it had taken me to travel from Amritsar to Lahore, there seemed to be an undeniable permanence about this boundary, reinforced by the complex procedures of immigration and customs, the endless paperwork of power.

But beyond all that I couldn't get over my own feeling of passing through an illusory barrier; it was almost as if I had walked through a wall. Though I was a foreigner, a "third country national," there was hardly any sense of alienation and I felt as if I hadn't really been away from India. Other than the brief and irritating harassment from the two customs inspectors, I had experienced no difficulty or inconvenience crossing the border at Atari. Altogether, it had taken me less than an hour, a stroll in the park compared to my train journey on the Samjhota Express.

In retrospect, I realize that like the group of Indian activists who held their candlelight vigil at Atari, I too wanted to erase that border, to turn back the clock to a time before Partition. Even now, as I attempt to record the experiences of my journey, I find myself denying some of those historical realities. Instinctively I keep using terms like "South Asia" and "the subcontinent," in an effort to express that unified vision of India that still persists in my imagination.

The problem is not so much an issue of geography but a more personal question of identity. Every border makes us a foreigner, no matter who we are. The restricting demands of nationalism force us to take sides, but like Manto's characters who are not as mad as they appear, there will always be those of us who choose to live "neither in India nor in Pakistan" but somewhere in between.

Air-conditioned coaches from Amritsar to Delhi operate only at night but since I wanted to travel during the day, I took an ordinary Punjab State Roadways bus. These are inexpensive and convenient, departing every few minutes for any number of destinations. My ticket to Delhi cost Rs. 123, less than three dollars, and when I calculated the various bus fares from Peshawar all the way to Delhi, they added up to the equivalent of eight dollars, for a distance of almost a thousand kilometers.

Most of the Punjab is a rural landscape, with a network of canals and fields of wheat, rice, corn, and sugar cane. Agriculture has brought prosperity to the state and there are almost as many tractors on the highway as buses and cars. Dairy farming is an important part of Punjab's economy and we passed several trucks loaded with brass canisters of milk. Painted on the back was a sign: "On Govt. Milk Duty." The largest industrial city in Punjab is Ludhiana. Though the air was clean for much of the journey, a thick layer of smog lay over the factories and workshops. Ludhiana is famous for the manufacturing of bicycles, which remain the most common form of transport in India. One of the most popular brands made here are Hero cycles.

With a prosperous middle class, many of the towns and cities along the highway project an ostentatious facade, representing a style of architecture sometimes referred to as "Punjabi baroque." One house that we passed at the side of the road was trimmed with intricate plaster molding and painted several different colors, like an ornate wedding cake. Topping it off was a full-scale model of a Mercedes car on the roof, perched there like a symbol of social mobility.

Plenty of other monuments have been erected along the GT Road. At one of the main crossings in Jalandhar stands the bronze statue of a Sikh officer who could easily have been Major Chandewala, the hero of the film *Border*. Freedom fighters and politicians also proliferated — a life-size cement likeness of Dr. Ambedkar, looking like a portly Rotarian in a bright blue suit and tie, busts of Shahid Bhagat Singh, Mahatma Gandhi, and Subhas Chandra Bose.

In the military cantonments of Amritsar, Jalandhar, and Ambala there were Pakistani tanks on display. Unlike the freshly painted and polished vehicles of war that I had seen in Peshawar, Nowshera, and Rawalpindi, these were old and rusted, punctured with bullet holes, their treads ripped off. Captured relics of the battles in 1965 and 1971, these enemy tanks are displayed as trophies at roundabouts and crossings. Though I could see no signs or plaques to explain their presence, the Urdu lettering and numerals on the gun turrets made it clear where they came from. Like the wreckage of highway accidents, they had a grim, derelict appearance compared to the whitewashed walls and polished brass insignia of the army messes and parade grounds.

The Grand Trunk Road passes from Punjab into Haryana before entering the union territory of Delhi. Being a national highway, kilometer posts alternate between four languages — Punjabi, Hindi, Urdu, and English. The state border between Punjab and Haryana is most evident in the roadsigns, which shift from Gurmukhi to the Devanagari script. The only other noticeable difference between the two states was the existence of prohibition in Haryana. Driving through the Punjab I saw a number of shops selling beer and "English wine," a euphemism for whisky, rum, vodka, or gin, as distinct from "country liquor," which is the poor man's drink. There were billboards advertising Aristocrat Whisky and Godfather Beer, whereas the country liquor shops had no need for brand names and signs. The proprietors simply tied bottles of the orange-colored spirits from the awnings of their stalls. As my bus approached the Haryana border the number of liquor stores increased dramatically, but as soon as we crossed over they disappeared.

As we neared Delhi the Grand Trunk Road passed by the ancient battlefield of Panipat, where the Mughal armies won three of their most decisive victories. Further on we passed the town of Kurukshetra, where the legendary conflicts in the *Mahabharata* took place, an epic war between brothers. At several points along the highway I could see masonry pillars built by the Afghan conqueror Sher Shah Suri, which marked the stages of his route to Delhi. The violent history of this highway predates the modern cantonments which now guard the GT Road. Instead of armored tanks the soldiers from earlier times rode in chariots or on the backs of elephants. But today the road warriors are drivers of Tata buses and trucks that do battle on the highway.

The mainstay of the Roadways fleet, Tata buses are rugged vehicles with very few frills. Unlike the ornately decorated buses and trucks in Pakistan, most of the public transport vehicles in India are painted drab colors and have a solid, functional appearance. Thinly padded seats are bolted to the chassis and the diesel engine has a low, unmuffled roar, belching clouds of noxious black smoke.

It didn't matter whether I was in Pakistan or India, the drivers were the same, oblivious of danger as they jockeyed for position. More than once I saw a truck bearing down on us with its headlights flashing, both drivers swerving at the last possible instant. Every few kilometers we passed the remains of an accident, an overloaded truck lying on its side or two buses which had collided, the impact welding them together in a grotesque tangle of steel and broken glass. Just as we entered Kurukshetra, we came upon a fresh casualty of these highway battles. A cyclist had been hit and killed. His body lay in the middle of the road and a crowd of men stood around, staring at the anonymous corpse. Someone had placed a line of bricks across the road and our bus had to slow down and circle the scene of the accident. All of us looked out the window and stared at the crumpled figure, ribbons of blood flowing across the asphalt. His bicycle lay in a twisted heap ten feet away. For the next few kilometers our bus driver slowed his pace, sobered by the sight of death, but as we approached the outskirts of Delhi he sped up again, impatient to reach our destination.

10

DELHI Jubilee

The Government is issuing a new 50 paise coin to commemorate the golden jubilee of Indian Independence. The coin is to be released by the president, Mr. K. R. Narayanan, at noon on August 15. The reverse of the coin in ferritic stainless steel will bear the motif of "Dandi March," which depicts Mahatma Gandhi with a band of marchers. It will also bear the legend "50 years of Independence" in the lower periphery in Hindi on the left and English on the right.

On Independence Day morning, the Prime Minister, Mr. I.K. Gujral will release a postage stamp depicting three INA stalwarts — Shahnawaz Khan, Prem Kumar Sehgal and G.S. Dhillon — with the backdrop of the room in Red Fort where a case involving them for sedition against the British Empire was held.

The Railways will be running two exhibition trains that will span the length and breadth of the country. They will pictorially depict the freedom struggle as well as the strides made by the country during the past five decades.—*The Hindu*, 14 August 1997

W hat is there to celebrate?" asked a close friend of mine in Delhi, echoing the sentiments of many Indians. She went on to list the failures of the government, from widespread poverty to crime, corruption, and communal violence.

Driving through the capital late at night, less than twenty-four hours before the festivities began, my taxi driver pointed to the shrouded forms of pavement dwellers sleeping on the road dividers. "Here's their Jubilee," he said.

"Is this what the father of the nation struggled for?" read a newspaper advertisement, with a picture of Mahatma Gandhi's wire-rimmed spectacles and a list of disheartening statistics: "India ranks 135 out of 174 countries (Human Development Index). 46% of Indian population survive in absolute poverty. Only 53% of adults are literate. 62 million children, under the age of five are malnourished. 226 million lack access to safe drinking water. Of the total prostitutes in Delhi alone, 40% are minors."[1]

Even the government, preoccupied with political instability and wrangling, corruption scandals and economic woes, seemed initially ambivalent about the Jubilee celebrations. When I first arrived in Delhi, on 21 July, nobody really seemed to know what festivities had been organized. But as the fiftieth anniversary of India's Independence approached momentum had begun to build. Bureaucrats and lawmakers, educators, social activists, and business leaders suddenly seemed energized by the impending event, and when I returned to Delhi on 13 August the city and the nation was in a more celebratory mood. Cynicism remained but even the most staid Delhites seemed ready to have a party. For a city that has always been ridiculed for its nonexistent nightlife — the streets of Delhi fall silent by nine o'clock — the unusual excitement of the midnight hour was approaching.

Elsewhere in the country there were fears that the celebrations might get out of hand. In Bangalore, for instance, moralistic politicians in both the Bharatiya Janata and Congress parties protested the fact that the government had allowed liquor shops to remain open for the Jubilee.

The 50th anniversary of Independence is not an occasion for merrymaking and the citizens should realize its solemnity, is the message sent out by members of the Legislative Assembly [who were] . . . provoked by the advertisements issued by the managements of some hotels, clubs and holiday resorts in and around the city inviting people for merrymaking on August 14-15. The members averred that the solemnity of the day would be violated if people indulged in dining, wining and dancing.[2]

Despite the sobering realities facing the nation and the dour pronouncements of sanctimonious parliamentarians, there was clearly a desire on the part of many people in India to make this a memorable and momentous affair. In New Delhi the official celebrations would begin with a "March of the Nation," along Rajpath, the main avenue leading from India Gate to the ramparts of the central secretariat. Over a week in advance the main public buildings were illuminated with strings of electric bulbs, elaborate constellations of lights that turned the center of the capital into a dazzling galaxy. Fireworks displays, musical performances, and a laser show costing a reported eighty lakhs were planned by a special government secretariat established expressly for the Jubilee. Over fifty thousand people were expected to attend the outdoor events. Within the central hall of parliament, there would be a reenactment of freedom at midnight, with an address by the president and taped speeches by Mahatma Gandhi, Subhas Chandra Bose, and Jawaharlal Nehru. Bhimsen Joshi, one of India's greatest classical vocalists, would open the special parliamentary session by singing the freedom hymn "Vande Mataram," while the Hindi film industry's "melody queen" and legendary playback singer Lata Mangeshkar offered her own rendition of "Saare Jahan Se Achcha," a patriotic song composed by Mohammed Iqbal. Even though he was one of the first people to suggest the creation of a separate Muslim state, Iqbal is still revered by many Indians for his poetry. The title of his song, roughly translated: "Better than any place on earth, our Hindustan."

The plethora of national symbols which were in evidence made it clear that these celebrations were an effort to dramatize the unity of India, to create an illusion of solidarity within the country. The songs and slogans, the emblems and iconography of the freedom movement were prominently on display. Billboards carried these images at every crossroads, posters were plastered on every wall, banners hung from trees, and television screens were filled with lingering shots of the national flag or grainy black-and-white footage of Pandit Nehru releasing a dove. Even the Ambassador car, that pugnacious chariot of the Indian road, was promoted as a national symbol and motif of self-reliance. Manufactured by Hindustan Motors, the Ambassador or "Amby" as it is affectionately called, is a modified version of the Morris Oxford — a rugged, dumpy-looking car. For almost fifty years it has been the vehicle of choice for government officials in India and the white Ambassador with a fluttering tricolor on its bonnet remains an emblem of power and authority.

Yet all these symbols were open to interpretation. Long before the advent of computers and the manipulation of digital images, the Congress Party was refashioning the motifs of nationalism to project its own agenda. For instance, the chakra or chariot wheel which lies at the center of India's flag was transformed into Mahatma Gandhi's spinning wheel. Later this icon was replaced by the cow and calf, or the picture of an open hand which was Indira Gandhi's polling symbol. All this occurred despite legal restrictions on the misuse and unauthorized display of the national flag. For the Jubilee celebrations, however, these rules were temporarily lifted and the Home Ministry issued a statement, "There will be no objection to the hoisting of the national flag on all public buildings and houses in villages, towns and cities." It was noted however that "the display of the national flag on motor cars shall be strictly in accordance with the provisions of the flag code. The privilege of flying the national flag on motor cars will be limited to the dignitaries specified in the code."[3] Meanwhile, in the southern state of Andhra Pradesh, Naxalite leaders of the People's War Group, issued a diktat, demanding that the tricolor not be flown on Independence Day, as a protest against the repressive actions of the government and its "anti-people attitude."[4]

Perhaps one of the most symbolic and enduring controversies in New Delhi surrounds a monument on Rajpath, the venue for the "March of the Nation." After Independence the statue of King George V was removed from a stone pavilion opposite India Gate and there were proposals for installing a statue of Gandhi in his place. Immediately, a controversy arose because it was argued that the father of the nation should not be placed on an imperial pedestal, beneath a canopy which was designed to shelter the king emperor. Fifty years later the pavilion remains empty, while parliament continues to debate the issue and appoint committees to study the question.

Even India's freedom fighters are not entirely secure on their own pedestals. This was clear in Uttar Pradesh, where the newly elected chief minister, Mayawati, was indiscriminately promoting Dr. Ambedkar, the author of India's constitution and hero of the Dalit communities. Mayawati had erected his statues throughout the state and renamed many streets, parks, and institutions in his memory. As one commentator complained, this led to the toppling of other heroes, including Chandrashekar Azad, who is considered one of the martyrs of the freedom struggle.

It is evident that today's political class is incapable of defending even the nation's symbols, leave alone anything else. . . .

In her overzealousness [Mayawati] has not spared even Chandrashekar Azad. She has decided to rename a college in Etawah and a university in Kanpur — that were named after the revolutionary hero of the 1920's — after Ambedkar.

What is worse is that Mayawati, with scant respect for history, sought to justify the dropping of Azad's name from the two institutions on the ground that he was "merely a terrorist." There cannot be a graver travesty of truth.[5]

Political and communal sensitivities regarding the conflicting narratives of Independence were best demonstrated in an incident in Maharastra, where the chief minister, Manohar Joshi, dismissed a senior civil servant, for referring to Mohammed Ali Jinnah as a "great freedom fighter." Govind Swaroop, head of the Culture Department in the state government, had made this "inadvertent remark," on a videotaped documentary about the Jubilee. Joshi, who is a Hindu nationalist and member of the Bhartiya Janata Party declared, "I cannot accept such remarks. The statement was not only irresponsible but it was dereliction of the highest order. I am transferring him with immediate effect. At the same time, I have directed that Govind Swaroop's remarks should be deleted from the official videocassette."[6]

In the course of the Jubilee celebrations, national symbols were also shamelessly exploited for commercial gain. Even the multinational corporations took advantage of the anniversary. Johnson & Johnson ran the following advertisement, which covered three quarters of a page in the *Times of India*.

> In 1947, Indians were left behind
> with some indelible scars.
> General Robert Wood Johnson knew
> it was time to provide the healing touch.
>
> It was not the best of times.

> When General Robert Wood Johnson introduced Johnson's Baby Powder in India in 1947, he faced two hurdles. One, he was selling an unknown foreign product. Two, he was a foreigner himself (and white).
>
> But thankfully for Gen. Johnson, the product's inherent qualities quickly converted hostility into total acceptance. Soon life became much more comfortable for newly born, post-independence Indians.[7]

On a somewhat less patronizing but unhealthier note the Dhariwal Tobacco Company advertised its Manikchand Gutka chewing tobacco with the motto: "Many Countries, Many Attires, Many Tribes — And One Unifying Choice? It isn't strange. Muktichand Gutka."[8] Under this enigmatic slogan was a picture of India's flag with a tobacco sachet in place of the chakra. Employing a copywriter's license, Vimal Suiting proclaimed itself "the fabric of the nation" while Bajaj presented their scooters as the vehicle of freedom: "'Quit India' 'Simon Go Back' 'Chalo Dilli' 'Jai Hind' 'Vande Mataram' . . . A Million Passionate Cries. One Great Nation. One Great Scooter."[9] For the well-healed patriot, European watchmaker Louis Cartier announced a special limited-edition timepiece, commemorating the Jubilee, with a Sanskrit slogan, "Satyameva Jayate," inscribed on the dial. Only fifty of these were produced at a price of Rs. 3.4 lakh each (approximately $7,000).

Probably the most brazen exploitation of the Jubilee was an ad campaign undertaken by Canada Dry. The soft-drink company had bought rights to sponsor the telecast of celebrations inside parliament.

Though alcohol is not permitted within the sacred precincts, Canada Dry had designed bottles of ginger ale to look like champagne and the company's public relations department had arranged for Lata Mangeshkar to open one of these bottles after she finished singing "Saare Jahan Se Achcha."

In the weeks leading up to the celebrations, newspapers and television were full of ads promoting the "Canada Dry Freedom Salvo." Many people were outraged by such crass commercialism and the fact that freedom at midnight was being usurped by a foreign corporation.

> Since when has the Cadbury-Schweppes soft drink "Canada Dry" become a momento of the country's 50th anniversary celebrations? In fact it is almost incredible that the historic midnight session of Parliament on August 14 — studded with inspiring speeches by the heroes of the country's independence struggle — should come to a close with the Indian nightingale, Ms. Lata Mangeshkar, opening a bottle of the soft drink as a tribute to a special moment in Indian history.[10]

Criticism of this kind finally led to canceling of the "Canada Dry moment," despite the advertiser's last-minute claims that any revenues from the event were going to be donated to charity.

Celebrations in Delhi naturally focused on the theme of Independence, though Partition remained the dark side of this narrative, a depressing counterpoint to all of the patriotic fanfare. As Sunil Khilnani writes, "Partition is the unspeakable sadness at the heart of the idea of India: a *memento mori* that what made India possible also profoundly diminished the integral value of the idea."[11]

Among the large refugee population in the capital there was a general antipathy towards the pervasive mythology of nationalism. For every heroic freedom fighter and victorious act of satyagraha there was another story waiting to be told, the personal narratives of those who had been uprooted from the other side of the border.

In Bhisham Sahni's classic novel *Tamas*, which is set during Partition, there is a poignant scene in which the manager of a Refugee Relief Committee pleads with the displaced Hindus and Sikhs whose plight he is trying to record in a ledger.

"We want statistics, nothing but statistics," he says. "I don't want stories. I want the bare figures — how many died, how many were injured and the extent of the financial loss."[12]

Despite his pleas the refugees insist on telling their tales of horror, describing the property they left behind, the friendships that were betrayed, their fears of separation, the physical and emotional wounds they suffered.

Exact figures surrounding Partition are not available, and even if these statistics were on record they would never provide a complete picture of the events. Far more important are the personal narratives of these refugees. History exists in those voices and on the anniversary of Partition there were innumerable accounts of what happened. By telling and retelling the stories of their loss, the refugees sought to reclaim their memories and pass these on to another generation.

Most of the newspapers and magazines in India carried versions of these stories, each with a different set of voices, but all with a shared refrain of fear, nostalgia, and regret. In many ways it was like an oral epic, one huge story made up of hundreds of other stories, a cycle of narratives that recounted layers upon layers of experience. Some of the factual accuracy of these accounts may be called into question, for memories over time become blurred, but there remained an overwhelming truth in what was being told.

In an effort to collect these stories, Urvashi Butalia, has recorded and published an anthology of oral narratives, *The Other Side of Silence* about the trauma of 1947. It is perhaps the closest we will ever come to a personal history of these events, as told by the survivors of Partition. Butalia herself is the daughter of refugees; she describes her motivation in this project:

> My mother tells of the dangerous journeys that she twice made back there to bring her younger brothers and sister to India. My father remembers fleeing to the sound of guns and crackling fires. I would listen to these stories with my brothers and sister and hardly take them in. We were middle-class Indians who had grown up in a period of relative calm and prosperity, when tolerance and "secularism" seemed to be winning the argument. The stories — looting, arson, rape, murder — came out of a different

time. They meant little to me.

Then, in October 1984, the prime minister, Mrs. Gandhi was assassinated . . . For days afterwards Sikhs all over India were attacked in an orgy of violence and revenge. Many homes were destroyed and thousands died. In the outlying suburbs of Delhi more than three thousand were killed, often by being doused in kerosene and then set alight. . . . The stories from Partition no longer seemed quite so remote; people from the same country, the same town, the same village could still be divided by the politics of their religious difference, and, once divided, could do terrible things to each other.[13]

Pursuing the stories within her own family and amongst other refugees in India, Butalia presents a fascinating and disturbing collage of memoirs that reveal both the violence and bestiality as well as the compassion and humanity of that period.

I had planned to attend the March of the Nation with friends who lived in one of the southern colonies of New Delhi, but as it turned out the main streets were cordoned off, making it nearly impossible to get from one side of the city to the other except by way of a long detour. In a strange sense, it was like being stranded on opposite sides of a border with no way of crossing back and forth. By nightfall the crowds had started to gather and around nine o'clock I took an autorickhaw from my hotel to the press club. From there I walked across to the broad lawns that extend the length of Rajpath, one of the largest green spaces in the city, where people often picnic in the shade of the jamun trees. The police had erected barricades and fences to control the crowds but once I got past these it was easy to move about.

The night was warm but pleasant. People were milling about near the cold-drinks stands and food stalls selling chaat and other snacks. All of the buildings along Rajpath were decorated with lights and it was a dramatic sight, particularly the domed architecture of the central secretariat and the presidential estate, a beaded outline of yellow bulbs. Later I learned that other sections of the city had suffered power cuts so that this area could be lit up.

An open-air stage had been erected in Vijay Chowk, the main square in front of the secretariat and Lok Sabha. There was a special enclosure with chairs for VIP guests. The crowds seemed to be slowly drifting in that direction but, except for the special enclosure, the stage was too far away for anyone to see. Instead there were large video screens at intervals along the route of the parade; on one of these I was able to watch the dancers and musicians who were performing. Mrinalani Sarabhai, the doyen of Indian dance, had choreographed an Odissi performance, and pop idol, A. R. Rehman had composed a contemporary version of "Vande Mataram" that was played to the accompaniment of a light show and video montage.

A series of smaller stages had been positioned along the route and folk dancers from each of the different states of India were performing throughout the night. For a good part of the evening, I was standing closest to a stage where a troupe from Karnataka was putting on their show. Five drummers set the tempo and the decibel level was loud enough to shatter your eardrums. The dancers had elaborate headdresses and as they twirled about and stamped their feet, the colored ribbons whirled together in a dizzying blur of orange, white, and green.

The March of the Nation began with a military band and marching squads representing the army, navy, air force, and police services. These were followed by a fleet of jeeps carrying veteran freedom fighters, men and women who had been activists and organizers during the struggle for Independence. Most of them were in their seventies and eighties, waving paper flags as they went by. Freedom fighters have always held a position of privilege in the country, and as a gesture of recognition the prime minister had recently announced that their pensions would be doubled. The freedom fighters were followed by two floats, mounted on trucks, one of which depicted Gandhi's Salt March. The other consisted of a group of soldiers in foxholes, hiding behind artificial bushes and firing plastic rifles. The sound effects, broadcast at full volume, were like something out of a video arcade, with sharp explosions and the whine of bullets ricocheting. It took me a while to realize that this was a depiction of the Indian National Army, the militant counterpoint to Gandhi's campaign of nonviolence.

Except for the marching band and soldiers, the general atmosphere of the parade was relaxed and casual. From what I could see everyone seemed to be having a good time. There wasn't a great deal of patriotic fervor, except for one group of college students who had painted their faces with the colors of the Indian flag and run through the crowd shouting, "Jai Hind!" Though I had expected most people to be wearing handloom khadi clothes, a traditional symbol of Gandhi's defiance of British exploitation, the vast majority of men were in bush shirts and jeans while the women wore light cotton salwar kameez or printed saris. Most people seemed almost indifferent to the historical and ceremonial aspects of the event. They looked more like holiday crowds at a fair, eating, drinking, and wandering about with their friends. The majority were middle-class families and it was clear that what was being celebrated on the lawns of Rajpath was not so much the anniversary of Independence but a cautious sense of prosperity and hope for the future. These were the citizens of India to whom the advertisements in the newspapers were directed, those who would purchase Bajaj scooters, Vimal fabrics and Canada Dry ginger ale. Their sense of identity was as closely tied to these icons of material success as it was to the traditional symbols of nationalism.

Part of the ambivalence that I sensed on the lawns bordering Rajpath reflects changing attitudes towards nationalism in India, as described by Ashis Nandy in his essay "The Political Culture of the Indian State."

> While the idea of nationalism as a universal concept, with a universal content, takes hold of the Indian mind, more and more Indians seem to be losing confidence in their own version of patriotism and in their concepts of state, governance, and integration. The urban middle-class Indians, the ones with most exposure to the mass media and easy access to contemporary political ideas, now believe that those who do not follow the standard definition of nationalism are doomed to be dominated and marginalized in international affairs. These Indians are willing to depend on the nation-state to forge national unity and to shed the slogans of the earlier generations of political elites — such as "unity in diversity" and "coexistence" — as effete cliches.[14]

Various delegations were represented in the march, including labor unions and other social and cultural organizations. There was an eclectic mix of occupations, each with its own group of marchers — bank employees, nurses, farmers, government sweepers, and university professors. All of them had been issued souvenir jholas, shoulder bags which were decorated with the fiftieth-anniversary logo, and each group carried a banner identifying their constituency.

Several contingents of Boy Scouts and Girl Scouts were included in the parade, dressed in starched khaki with blue scarves knotted at their necks. Some of them were trying to march in unison but others, like a group of Girl Guides between eight and ten years old, kept breaking ranks and darting back and forth among themselves. Accompanying them was an officious scoutmaster, dressed all in white, who carried a swagger stick. He kept trying to make the girls stay in line but they ignored him, laughing and teasing each other. The scoutmaster, his shirt ringed with sweat, was obviously frustrated by their lack of discipline and kept shouting at the girls and waving his stick ineffectually.

Around eleven o'clock the parade came to a halt because the area near Vijay Chowk was jammed with people. The marchers stood about for awhile and many of them sat down on the road or wandered over to the lawns to watch the giant television screens. As dignitaries strutted about on the stage and intoned platitudes, the mood in the crowd remained lighthearted. There were speeches but hardly anyone was listening. After the prime minister and other members of parliament retreated into the Lok Sabha, there was a pyrotechnic display above the National Stadium with rockets and flares bursting like orange, white, and green comets against the night sky.

While the party carried on outside, the president and others were giving speeches inside the halls of parliament and tape recordings of Gandhi, Bose, and Nehru were played with appropriate reverence. By all accounts it was a dull affair. Even Lata Mangeshkar was a disappointment, sounding nervous as she sang "Saare Jahan Se Achcha" while reading the lyrics off a piece of paper. I was much happier to be outdoors, and when midnight eventually arrived there were more fireworks and cheers from the crowds along Rajpath. By this time the evening was cooler and the merrymaking went on for another hour or two before people dispersed for home.

No autorickshaws or taxis were available so I walked back to my hotel. The streets were mostly deserted, except for a few pavement dwellers who had slept through the festivities. Their shadowy forms lay on the sidewalk, some of them sprawled on straw mats, others curled into fetal positions. As I walked along Ashoka Road, I noticed a group of ten or twelve men painting a fence, part of the last-minute preparations for the Jubilee. In the early hours of Independence Day, the capital was still being tarted up. The gang of painters worked in silence, crouched in a line. Instead of using brushes they were dipping their hands in tins of yellow enamel paint and smearing it on the metal fence posts. As I passed these mute, anonymous figures they seemed to be performing a secret ritual under the cover of darkness, their hands gloved in yellow paint.

> The historiography of Partition, and of communalism in general, is dominated by a narrative in which the Indian National Congress is represented as being synonymous with the Independence movement. Denominational communalisms of Hindus and Muslims are said to have been discrete phenomena that arose on the fringes of the Indian society. In this narrative, the Congress is always portrayed as being secular, splendidly free of the communal virus. . . . The night on August 15 then becomes that magical moment when the Indian people finally arrive, in Nehru's famous phrase, at their "tryst with destiny." This triumphalist account of a nationalism that failed to protect a fifth of the territorial nation that it claimed to represent is credible only if the creation of Pakistan is seen as the severance of "the diseased limb" as Patel described it in 1946 while recommending the bloody surgery.[15]

Aijaz Ahmad, a political scientist and senior fellow at the Nehru Museum, goes on to question the factual basis of this narrative. In a provocative essay written especially for the Jubilee, he casts doubts on Congress Party claims of being untainted by communal prejudices. At the same time he argues that the creation of Pakistan was not inevitable and that the "diseased limb," a euphemism for Muslim polity in India, was never seriously in need of amputation.

The Jubilee festivities posed something of a dilemma for those who sought to manipulate these narratives. As Ahmad points out, so much of the freedom struggle is enmeshed in the mythology of the Congress Party, whether it is Mahatma Gandhi's ascetic purity, Sardar Patel's calculating pragmatism, or Nehru's visionary eloquence. On the fiftieth anniversary of Independence, however, Congress was out of power and the United Front coalition chose to temper the traditional narratives of freedom, with versions of their own. The prominence given to Subhas Chandra Bose and the Indian National Army was part of this retelling of history, but even more striking was the almost complete exclusion of Indira Gandhi and her two sons. Clearly, if Congress had been in control of the government, the Nehru dynasty would have featured much more prominently in the story of Independence but they were edited out of the script.

On this occasion, secularism was presented not as the exclusive monopoly of Congress but as an overarching national ideal, upheld by all but the most rabid fundamentalists. Time and again the prime minister, I. K. Gujral, was portrayed in the media as a man of secular principles and more than anyone he probably fit that role. His earlier associations with the Congress Party during the freedom struggle and his eventual split with Indira Gandhi in the 1970s, suggested that Gujral represented those national ideals which Congress had ultimately betrayed. Amongst Gujral's secular credentials was the fact that he had recently made serious attempts at rapprochement with Pakistan and even offered to enter into dialogue with the separatists in Kashmir (though this soon led to an embarrassing retraction). The prime minister's other trait, played up in the newspapers, was his fluency in Urdu and his penchant for reciting couplets in that language.

Meanwhile, the Congress Party, which had not been able to form a government following the last elections and eventually gave grudging support to the United Front coalition, was scrambling to rescue its reputation as the torch bearer of secularism and defender of minorities. But memories of the siege at the Golden Temple in Amritsar, the anti-Sikh riots following Indira Gandhi's death, and more recently the destruction of the Babri Masjid in Ayodhya were still clear in people's minds. The Congress leaders must have understood that they faced a crisis of credibility; on the eve of the Jubilee the party issued a statement apologizing for not protecting the mosque. This was received with skepticism. "Not a single Muslim organisation has greeted the Congress apology demonstrating the reservation of the community towards the belated gesture, while individual Muslims feel that the party should have committed itself to rebuilding the demolished mosque at the very site where it existed."[16]

While the various narratives of the freedom struggle were being recounted in the nation's capital, each of them attempting to coopt the spirit of secularism, there was little doubt that politicians of all persuasions had betrayed one of the fundamental principles on which India's democracy was founded. A more extreme view was expressed by commentators like Aijaz Ahmad, who argued that the Congress Party was essentially founded on "communal" principles, reflecting social structures, which were imposed by colonialism, caste, and Hindu reformist movements.

> . . . the national movement itself, including the majority of the Congress under Gandhi, was deeply complicit in a transactional mode of politics which involved bargaining among the elites and a conception of "secularism" which was little more than an accommodation of the self-enclosed orthodoxies. Given the immensity of this historical weight, the wonder is not that there was a partition but that there was only one.[17]

After four hours of sleep I didn't want to get out of bed when my alarm clock rang at five o'clock in the morning on August 15th. I had arranged to attend the flag-raising ceremony at the Red Fort with my cousin Marty and her husband Lincoln, who had flown into Delhi a few days earlier to attend the Jubilee celebrations. Through friends in the government they had been able to get special invitations to the midnight session of parliament as well as the flag raising. Though I didn't have a pass myself, I figured that I would tag along with them and see if I could get a seat in the VIP enclosure. If that didn't work I could always join the less privileged crowds on the periphery.

We had been warned that security was going to be tight and we needed to allow plenty of time to reach our seats. The car which picked us up at six o'clock was a white Ambassador, with an official sticker that allowed entry into the parking area for dignitaries. As we drove past India Gate, the police barricades were still in place, but there was no sign of the crowds from the night before. Circling the main roundabout, past the pedestal where George V's statue used to stand, I noticed three other white Ambassadors with tinted windows, cutting in front of us. They were traveling together and obviously headed to the flag-raising ceremony. At one of the main crossroads the three cars tried to drive through a red light when a Delhi Transport Corporation bus came roaring in from the right and almost collided with the lead Ambassador. Everyone braked at once and immediately the doors on the car in front of us flew open. Two "black cat" commandos with sten guns jumped out and positioned themselves on either side of the lead vehicle, while a plainclothes officer with a walkie-talkie ran up to the bus and started gesticulating frantically. The distinguished passenger in the car ahead of us must have been a senior cabinet member or perhaps a former prime minister, though we couldn't see who it was on account of the tinted windows. Since the early eighties, armed bodyguards and security details have become a status symbol in Delhi. During the height of the separatist agitation in the Punjab it was a necessary precaution, but now the commandoes in their forbidding black uniforms seem to serve the paranoid delusions of the ruling elite.

I was anticipating problems getting into the VIP enclosure without an invitation, but in the end nobody stopped me as I walked through the security gate and the metal detectors. We had arrived in plenty of time and were able to get seats near the front, directly under the sandstone ramparts of the fort. The Independence Day ceremony has been held on this site for the past fifty years. It is an occasion on which the prime minister addresses the nation and the speech is carried live on radio and television all across the country. Jawaharlal Nehru used it as a platform to outline his vision of modern India, while Indira Gandhi harangued the nation from these same ramparts. Once again, it is a patriotic ceremony, carefully staged as a tableau of national unity, played out against the backdrop of the Red Fort. It is significant that the flag raising is held in front of this sandstone citadel from which the Mughal emperors once ruled India. Directly opposite is the Jumma Masjid and the Muslim quarter of the city. Most important of all, there is no evidence of Lutyens's colonial architecture.

Near the VIP enclosure was a massed choir of schoolchildren who sang songs in all the different languages of the country, a symbolic chorus of national harmony. A few hundred yards from the fort stood an enormous hot air balloon in the shape of the Ashokan capital, the three lions which appear on everything from one-rupee coins to official government stationery. Inflated to a height of fifty feet, the balloon rose over the thousands of spectators who had gathered for the ceremony.

The flag raising was organized by the Ministry of Defence and there was a military punctuality to the occasion which was noticeably different from the March of the Nation. The programs, which had been handed out at the gate, listed the Guard of Honor forming at 7:10, fanfare for the prime minister at 7:24, and his arrival at the ramparts timed precisely for 7:29, so that he could unfurl the flag at exactly 7:30. Just before 7:00 there was an announcement over the loudspeaker system asking all officials to synchronize their watches.

The honor guard consisted of Sikh soldiers, every one of them over six-feet tall, with several inches of red turban on top of that and circlets of polished steel. A military band played the national anthem "Jana Gana Mana," followed by a twenty-one-gun salute and a flypast of fighter jets, all precisely choreographed into the schedule. The jets left colored vapor trails — orange, white, and green. A couple minutes later three military helicopters came in low over the crowd and showered us with rose petals and marigolds. The helicopters caused the only mishap of the morning when a rush of wind from their rotor blades shook the hot air balloon. The Ashokan lions swayed precariously and as the crowd gasped, one section tore open and the balloon deflated rapidly.

Despite this distraction the ceremony continued on schedule and after the flag was unfurled I. K. Gujral began his speech. By this time the sun was beating down on the Red Fort and the temperature was climbing into the upper nineties. Though he raised a number of important points, the speech was much too long, an hour and twenty minutes. The crowd grew restless and many of the spectators began to disperse. In the VIP enclosure many of the dignitaries eventually got to their feet and started to mill about, greeting each other and chatting while the speech continued. Meanwhile, the choir of schoolchildren fidgeted in the sun, but they were restrained by an officious man, dressed all in white, like the scoutmaster I'd seen the night before. He must have been the choir director, for instead of a swagger stick he carried a baton in one hand. Every few minutes, after the prime minister made a particular point, the man in white raised his baton and the children obediently applauded. By the end of the speech they were the only ones who were clapping.

As he had done on earlier occasions, the prime minister emphasized the need to root out corruption in Indian society and announced a "satyagraha" on the issue. The irony was that amongst the rows of dignitaries seated on the ramparts of the fort there were quite a few politicians who were presently being investigated for bribery and money-skimming, including former prime minister Narasimha Rao. One of the notable omissions in the speech was that Gujral did not mention Indira or Rajiv Gandhi even once, though Sonia Gandhi was seated in the front row of dignitaries. Possibly the most forceful moment in the speech came when the prime minister made a pledge to improve relations with Pakistan, reiterating his commitment to carrying on a bilateral dialogue. There was an emotional resonance in I. K. Gujral's voice at this point, amplified by his choice of Urdu phrases and the acoustics of the huge, sandstone archway in front of which he stood. After all, this was the Lahore Gate of the Red Fort, which faces in the direction of the border.

EPILOGUE

Between the time I completed my journey and the writing of this book, several important events have occurred. None of these has made me want to change anything that I have written. In fact, recent headlines only serve to reinforce many of my own impressions and beliefs about the border which divides India and Pakistan. Partition was undoubtedly a mistake but once it had been carried out there was little or no chance of reconstituting a unified India, if indeed such a mythical homeland ever existed.

Because of this border there will continue to be conflict in South Asia, not only on a communal or sectarian level but also between two nations and their military establishments. The bloodshed and hatred that accompanied Partition might well have occurred even if the British had not drawn their lines on the map, but the creation of two separate, independent states clearly exacerbated and extended the conflict. What is happening now, over fifty years later, is the result of irreversible decisions taken in 1947, by colonialists and freedom fighters alike. Breaking India apart led to the spontaneous release of unprecedented violence and hostility which has poisoned relations between the two countries ever since. Under present circumstances the analogy of splitting the atom is frighteningly appropriate.

On May 11, 1998, less than one year after the Jubilee, India exploded a nuclear device. The Pokhran test site, where this and four subsequent explosions were detonated, is located in the deserts of Rajasthan, about 125 kilometers from the border. In a defiant display of technological and military bravado, the prime minister, Atal Bihari Vajpayee, announced India's intentions of becoming, "a nuclear weapons state," even though he claimed that the nation's motives were peaceful and said that, "Ours will never be weapons of aggression."[1]

Euphoric crowds danced in the streets of Delhi, as if the nation had just won a cricket match. While the scientific research and development of nuclear technology that made these tests possible had been going on for many years, it was no coincidence that the Bharatiya Janata Party had recently come to power. Dominated by ardent Hindu nationalists, the BJP has always promoted India's nuclear capabilities as part of its electoral campaigns. Emphasizing both real and imagined threats from Pakistan and rejecting nonproliferation treaties as an encroachment on India's national sovereignty, the party played its "nuclear card," without hesitation. Widespread public support for this decision helped Vajpayee bolster his own precarious position at the head of a fractious coalition government. Once again, political expediency rather than rational or moral judgement seemed the rule of the day.

Worldwide condemnation of the nuclear tests was accompanied by a few isolated voices in India protesting the government's decision. For the first time since the end of the Cold War, the frustratingly familiar arguments between deterrence and Armageddon were bantered about in the media. The specter of nuclear war in one of the most populous regions of the globe made the destruction of Hiroshima and Nagasaki, or the death and displacement of Partition, seem almost insignificant by comparison. Regardless of the existence of nuclear arsenals in other countries and the scale of public approval in India, there can be no ethical justification for weapons of mass destruction that would kill hundreds of thousands of people and reduce much of the subcontinent to a toxic wasteland. Perhaps the only thing that might survive such a war is the border itself — that invisible, intractable line in the sand.

Two weeks after India conducted its tests, Pakistan retaliated by exploding five nuclear devices of its own. Unable to resist the wave of public sentiment in his country, prime minister Nawaz Sharif gave in to pressure and declared that Pakistan had "settled the score." With xenophobic demonstrations of patriotism, including the burning of effigies and flags in cities on both sides of the border, the frenzy of accusations and paranoia reached a fever pitch. Countries like the United States and Britain issued warnings and calls for peace, but having similar weapons of their own, they lacked the moral authority to force Pakistan and India to back down. Instead, some of the Western nations imposed economic sanctions, which have been largely ineffectual and are now in the process of being repealed.

Though the devices that were exploded did not amount to actual bombs or warheads, it was clear that the two nations possessed the capability to build and "deliver" these weapons within a very short period of time. India had already tested a ballistic missile, code named Agni, after the Hindu god of fire, while Pakistan had its Ghaznavi and Ghuri rockets, named after two of the first Muslim conquerors of India. These missiles have more than enough range to reach either Islamabad or Delhi and beyond.

Fortunately the initial hysteria and hyperbole which accompanied the nuclear tests eased within a few months. This cooling-off period was followed by claims from leaders on both sides, reasserting that they had no intention of using nuclear weapons as a "first-strike option" and that their missiles were intended purely for defense. As hostile posturing gave way to diplomacy in the months following the nuclear tests the two nations attempted to defuse tensions.

Early in February 1999, it was suddenly announced that an agreement had been reached for a bus service between Delhi and Lahore. Since the war in 1965 there had been no regular road transport along this route and the only means of travel for citizens of India and Pakistan was by air or train. This gesture of goodwill became all the more dramatic when Prime Minister Vajpayee announced that he would be the first passenger to ride on the bus and that his journey would culminate in a summit meeting at Lahore with Pakistan's premier. On 20 February, Vajpayee boarded the bus in Amritsar and drove through the Atari checkpoint, accompanied by an entourage of journalists and dignitaries. He was met on the other side by Nawaz Sharif, and flown to Lahore by helicopter, where discussions were cordial but inconclusive.

The inauguration of this bus service does not negate the serious problem of nuclear arsenals but it did serve to temporarily disarm some of the tensions between India and Pakistan. It is significant that the two nations chose this particular gesture as a symbolic first step towards reconciliation, putting emphasis on the notion that peace can be achieved by the crossing of national boundaries. Painted on either side of the bus were the words "Sada-e-Sarhad" — call of the border. Both the flags of India and Pakistan were prominently displayed on the bus and two veteran Delhi Transport Corporation drivers were handpicked for the inaugural journey, one of them a Hindu and the other a Muslim. Regular passenger service along this route began soon afterwards, with a single luxury coach that completes the round-trip journey four days a week. Seating is limited to thirty-seven passengers and the tickets, at Rs. 800 each, are far more expensive than train fare on the Samjhota Express.[2]

Given the price, most travelers will continue to make the journey between Delhi and Lahore by train and those who have money are still likely to go by air. However, the bus service will undoubtedly carry more people across the border and that can only be seen as a positive change. Aside from all the symbolism and fanfare, the option of road transport does make it easier to travel between India and Pakistan. In and of itself this may seem a minor development, especially in comparison to the proliferation of nuclear weapons, but it is important to recognize that each time a traveler crosses that border this helps to diminish its impermeable nature and dispel the tensions that lie between these two countries. Every visa, every entry stamp and exit permit, every signature on a customs or immigration form, every exchange of currency represents a concession by the governmental authorities, allowing people the freedom to move back and forth across that line. If there is to be any hope of lasting peace and reconciliation in South Asia, it can only occur when the people of these two nations are allowed to meet and mingle with each other, instead of being isolated behind national boundaries.

The most insidious legacy of Partition has the been the wholesale separation of identities, the exclusiveness of citizenship and an opposing sense of national allegiance. Ethnic, cultural, and religious conflicts have always existed, but with the imposition of borders these differences have been brought into sharper contrast. Throughout the twentieth century, as colonial powers divested themselves of conquered territory, there was an underlying assumption that borders were needed to divide people according to their race, their language, their history, and their faith. Simply because the Europeans found their colonial subjects to be "ungovernable," decisions were made to segment the globe into discreet and often disputed territories. The traditional adage "divide and rule," was conveniently changed to, "divide and retreat." Wherever the principle of Partition has been applied — whether in India, Ireland, Vietnam, Palestine, or Rwanda — there has been a history of bloodshed. Those who might argue that good borders make good neighbors would be hard pressed to give an example of an international boundary, created after 1900, that has not led to controversy and conflict. Yet even as we leave behind the past, violent century, world leaders seem incapable of understanding or accepting the failure of these policies and borders continue to be drawn in places like Bosnia and Kosovo.

There is something perverse about the notion that human beings can only coexist with people of their own kind and that national boundaries should be used to separate ethnic and religious communities. If this logic were to prevail, the world would ultimately be fragmented into smaller and smaller units, each with its own chauvinistic agenda and its own set of enemies and allies. This is the fundamental problem with most separatist movements in the world today. They seek to create new borders on the basis of exclusive identities, fomenting suspicion, prejudice, and hatred. At the other extreme, however, many governments misinterpret the concept of national unity as justification for enforcing homogeneity and centralized power. In the process, minorities are often brutally abused and disenfranchised, while any form of regional or cultural autonomy within the territorial limits of a nation is conceived as a threat. Ultimately, the symbolic importance of national boundaries is exaggerated to a point where even the most remote and inhospitable regions of a country become the focus of aggression and animosity.

On 8 May 1999, the Indian Army announced that it had begun operations to flush out Pakistan-backed infiltrators who had crossed the Line of Control in the Kargil region of Ladakh. Artillery battles and small arms fire had been going on in this area for years but these recent incursions were considered much more serious because the attackers had penetrated several kilometers inside Indian territory and captured a number of strategic peaks and ridges, from which they could threaten the main highway through Ladakh.

Initially, there was a great deal of confusion over the exact identity of these intruders. Conflicting reports listed them as Kashmiri separatists, Afghan and Pathan mercenaries, or Pakistani troops. Whoever they were — probably a combination of all three — the government of India was determined to push them back across the Line of Control. This was easier said than done, for most of the area which had been captured was at altitudes above twelve thousand feet and virtually inaccessible. As casualties began to mount on both sides, Indian Air Force fighters and helicopter gunships entered the fray in an effort to dislodge the intruders. Tensions escalated when two Indian jets, one of which was shot down by a shoulder-fired missile, crash-landed in Pakistani territory. One pilot was killed and the other captured, then later released. Virtually all the fighting was restricted to the Indian side of the Line of Control, though artillery fire was exchanged between the two countries and some of the dead were identified as regular Pakistani soldiers.

Both countries refrained from officially declaring war, though army commanders described "warlike conditions" in the region and close to a thousand men were killed before the fighting tapered off. The government of Pakistan reluctantly withdrew its support for the insurgents after diplomatic pressure was exerted by the United States. The onset of winter also helped put a stop to the bloodshed, as snowfall and subzero temperatures sealed off the mountains and made them uninhabitable for another eight months of the year. But the political consequences of this border conflict will be felt for quite some time. In India, Atal Bihari Vajpayee and the BJP claimed victory for their hard-line stance against the incursions. With the party's gains in nationwide elections, Vajpayee established a more secure tenure in the prime minister's seat. On the other hand, Nawaz Sharif was branded as a traitor in Pakistan for having capitulated in Ladakh. He was soon ousted in a coup led by General Pervez Musharif, one of military commanders who masterminded the incursions across the Line of Control.

Each of these events — the explosion of nuclear devices, the inauguration of a bus service from Delhi to Lahore, the recent battles in Ladakh, and the dramatic shifts in political power in both countries — demonstrate the volatile and unpredictable relationship that exists between India and Pakistan. Through all of this upheaval and conflict runs the border, an artificial fault line that has created a rift in the subcontinent, an unstable and invisible barrier that stands between people who have shared the same landmass for more than a millennium.

GLOSSARY

amrit, nectar.

bidi, small cheroot made of tobacco wrapped in a bidi leaf.

bourka, garment worn by Muslim women covering them completely.

chaat, variety of savory snacks, usually served with sauce.

challi, roasted corn on the cob.

channa, chickpeas, often eaten roasted.

chewda, mixture of dry savory snacks and nuts.

dharamshala, resthouse for pilgrims.

dupatta, long scarf worn by women, usually with salwar kameez.

farishta, angel.

Gangajal, sacred water from the River Ganga.

garam, hot.

ghazal, form of Urdu poetry, often set to music.

goonda, thug or hoodlum.

gurdwara, Sikh temple.

halal, butchering process that involves a short prayer by a Muslim cleric and bleeding of the animal.

halwa, sweetmeat or pudding, often made with semolina.

hijira, eunuch.

jamun, purple fruit, the size of a small plum.

jatka, butchering process that involves the cutting of an animal's throat.

jhalfrezi, form of meat curry.

jhola, shoulder bag.

jirga, a meeting of Pathan elders.

juggi, temporary huts or shanties, often made of mud or thatch.

kajal, antimony, used to outline the eyes, like mascara.

kanga, comb.

kara, steel bracelet worn by Sikhs.

kar sewak, volunteer engaged in religious service.

kes, uncut hair, one of the primary tenets of Sikhism.

khadi, handspun and handwoven fabric, usually cotton, popularized by Mahatma Gandhi during the freedom struggle as a symbol of self reliance.

khasedar, tribal militia in the Khyber Agency.

khwabgah, dream chambers, royal bedrooms in Mughal forts.

kikad, a species of acacia.

kirpan, sword or dagger carried by Sikhs.

kirtan, religious hymns.

kullar, clay cup, also refers to a conical cap sometimes worn under a turban.

kurta, loose, long sleeved shirt.

kutcha, underpants.

langar, charitable kitchen at Sikh shrines.

lathi, cane or staff, usually made of bamboo.

mazdoori, daily wages.

muhajir, refugee, generally refers to Muslims who migrated to Pakistan at the time of Partition.

naan, form of leavened bread baked in a clay oven.

neem, common species of tree, prized for its shade and medicinal properties.

Odissi, classical Indian dance form.

paan, heart shaped leaf in which betel nuts, other ingredients, and sometimes tobacco, are wrapped and eaten.

pakora, deep fried, savory fritters.

parikrama, concourse surrounding the Golden Temple and sacred tank of water.

pipal, species of tree, considered sacred by Hindus.

prasad, food or sweets offered to worshippers at a temple.

pulloo, end of a saree which is wrapped around a woman's shoulder and sometimes used to cover her head.

roti, wholewheat bread.

salwar kameez, two-piece outfit worn by both men and women, consisting of a long shirt over loose pantaloons.

samadhi, memorial shrine, usually on the site of a cremation.

saree, long, unstitched garment worn by women in India.

satyagraha, literally truth-force, nonviolent form of civil disobedience practiced by Mahatma Gandhi and his followers.

sepoy, archaic term for infantry troops in the Indian army.

sharbat, sweetened drink, sometimes made with milk and almonds.

shesham, species of hardwood tree, sometimes called Indian teak.

tabla, a pair of drums used in North Indian music.

thanda, cold.

NOTES

1 New Delhi

1 Edward Said, *Culture and Imperialism* (New York: Vintage, 1993), 336.
2 V. S. Naipaul, *India: A Million Mutinies Now* (Delhi: Rupa, 1990), 420.
3 Salman Rushdie, *Imaginary Homelands* (London: Granta, 1991), 10.
4 Ibid., 14.
5 Sunil Khilnani, *The Idea of India* (New York: Farrar Straus, 1998), 129.
6 Amrita Pritam, "My City, a World City," *Times of India*, 15 August 1997, 25.
7 Sudhir Kakar, *The Colours of Violence* (Delhi: Viking, 1995), 250.

2 Mussoorie

1 Kushwant Singh, *Kushwant Singh's View of India* (Bombay: IBH, 1976), 165.
2 Nirad C. Chaudhuri, *The Continent of Circe* (Bombay: Jaico, 1966), 291.
3 "Decadent India," *India Today*, 28 July 1997, 88.
4 Chaudhuri, 108.
5 Ibid., 300.
6 Ibid., 1.

3 Amritsar

1 M. J. Akbar, *India: The Siege Within* (Delhi: UBSP, 1996), 107.
2 Ibid., 110.
3 Naipaul, 448.

4 Ibid., 450.
5 Akbar, 113.
6 Ashis Nandy, "The Political Culture of the Indian State," *Daedalus* (Fall 1989), 23–24.

4 Wagha

1 Henri Cartier-Bresson, *Henri Cartier-Bresson in India* (Ahmedabad: Mapin, 1987), 8.
2 Saadat Hasan Manto, *The Best of Manto*, ed. and trans. Jai Ratan (Lahore: Vanguard, 1990), 49.
3 Bhisham Sahni, *We Have Arrived in Amritsar and Other Stories*, trans. Jai Ratan (Delhi: Orient Longman, 1990), 112.

5 Lahore

1 Samuel Purchas, *Purchas His Pilgrimes*, cited in Muhammad Baqir, *Lahore: Past and Present* (Delhi: Low Price Publications, 1993), 327.
2 Ibid., 333.
3 C. E. Luard and H. Hosten, *Travels of Fray Sebastien Manrique, 1629–1643*, cited in Baqir, 339.
4 Jean-Baptiste Tavernier, *Travels in India*, cited in Baqir, 335.
5 Niccolao Manucci, *Storia Do Mogor*, cited in Baqir, 340.
6 Ibid.
7 J. H. Thornton, *Lahore*, cited in Baqir, 341.
8 Charles Masson, *Narrative of Various Journeys in Baluchistan, Afghanistan, the Panjab and Kalat*, cited in Baqir, 343.
9 "Islamabad Warns of Missile Race," *Dawn*, 1 August 1997, 1.
10 *Dawn*, 26 February, 1948, cited in Aijaz Ahmad, *In the Mirror of Urdu* (Simla: Indian Institute of Advanced Study, 1993), 13.
11 Iqbal Singh, *The Ardent Pilgrim: An introduction to the Life and Works of Mohammed Iqbal* (Delhi: Oxford University Press, 1997), 89–90.
12 William Jordan, "The Poetry of Iqbal," *Tributes to Iqbal*, ed. Mohammad Haneef Shahid (Lahore: Sangemeel, 1977), 239.
13 Intizar Husain, "Still Waters," *Dawn*, 7–13 August 1997, 7.
14 Faiz Ahmad Faiz, "Nowhere, No Trace Can I Discover," *Penguin Book of Modern Urdu Poetry*, ed. and trans. Mahmood Jamal (Harmondsworth: Penguin, 1986), 22.
15 Baqir, 428–33.
16 Rudyard Kipling, *Kim* (New York: Bantam, 1983), 1.

6 Peshawar

1   Mohammad Nawaz Khan and Alamzeb Gandapur, "The Jirga System II," *The Frontier Post* (Peshawar), 4 August 1997, 8.

2   Ibid., 8.

3   D. Emmet Alter, *Mann of the Border* (Grand Rapids, Mich.: Eerdmans, 1937).

4   *Frontier Post*, 4 August 1997, 1.

5   Sara Suleri, *Meatless Days* (Chicago: University of Chicago Press, 1989), 31–32.

6   Mahnaz Z. Ispahani, *Roads and Rivals: The Political Uses of Access in the Borderlands of Asia* (Ithaca, N.Y.: Cornell University Press, 1989), 144.

7   Ibid., 2.

8   John Keay, *The Gilgit Game* (London: John Murray, 1979), 1.

9   Ispahani, 223.

7 Rawalpindi and Islamabad

1   Minoo P. Bhandara, "Mutually Assured Destruction," *Dawn*, 20 August 1995.

2   Salman Rushdie, "A Land of Plenty," *Time*, 11 August 1997, 21.

3   Anthony Spaeth, "The Price of Freedom," *Time*, 11 August 1997: 19.

4   Amitav Ghosh, "India's Untold War of Independence," *New Yorker*, 23 and 30 June 1997, 116.

8 Murree

1   Keay, 15.

2   Akbar, 231.

3   Ibid., 235.

4   Percival Spear, *A History of India,* vol. 2 (Harmondsworth: Penguin, 1973), 242.

5   Jawaharlal Nehru, *Jawaharlal Nehru, An Anthology*, ed. Gopal Sarvepalli (Delhi: Oxford University Press, 1980).

6   Akbar, 244.

7   Amitav Ghosh, *Countdown* (Delhi: Ravi Dayal, 1999), 44.

8   *Dawn*, 7 August 1997, 1.

9   Ibid., 6.

10 James Buchan, "Kashmir," *Granta* 57 (Spring 1997), 62.

9 Atari

1   Ahmed Rahi, "Listen to an Exile" (interview), *Seminar* (August 1994), 15–16.

2   Ajay Bharadwaj, "This Shrine Unites All Despite Partition, Wars," *Times of India,* 15 August 1997, 13.

3   Urvashi Butalia, "Blood," *Granta* 57 (Spring 1997), 22.

4   Satinder Bains, "Candlelight Vigil at Wagha Border," *Indian Express*, 16 August 1997, 9.
5   Saadat Hasan Manto, "Toba Tek Singh," *Kingdom's End and Other Stories*, trans. Khalid Hasan (Delhi: Penguin, 1987).
6   Khilnani, 198.

10 Delhi

1   *Times of India*, 15 August 1997, 27.
2   *The Hindu*, 14 August 1997, 5.
3   Ibid., 6.
4   Ibid., 5.
5   Neerja Chowdhury, "Martyr Azad Is a Terrorist for Mayawati," *Indian Express*, 16 August 1997, 1.
6   *Indian Express*, cited in *Dawn*, 7 August 1997, 20.
7   *Times of India*, 15 August 1997, 7.
8   Ibid., 12.
9   Ibid., 15.
10 *The Hindu*, 14 August 1997, 2.
11 Khilnani, 201–2.
12 Bhisham Sahni, *Tamas (Kites Will Fly)*, trans. Jai Ratan (New Delhi: Vikas, 1981), 232.
13 Butalia, 14–15.
14 Nandy, 13.
15 Aijaz Ahmad, "'Tryst with Destiny' — Free but Divided," *India!*, special supplment, *The Hindu*, 15 August 1997, 21.
16 *The Hindu*, 14 August 1997, 4.
17 Ahmad, "'Tryst with . . .,'" 28.

Epilogue

1   Atal Bihari Vajpayee, interview, *India Today*, 25 May 1998, 39.
2   Joy Purkayastha, "Bus to Lahore Leaves on Historic Journey," *Indian Express*, 19 February 1999, 1.

WORKS CITED

Ahmad, Aijaz. *In the Mirror of Urdu*. Simla: Indian Institute of Advanced Study, 1993.
——. "'Tryst with Destiny' — Free but Divided." *India!*, Special supplement, *The Hindu*, 15 August 1997 21–28.
Akbar, M. J. *India: The Siege Within*. Delhi: UBSP, 1996.
Alter, D. Emmet. *Mann of the Border*. Grand Rapids, Mich.: Eerdmans, 1937.
Bains, Satinder. "Candlelight Vigil at Wagha Border." *Indian Express*, 16 August 1997, 9.
Baqir, Muhammad. *Lahore: Past and Present*. Delhi: Low Price Publications, 1993.
Bhandara, Minoo P. "Mutually Assured Destruction." *Dawn*, 20 August, 1995.
Bharadwaj, Ajay. "This Shrine Unites All Despite Partition, Wars." *Times of India*, 15 August 1997, 13.
Butalia, Urvashi. "Blood." *Granta* 57 (Spring 1997): 13–38.
——. *The Other Side of Silence: Voices from the Partition of India*. Delhi: Penguin, 1998.
Buchan, James. "Kashmir." *Granta* 57 (Spring 1997): 59–83.
Cartier-Bresson, Henri. *Henri Cartier-Bresson in India*. Ahmedabad: Mapin, 1987.
Chaudhuri, Nirad C. *The Continent of Circe*. Bombay: Jaico, 1966.
Chowdhury, Neerja. "Martyr Azad Is a Terrorist for Mayawati." *Indian Express*, 16 August, 1997, 1.
"Decadent India." *India Today*, 28 July 1997, 88.
Faiz, Faiz Ahmad. "Nowhere, No Trace Can I Discover." *Penguin Book of Modern Urdu Poetry*, ed. and trans. Mahmood Jamal. Harmondsworth: Penguin, 1986.
Amitav Ghosh. *Countdown*. Delhi: Ravi Dayal, 1999.
——. "India's Untold War of Independence." *New Yorker*, 23 and 30 June, 1997, 104–21.
Husain, Intizar. "Still Waters," *Dawn*, 7–13 August, 7–8.
"Islamabad Warns of Missile Race." *Dawn*, 1 August 1997, 1.
Ispahani, Mahnaz Z. *Roads and Rivals: The Political Uses of Access in the Borderlands of Asia*. Ithaca, N.Y.: Cornell University Press, 1989.

Jordan, William. "The Poetry of Iqbal." *Tributes to Iqbal*, ed. Mohammad Haneef Shahid. Lahore: Sangemeel, 1977.

Kakar, Sudhir. *The Colours of Violence*. Delhi: Viking, 1995.

Keay, John. *The Gilgit Game*. London: John Murray, 1979.

Khan, Mohammad Nawaz and Alamzeb Gandapur. "The Jirga System II." *Frontier Post* (Peshawar), 4 August 1997.

Khilnani, Sunil. *The Idea of India*. New York: Farrar Straus and Giroux, 1998.

Kipling, Rudyard. *Kim*. New York: Bantam, 1983.

McGirk, Tom. "Making the Final Cut." *Time*, 11 August 1997, 30–31.

Manto, Saadat Hasan. *The Best of Manto*, ed. and trans. Jai Ratan. Lahore: Vanguard, 1990.

——. "Toba Tek Singh." *Kingdom's End and Other Stories*, trans. Khalid Hasan. Delhi: Penguin, 1987.

Naipaul, V. S. *India: A Million Mutinies Now*. Delhi: Rupa, 1990.

Nandy, Ashis. "The Political Culture of the Indian State." *Daedalus* (Fall 1989).

Nehru, Jawaharlal. *Jawaharlal Nehru, An Anthology*, ed. Gopal Sarvepalli. Delhi: Oxford University Press, 1980

Pritam, Amrita. "My City, a World City." *Times of India,* 15 August 1997, 25.

Purkayastha, Joy. "Bus to Lahore Leaves on Historic Journey." *Indian Express*, 19 February 1999, 1.

Rahi, Ahmed. "Listen to an Exile" (interview). *Seminar,* August 1994, 15.

Rushdie, Salman. *Imaginary Homelands*. London: Granta, 1991.

——. "A Land of Plenty." *Time*, 11 August 1997, 20–21.

Sahni, Bhisham. *We Have Arrived in Amritsar and Other Stories*, trans. Jai Ratan. Delhi: Orient Longman, 1990.

——. *Tamas (Kites Will Fly)*, trans. Jai Ratan. Delhi: Vikas, 1981.

Said, Edward. *Culture and Imperialism*. New York: Vintage, 1993.

Shahid, Mohammad Haneef, ed. *Tributes to Iqbal*. Lahore: Sangemeel Publications, 1977.

Singh, Iqbal. *The Ardent Pilgrim: An Introduction to the Life and Works of Mohammed Iqbal*. Delhi: Oxford, 1997.

Singh, Kushwant. *Kushwant Singh's View of India*. Bombay: IBH, 1976.

——. *Train to Pakistan*. London: Fontana, 1961.

Spaeth, Anthony. "The Price of Freedom." *Time*, 11 August 1997: 14–19.

Spear, (Thomas George) Percival. *A History of India*, vol. 2. Harmondsworth: Penguin, 1973.

Suleri, Sara. *Meatless Days*. Chicago: University of Chicago Press, 1989.

Vajpayee, Atal Bihari. Interview. *India Today*, 25 May 1998, 39.

INDEX

ACKNOWLEDGMENTS

This book was made possible by two research and travel grants I received from the Massachusetts Institute of Technology. My sincere thanks to Philip Khoury, Dean of Humanities, Arts and Social Sciences, Jim Paradis, Head of the Program in Writing and Humanistic Studies, and Alan Brody, Associate Provost for the Arts, each of whom helped fund the project. I would also like to thank Anita Desai and Alan Lightman for their encouragement and support. Susanne Martin, Nicholas Altenbernd, and Maya Jhangiani have offered assistance throughout, for which I am extremely grateful. My thanks also to Jill Grinberg, Patricia Smith, Kavi and Devika Singh, Robert and Ellen Alter, and Jonathan Addleton, as well as the many people I met on my journey, who offered their insights and hospitality.